Dyslexia, Dyscalculia and Math

Dyslexia, Dyscalculia and Mathematics will be an essential resource for teachers, classroom assistants and special educational needs co-ordinators (SENCOs) who help dyslexic and dyscalculic children with their understanding of mathematics. Written in an accessible style with helpful illustrations, this practical book reveals helpful ways in which to tackle both simple and complex concepts with students of all ages.

This second edition has been updated to include references to using technology that will help children with dyslexia and dyscalculia reinforce their mathematical skills, and also contains a number of photocopiable resources that can be used in the classroom. Written by Anne Henderson, who is experienced in teaching language and mathematics to pupils with dyslexia and dyscalculia, this book outlines current thinking in the field and shows how the research methods that have been proven successful can be used with whole classes of children.

This book encourages flexible methods and gives teachers the confidence to discuss alternative solutions with their pupils and help them achieve success. It is an ideal handbook for parent–teacher programmes and is also suitable for in-service training.

Anne Henderson is a lecturer in Mathematics and Dyslexia for Masters and Diploma courses at UCW Bangor, Wales, as well as Educational Consultant for BEAM mathematics and Numicon. She has provided training all over the world.

For my lovely grandchildren,
Callum, Ross, Euan, Ffion, Haf and Leo

Dyslexia, Dyscalculia and Mathematics

A practical guide

Second edition

Anne Henderson

LONDON AND NEW YORK

First edition published as *Maths for the Dyslexic*
by David Fulton Publishers 1998

This edition published 2012
by Routledge
2 Park Square, Milton Park, Abingdon, Oxon OX14 4RN

Simultaneously published in the USA and Canada
by Routledge
711 Third Avenue, New York, NY 10017

Routledge is an imprint of the Taylor & Francis Group, an informa business

© 2012 Anne Henderson

The right of Anne Henderson to be identified as author of this work has been asserted by her in accordance with sections 77 and 78 of the Copyright, Designs and Patents Act 1988.

All rights reserved. The purchase of this copyright material confers the right on the purchasing institution to photocopy pages which bear the photocopy icon and copyright line at the bottom of the page. No other parts of this book may be reprinted or reproduced or utilised in any form or by any electronic, mechanical, or other means, now known or hereafter invented, including photocopying and recording, or in any information storage or retrieval system, without permission in writing from the publishers.

Trademark notice: Product or corporate names may be trademarks or registered trademarks, and are used only for identification and explanation without intent to infringe.

British Library Cataloguing in Publication Data
A catalogue record for this book is available from the British Library

Library of Congress Cataloging in Publication Data
A catalog record for this book has been requested

ISBN: 978-0-415-68311-1 (pbk)
ISBN: 978-0-203-80388-2 (ebk)

Typeset in Helvetica
by Saxon Graphics Ltd, Derby

Contents

Acknowledgements

I would like to thank my daughter Bethan, a health psychologist who, even in the middle of a further doctorate to become a clinical psychologist, has found time to share her knowledge and expertise, and my dyslexic son Gareth, a consultant petrophysicist who from distant Kazakhstan has helped so very much. Both of them gave me encouragement to complete this project. Thanks also to my sister Vera, her daughter Davina Perry and my friend Ann Harrison, who are all teachers leading busy lives, but have found time to discuss their experiences about numeracy so willingly.

I also thank Nicky Silcocks, Suzanne Keith, Margaret Haseler, Silke Vanatter, Lee Khiang Kong, Lee Chew Ing, Melody Appleton, Tony Wing, Gwynfor Parry, Nick Dowrick, Yvonne Panteli, Jean Robertson, Romey Tacon, Ruth Atkinson, Penny Manning and her team (Hayley Roberts, Natalie Hough, Jo Bain, Hilary Glover, Katherine Sinclair, Karen Strowbridge, Natalie Goodwin, Ruth Ashworth and Samantha Joy), whose views changed and directed the course of the script.

A special thanks to Ann Cooke and the Miles Dyslexia Centre, Bangor University, for allowing me over the years to work with so many interesting and gifted students.

I wish to thank Edge Hill University for permission to include details of the Numbers Count Intervention Strategy also Oxford University Press for their permission to include details of the Numicon programme. Images of Numicon materials on pages 48–50 are reproduced with kind permission of Oxford University Press, Numicon © Oxford University Press 2010.

Preface

In the fourteen years since the first edition of this book the knowledge of the mathematical difficulties of dyslexic and dyscalculic children has grown considerably. Research on various numerical skills has increased as neuroscientists using brain scans have identified differences between the so-called 'normal' brain and those of the dyslexic and dyscalculic. This evidence provides proof that some children struggle to compensate for a physical difference, so therefore the majority of teachers will be reluctant to describe a child as 'lazy' or 'not trying' when obviously the child is struggling with a physical difficulty.

In addition, my own experiences working, providing training and lecturing throughout the United Kingdom and many countries around the world (Australia, Brazil, Chile, Ireland, North America, Korea, New Zealand, Luxembourg, Spain, Malaysia, Singapore and Hong Kong) have given me a greater insight into these difficulties. Talking and working with teachers and educationalists showed me clearly that it is impossible to ignore the importance of the early years, and it is for this reason I have included a section on early numeracy skills in this book.

Although I was a teacher of mathematics, I spent ten years teaching dyslexic children of all ages with literacy difficulties, familiarizing myself with ways to help them spell, read and write. This was an excellent experience but a steep learning curve for me. I was aware that these children had a hidden handicap which magnified the problem, because it is always easier to be more understanding if a child has a visible handicap, perhaps in a wheelchair or a broken arm, than if they have one that cannot be seen. As I became confident in my own ability to help these children, I moved on to helping dyslexic/dyscalculic children at primary level to acquire basic number skills. This initial teaching experience in such a specialist field enabled me subsequently to work for many years with older dyslexic and dyscalculic students in a secondary setting, and eventually with supporting adults in the workplace.

I learned alongside my students which strategies worked, thus increasing my own knowledge of the difficulties that both younger and older dyslexic and dyscalculic children face in mathematics. In time, I realised that all the skills I had acquired in helping students with literacy problems, consolidating basics, multi-sensory teaching, improving visualisation skills, looking at learning styles and building on strengths, were just the skills needed to help them in mathematics.

Based on these intervention strategies I have provided photocopiable **memory cards,** the size of credit cards, in the Appendix. These may be copied onto card, cut out and placed into a credit card wallet. These cards can be personalised by encouraging children to draw, colour, or write something specific to them on the reverse of the card to help them remember the information the card has provided. Children of all ages have found these memory cards invaluable as they are easy to carry and simple to use as memory joggers.

Helping these children with mathematical difficulties day in and day out was the perfect way to develop the best teaching styles that would assist them. Therefore, the prime aim of this book has been to document these successful multi-sensory approaches, and pedagogical techniques that have influenced me most in my teaching.

Anne Henderson
2012

1 Dyslexia and dyscalculia

Section A: Success in mathematics

For many children, success in mathematics can be elusive for a variety of reasons. These could include absence from school when vital parts of a topic are missed, ineffective teaching and difficult home circumstances. In addition slow language acquisition, poor health and other disabilities may affect learning. Before starting school young children have a variety of mathematical experiences that are specific to themselves, whether it is counting toys, seeing numbers on buses or travelling in different time zones on planes. Once in school, they begin structured play and start to learn about numbers. Some children easily acquire skills, see patterns and become good at maths. Many others do not. These children struggle with the basics, and cannot see similarities or make connections, so already they are beginning to fail in maths. They try to keep up with others in the class who seemingly do maths without much effort. In fact, many adults who find maths difficult in everyday life admit that their troubles started at a very early age when they began to 'fail' in maths. They were not able to keep pace with their peers and had never caught up.

Individual differences

Individual differences in mathematics have to be considered in order to help children find success. All children have strengths and weaknesses, so teaching has to be tailored to allow for these differences. Strengths in one field and weaknesses in another produces a spiky profile which is almost always present in both the dyslexic and the dyscalculic student. Perhaps the statement by Thomas West (1991) that 'for some dyslexic children, "easy" is hard and "hard" is easy' could be responsible for the spiky profile often associated with learning differences.

Unless these differences are taken into account children become discouraged, lose confidence and begin to hate maths. Mathematics involves many skills and concepts that are connected, and children need the ability to understand these connections. Memory, language, sequencing and ordering are some of the important functions that all play a part in enabling children discover success. To progress in mathematics these functions must work together, as new ideas and concepts are continually integrated into problem-solving strategies. Some dyslexic and dyscalculic children are hesitant when trying to give answers to questions because they are using inefficient counting strategies to remember maths facts. Others lack strategies for coping as they do not seem to have grasped how the number system works or recognise the patterns within it. This lack of 'number sense' if not dealt with in early years persists through adolescence and adulthood, causing severe problems in the quality of life.

It is important to understand that children who perform badly in mathematics do so not because they do not try, not because parents or teachers have failed, but because of their individual differences with regard to mastering the number system. It is imperative to remember that mathematical ability is not set in stone, so it is possible to intervene successfully provided help is focused on the weakest components.

Section B: Dyslexia

What is dyslexia? Here is one useful definition:

> *Dyslexia is best described as a combination of abilities and difficulties which affect the learning process in one or more of reading, spelling, writing and sometimes numeracy. Accompanying weaknesses may be identified in areas of speed of processing, short-term memory, sequencing, auditory perception, visual perception, spoken language and fine or gross motor skills. Some dyslexic people have outstanding creative skills, others have strong oral skills. Whilst others have no outstanding talents, they can still have dyslexia. Dyslexia occurs despite normal intellectual ability and conventional teaching. It is independent of socio-economic or language background.*
>
> **(Miles Dyslexia Centre, Bangor University, 2012)**

It is estimated that 10 per cent of dyslexic children are gifted mathematically. The British Dyslexia Association (2011) suggests that 40 to 50 per cent have no signs of problems, which leaves the remaining 50 per cent showing difficulty with some aspects of mathematics. In spite of this Miles and Miles (2004) stated that a high level of success is possible for these children provided they are given appropriate help.

Children who receive teaching that is geared to their learning style are able to master concepts, then whole topics, finally moving on to more advanced work. They become enthused by the magic of patterns within mathematics and begin to love the thrill of solving problems. Sometimes these blossoming mathematicians are not seen in school, but if it was possible to see into the future, it would become clear that all efforts by teachers to make mathematics exciting would have not have been in vain.

Students with specific learning difficulties often reach their potential long after they have left schools and colleges, but it is usually in these places of learning that the spark of their brilliance was lit. Many seem to have potential that is somehow bogged down, stuck in the chaos of simple mathematics. If correct teaching is provided that allows them to understand mathematics, the world will benefit from their great contribution. Enabling dyslexic and dyscalculic children to reach their own fulfilment in mathematics has been the aspect of teaching that personally has been most enjoyable for me.

How dyslexia affects mathematics

Dyslexia is a cluster of symptoms that impede a child's learning ability. The main difficulty is the language of mathematics: reading, spelling, writing, understanding difficult maths words and understanding written problems. Other symptoms include poor memory, perseveration (see page 3), sequencing, directional and organisational difficulties.

Organisation problems

Dyslexic children struggle with organising themselves, often forgetting the day and the time as well as their maths books and equipment. These children often end up with messy pages that no one can read or interpret when they write down answers to maths problems.

Perseveration

The Oxford Dictionary (2012) defines perseveration as 'to repeat or prolong an action, thought, or utterance after the stimulus that prompted it has ceased'. It describes the action when children look back over a previous completed question to check methods, and in error copy the answer. Professor Miles always described this as being like a song you hear in the morning, and for some unknown reason it plays inside your head all day long.

In reality it is very frustrating because what happens is that children complete problems on a topic (say, length) and some find an answer of, let us say, 46.3 cm. They continue with the rest of the problems, performing different calculations, but recording the same answer, 46.3 cm, for each separate problem. When one very bright student realised that the five complex calculations on Pythagoras he had just completed had identical answers, he described his actions as 'mad'. The best way to avoid perseveration happening is to look back over work, cover it up completely with a piece of card, then concentrate on the new problem and reach an answer before rechecking. This simple, yet successful, technique has saved a great deal of anguish with many children.

Section C: Dyscalculia

Overview of the problem

Dyscalculia is a specific learning disability that affects approximately 6 per cent of the population. While children with dyscalculia struggle to learn mathematics and lack an intuitive grasp of number, they are not unintelligent and may excel in non-mathematical subjects. It is thought that dyscalculia is caused by a difference in brain function. An interesting statement from Butterworth (2011) provides us with fuel for thought. He says that for dyslexia, when there are the right kinds of intervention, patterns of activation in the relevant part of the reading brain change, making brain activity more normal. By comparison, for dyscalculia, if there is correct intervention will the dyscalculic brain become more normal, or will the dyscalculic learner just find a different way of doing the same task? Obviously more research into this will provide us with an answer.

Reeve (2011) describes dyscalculia like this:

> *It is often co-morbid with other problems such as dyslexia; sometimes it is very different from dyslexia. I think that the general agreement now is that there is a pure form that is not associated with other learning difficulties. We suspect that it is genetic, or at least a neurological problem in some respects.*

Dyscalculia could be compared to having dyslexia with numbers instead of letters. Research into dyscalculia is still far behind the research into dyslexia. A child who struggles in maths lessons often begins to develop a fear of maths which leads to much anxiety and loss of self-esteem. When this occurs it can affect all aspects of life, not just maths, so it is essential that we recognise dyscalculia as soon as possible, before it impacts negatively on self-esteem. Chinn (2007) recognises dyscalculia thus:

> *As a basic indicator, the child will be performing below expectations for no obvious reason .... This underachievement may manifest itself in specifics such as problems with knowing the value of numbers ... not realising that 9 is one less than 10, or being able to rapid recall basic number facts.*

Just as there is no single set of signs that characterise dyslexia, there is no one cause of dyscalculia. Those who have dyscalculia usually have great difficulties with many aspects of basic numbers, often described as number sense. Without having a firm base or a strong foundation on which to build a number awareness, these children may struggle all their lives to deal with numbers and our number system.

Warning signs

If a child:

- has a poor sense of direction and keeps getting 'lost' in school;
- struggles with any kind of mental maths;
- is unable to estimate number quantities;
- seems to be acquiring good reading, writing and speaking skills, but is slow with counting, knowing when to add, subtract, multiply, divide when solving maths problems
- struggles reading numbers and recalling numbers in sequence;
- has problems with telling the time, finishing work in time and estimating passage of time;
- is not able to record their work properly;
- struggles with money, understanding the value of coins and shopping.

Difficulties for dyslexic and dyscalculic children

Almost all dyslexic and dyscalculic children use immature and inconsistent methods to calculate, and even when they have mastered a method in one topic they are unable to transfer those skills to another topic.

Dyslexic children have difficulties reading accurately written maths problems and numbers written in words, while many dyscalculic children are able to do this easily. However, both groups struggle to read, for example:

- speed on a speedometer
- temperature on a thermometer
- directions correctly from a map
- and understand that 13 is thirteen and 31 is thirty one.

Dyslexic children struggle with remembering how to spell and write maths words, and both groups struggle with all or some of the following:

- the order and value of numbers in the number system
- counting accurately
- copying numbers correctly often reversing them
- patterns in the number system (1 + 2 = 3, 11 + 2 = 13, 21 + 2 = 23)
- basic number bonds (2 + 8 = 10)
- estimation
- knowing that the maths symbol + means add
- left and right
- times tables
- recognising where numbers are on a clock face

- telling the time on an analogue clock face
- using a calculator correctly
- a formula and how to use it
- place value, recognising or seeing a decimal point
- fractions and percentages.

'Pure dyslexia' and 'pure dyscalculia'

It could be said that those with 'pure dyslexia' have no problems with numeracy and those with 'pure dyscalculia' have no difficulties with literacy. However, if we look at the above list it is easy to see that there are many overlapping difficulties that these two groups share. Figure 1.1 illustrates how I see children with dyslexia and dyscalculia.

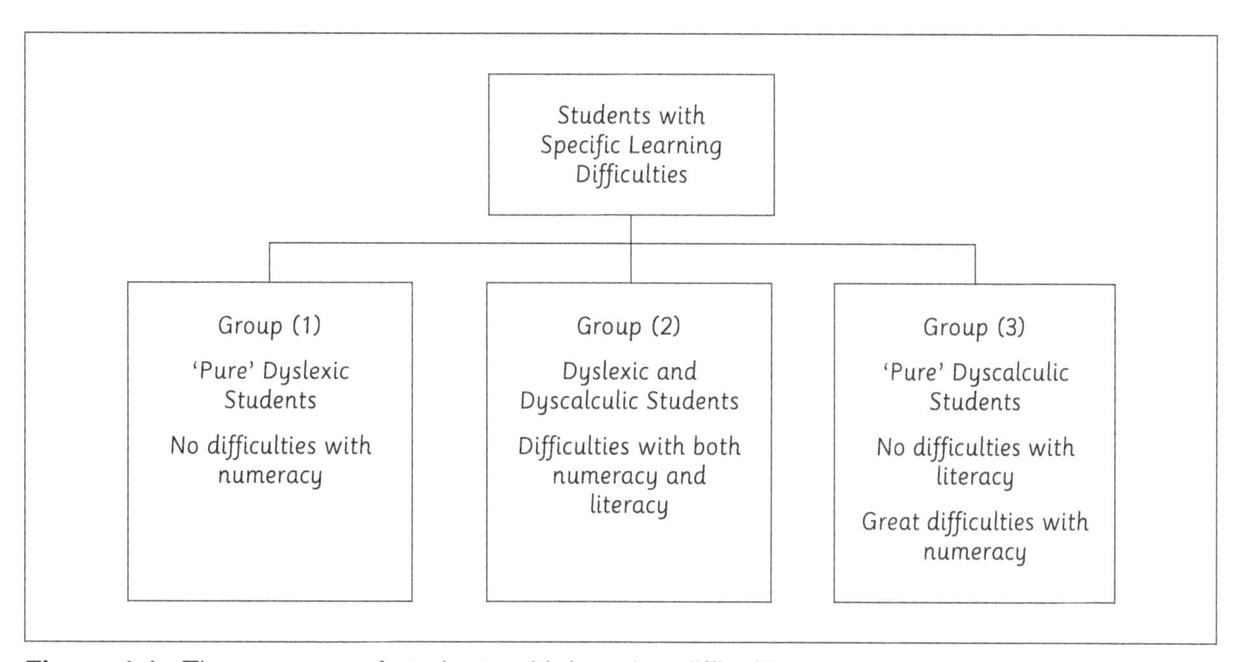

Figure 1.1 Three groups of students with learning difficulties

The percentages of children with difficulties in mathematics seem to change depending on which research papers are read, but almost all seem to agree that 10 per cent of dyslexics are high flyers in maths. Therefore this book is for teachers and parents whose children have difficulties in both numeracy and literacy, and 'pure dyscalculic' children.

Experiences of some dyscalculic children

Several children I have taught personally have been in the 'pure dyscalculic' category. These children were good readers, spellers and fluent writers, but their organisational and sequential ability, directional awareness and timekeeping were as impaired as their mathematical ability. The following quotes from dyscalculic children seem to highlight certain difficulties:

> *'When I do maths I see maths words in different colours and this distracts me from the maths problem question.'*
>
> *'Concentrating on mathematics is extremely difficult so my brain takes "time out" and my imagination takes over. I daydream then.'*
>
> *'I am sick of getting all the answers wrong. I seem to make mistakes even when I am trying. Teachers think that I am not trying, that somehow I am doing it on purpose!'*
>
> *'Talking to the other children who are struggling really helps. Sometimes they explain their way of getting an answer or maybe I can tell them how I have done it and it helps me to sort out my thoughts.'*

These children do not only have to deal with the mathematical problems that are mandatory in a school environment, they often struggle to become confident, competent shoppers. They find shopping a nightmare because they do not fully understand the amounts of money involved, so do not know how to offer the correct amount. As a result of this they like to pay with notes. They then end up with purses and pockets full of change, which is very heavy. Technology leads to additional difficulties, from remembering PIN numbers to obtain cash at ATM machines to copying flight numbers correctly if they wish to do an early self check-in for flights at airports.

How to help

An understanding tutor is needed to help children:

- simplify daily, weekly and monthly diaries to assist organisational problems;
- use lots of colour coding to help with correct reading of numbers;
- create meaningful rhymes and mnemonics to clarify sequences.

A dyscalculic student recalled times when he reversed the number of a bus, resulting in his travelling to the wrong part of town. When trying to catch a train at a station he read not only the time but also the platform number incorrectly, so he travelled a hundred miles by rail to a strange destination. On some of these 'bad days', when for dyscalculic person everything seems to be going wrong, their only recourse is to enlist the help of a good travelling companion or a good support network of helpers on Facebook or Twitter.

Many students who have left school still use the little tips learned in school to cope in situations where mathematical skills are needed. One student uses a watch to add, subtract, multiply and do fractions on, as well as a timepiece. Children who need to remember specific mathematical processes repeat certain procedures, eventually devising strategies to cope. Dyscalculic children need appropriate interventions to learn maths, just like the intervention strategies that are used to help dyslexic children to read.

What works with children with mathematical differences

The National Strategies Primary publication 'What works for Children with mathematical Difficulties?' (Dowker, 2009) states that Gross (2007) proposed a 'pragmatic stance on the emerging dyscalculia label' whereby:

> *Educational psychologists might want to adopt the scientifically less interesting but educationally more useful approach of taking dyscalculia by its literal meaning (an inability to calculate). They can then start from the assumption that all children who struggle with numbers of the number system are to some extent dyscalculic.*

The British Dyslexia Association (2011) reports that:

> *In summary, dyscalculia and dyslexia occur both independently of each other and together. The strategies for dealing with dyscalculia will be fundamentally the same whether or not the learner is also dyslexic.*

2 Factors affecting learning

Section A: Specific difficulties

Anxiety

Most children at some time mention that they are afraid of mathematics and dread the lesson, always feeling that they will never understand anything. Children who are failing in mathematics often say, 'I'm not thick, but I can't do maths. You see I can't remember what to do when I'm in a test, so I always come last.' Anxiety through constant failure causes them to hate the subject, and this can begin from a very early age. The mismatch of child perceptual preference and instructional activity mode appears to contribute to maths anxiety. However, the use of manipulative, concrete materials for mathematics instruction has also been found to reduce mathematics anxiety. Even though mathematics anxiety is not fully understood, its roots may be in instructional methods that cause the child to begin to develop a dislike or dread of mathematics.

Factors affecting confidence

Lack of basic skills with times tables, in telling the time and making simple number bonds almost always causes difficulties.

Mathematics is a precise subject that most often requires one correct answer. (This does not apply to open-ended questions.) Dyscalculic children who are failing always seem to find the wrong answer. This means that they are almost always 'bottom' of the class and they become afraid of failing again.

They become afraid of failing so begin to fear the lessons.

Regular mental tests (maths teachers love them!) mean that they are being tested on all those skills they have not mastered, so once again everyone will know how hopeless they are.

Mathematics teachers who think that dyslexia only affects literacy skills do not help to allay fears in this numeracy-based subject.

If children are afraid of failing then it is difficult for them to learn, because they cannot seem to concentrate hard enough on new ideas; so once again, they are left behind and their anxiety about the subject grows. They fear that they are not only failing themselves but also teachers and parents, who are often impressed by children who learn quickly and well. This is a particular difficulty for children who up to that time have been achieving quite well, working hard in mathematics and appearing confident. However, as soon as they have to demonstrate their expertise in manipulating simple number bonds or remembering the times tables in order to complete a calculation, they disappoint everyone. When there are too many processes involved, their anxiety inhibits their accuracy and in some cases paralyses their thoughts.

Dyslexic children know that they will always have some problems with literacy in their lives, but the realisation that they are dyscalculic as well might make them despair of ever achieving well in school.

Importance of a good working relationship

Children who are failing in mathematics will initially need one-to-one teaching. To make this support successful, it is vital to develop a good working relationship with a tutor so they are able to talk about aspects of topics they find worrying. Sometimes a discussion can help them see a way through a specific problem, and this then enables them to concentrate on the concept being taught. An easy atmosphere during the lessons allays fear and actively encourages children to explain informally how they have found a solution with no fear of ridicule from other children, which can happen in a class situation.

Example (1)

Matilda worked out a quick way of multiplying by 5.
If the number was even she halved it and added 0.
(a) What is 12 times 5? Halve 12 = 6 add 0 answer is 60
If the number was odd she took off 1 from the number, halved it then added a 5
(b) What is 11 times 5? 1 from 11= 10 halve it = 5 add 5 answer is 55

Example (2)

Ross said that he found subtraction difficult, especially if odd numbers were involved. With specific examples he demonstrated a strategy by simply subtracting the smaller number each time to avoid any 'borrowing and paying back', as he had never understood that procedure. For example:

  81
– 36

Starting with the units — 6 take away 1 = 5
Then tens — 8 take away 3 = 5 (this is 50)
50 take away 5 = 45

Answer is 45

(b) 727
– 358

Starting with the units — 8 take away 7 = 1
Then tens — 5 take away 2 = 3 (this is 30)
Then hundreds — 7 take away 3 = 4 (this is 400)
400 take away 30 = 370
370 take away 1 = 369

Answer is 369

Once this relationship has grown, children will come to talk about problems they are having with maths right across the curriculum. Teachers are then able to offer appropriate help or point them in the direction of someone who can help. These lessons should be individually tailored for each child to cater for their particular needs. This method allows for both child and teacher to work together in harmony, developing the child's skills so that they are able to deal eventually with varying levels of mathematics. It is always possible to go back to basics, regardless of the age and intelligence of the child, providing the teacher is aware that the approach used meets the child's needs.

Memory difficulties

Memory seems to have a big impact on success in mathematics for those with learning differences, as many different kinds of memory are used in problem solving. Children need to know where to start when working through a problem and then remember what to do next, and that means remembering which sequence and procedure to follow. They need a good active working memory to 'hold facts and figures 'in their heads while finding an answer. In addition, they need to recognise a problem by its pattern, remember that pattern, then connect it to a similar problem they have experienced before. Finally there is a need to apply appropriate rules to reach a successful answer. If a child has a poor prospective memory, it will impact on their mathematical ability.

Memory and mathematics

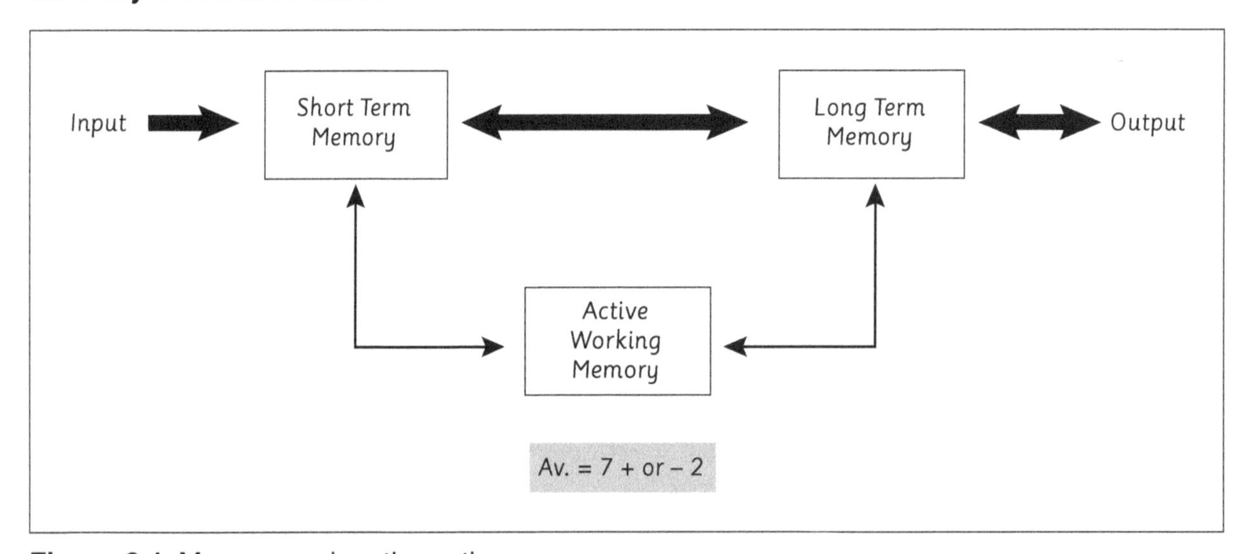

Figure 2.1 Memory and mathematics

Short-term memory

A child's poor short-term memory may be compared to a shelf that is not secure and may tip sideways easily. On average seven units of thought can be stored on the short-term memory shelf, but for an individual child the number could be five or nine. This means there will be some children in a class who can remember a great deal of information while others will be struggling to remember very little.

Example of short-term memory usage: Calculate 10 + 4

Unit 1: How big is 10? (It is one bigger than nine.)
Unit 2: The plus sign means add together
Unit 3: Four – I know how big that is
Unit 4: Ten and four more – count on
Unit 5: The answer is 14

If however, too much is taught too soon, in an haphazard way, building on a teacher's needs (for example because of shortage of time or pressure of the syllabus) then the wobbly shelf will tilt and absolutely everything will slide off, so nothing is remembered. It is better to provide information in small chunks to meet these criteria, because if the short-term memory shelf is not overloaded then it will stay level, and information can then be passed into the long-term memory shelf from where it can be retrieved, especially if it is filed near well-remembered information. *(Motto: avoid overload!)*

Active working memory

The size of active working memory has an almost direct correlation with the child's ability in mathematics, and the good thing is that we can improve its size. To do this it is essential to concentrate on developing mental maths, which is such a focal point in the National Curriculum. By teaching mental and visualisation skills we are enabling children to develop their ability in mathematics generally.

Strategies to help with memory problems

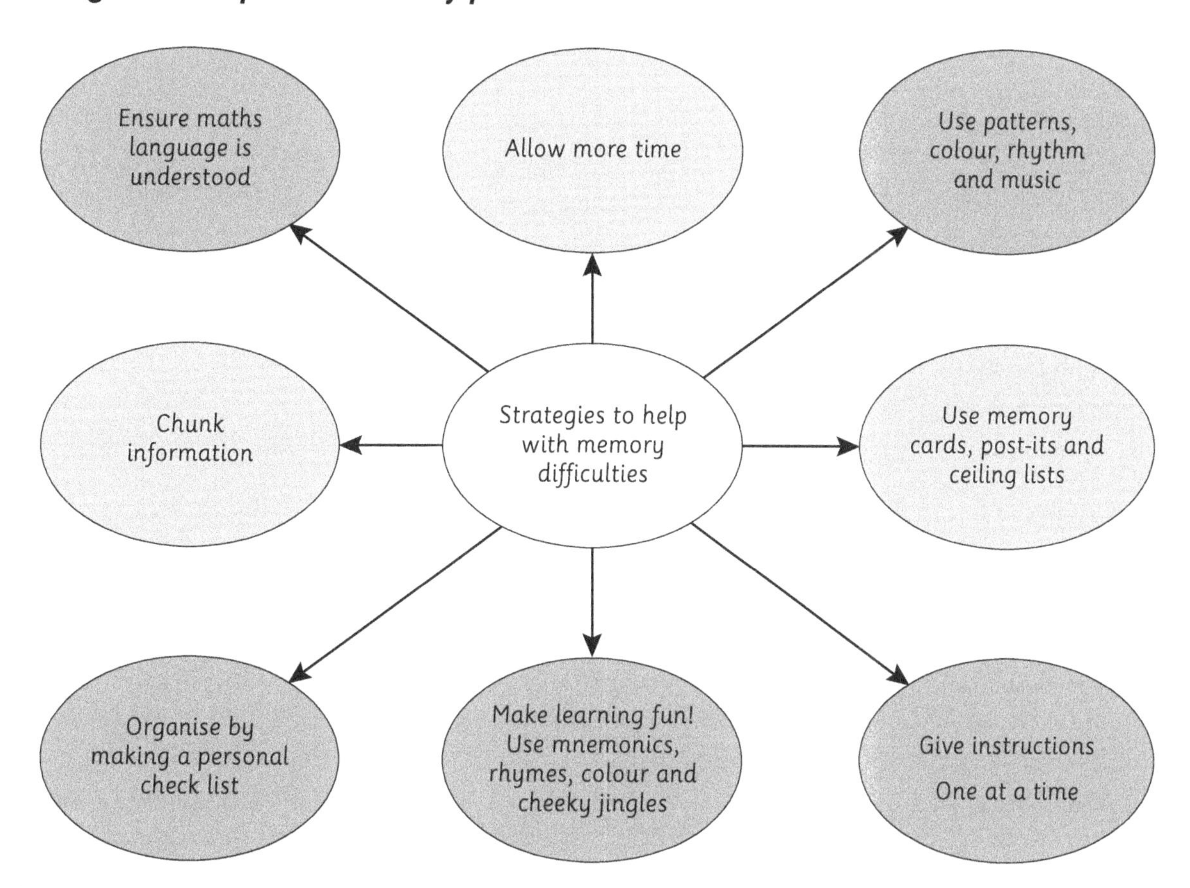

Figure 2.2 How to help with memory problems

Section B: Thinking and learning styles

The assessment of learning styles is important because once children's styles are identified, a teacher will be better able to cope with their learning differences. Dr Steve Chinn and colleagues' test of cognitive styles in mathematics (in Bath, Chinn and Knox, 1984) is an easy test to administer. It seeks to identify' Inchworm' (quantitative) and 'Grasshopper' (qualitative) learners. The differences in these learning styles are shown in Table 2.1.

Table 2.1 Inchworm or grasshopper?

Inchworm (quantitative)	Grasshopper (qualitative)
Prescriptive Finds formula Has recipe for solution Adds down a column Analytical Looks for facts Tends to do + and – Writes info down Unlikely to verify Rarely estimates	Intuitive Forms concepts Uses controlled exploration Reverses back and adjusts Holistic Estimates Tends to do × and ÷ Solves inside head Likely to verify Rarely writes info down
Number lines Paper and pencil Counting blocks Numicon apparatus	Some number lines Graph paper and grids Number rods Numicon apparatus

Not all children fall clearly into a particular category. Some are in the middle (perhaps they should be called inchhoppers or grassworms), using one method to do one type of problem and a completely different one to solve another. It is the children at the extreme ends of the spectrum on this test who experience the worst sort of problems, because they are set too rigidly into one way of working. However, once these styles are identified, teachers will realise that to meet the needs of all the children in the class they have to change certain aspects of their teaching.

The main difficulty for the dyscalculic inchworms is that as they are unable to see the whole of a problem they become too bogged down with details. Very often in an examination situation they will never finish a paper, limiting greatly their chances of getting a good mark. Grasshoppers, on the other hand, will 'leap' through any examination paper but will possibly have put down the answers only. They might see a question, think of a way of finding a solution, probably use a calculator, write down an answer and then move on. In fact on one occasion a child was encouraged to go through a paper writing down all the answers, and then to go back to the beginning to see if she could put down a method that would fit in with the answers she had already written.

How learning styles affect teaching

The main issue that emerges from the Chinn test is that inchworms and grasshoppers do not think in the same way. Grasshopper teachers, while they follow the curriculum, would prefer to show children the methods they like to use themselves to deal with maths questions, but if there are inchworm children in class, they will not always follow these methods or even like the apparatus being used. Therefore teachers with a different learning style from their children must be aware of the difference and adjust their teaching accordingly.

Awareness of a different way of learning enables teachers to present material in several different ways, for instance using two-dimensional diagrams, three-dimensional pictures, information on audio or video recorders, interactive white boards, TV and using computer-assisted learning wherever possible. In addition, different learning styles require different resources to maximise the opportunities in a teaching situation. Teachers who naturally lean towards particular apparatus (say, Numicon shapes as opposed to multilink) need to practise their own skills before trying to give a dynamic lesson with their non-preferred apparatus, since they might not be sure of its capabilities and limitations.

Teachers need to assess what apparatus children have used earlier so that any materials associated with failure will not be used again. If they make use of different apparatus, incorporating computer software and interactive white boards old concepts that previously were not understood can be revisited to allow the child to achieve success.

Observation of others' learning styles

Are they visual learners who remember what they see?

If so they probably like tidy work, plan ahead, like detail, daydream, prefer images to words, maybe draw, scribble and doodle, and learn best through two-dimensional pictures – so computers are great for these learners.

Are they auditory learners who remember what they hear?

If so they probably talk to themselves, listen well, spell out loud, prefer verbal instructions, are easily distracted by noise, enjoy rhythm, rhyme and love to talk. Sometimes by listening to children, sometimes by being sympathetic and making allowances for children's emotional state, we are able to help. In fact we ourselves need to recognise the importance of 'talk' in learning mathematics.

Are they kinaesthetic learners who remember when they use touch or movement?

If so they probably move a lot, use gestures, fidget, like physical activity, may need to visit a place to remember it and learn best through three-dimensional apparatus.

Do the children like maths?

If they do, they will be eager to solve problems by making the correct connections.

If children are given help at the right time, then far from saying, 'I hate maths!' they will begin to realise that they have some mathematical ability and find that maths 'isn't so bad after all'. While specialist teaching is always multi-sensory, it is essential to use first the child's preferred modality of learning to maximise the impact of teaching. Tutors should try to ascertain, through a series of observations, the methods that children prefer, keep a record and use them first to focus and build strengths.

In which order do children problem solve?

Do they read, think, visualise, write, draw, talk, and decide what to do?

Once you have sorted out a child's preferences, make a logo (see Figure 2.3) to show their thinking style, put on a memory card (number 1, see page 141) and save it on a computer so it can be reproduced as often as required.

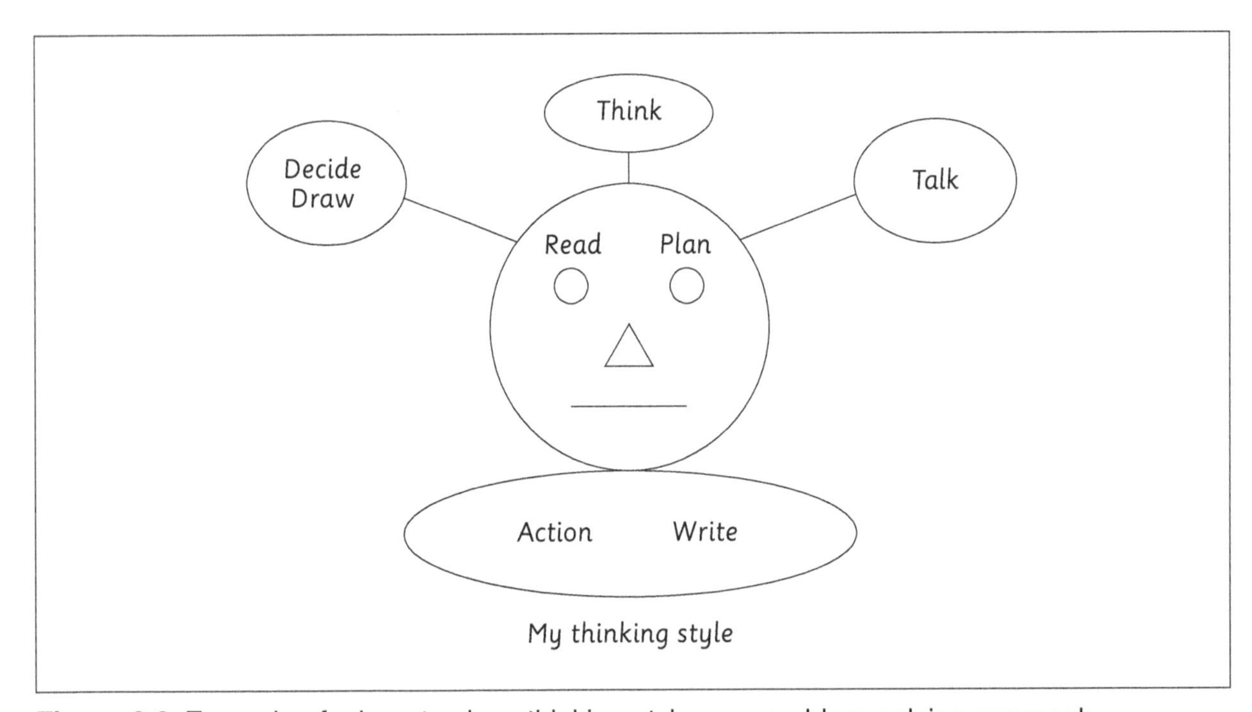

Figure 2.3 Example of a logo to show thinking styles – a problem-solving approach

3 The language of mathematics

Section A: Reading difficulties

Dyslexic children who have difficulties with reading will almost always have problems with reading mathematical text. Mathematics books and examinations have 'word' problems that have to be read correctly or there is no way that an accurate answer will be found. 'Pure' dyscalculic children may be able to read the words, but they interpret them wrongly, so very little of the question will make any sense to them. For example a student read a question on shape that included the word 'parallelogram'. He stopped, looked carefully at the drawing, then said, 'This word ends in gram but the question is nothing to do with weight, so what does this word mean?'

In mathematics accurate reading is essential. Those children who have been taught to speed read, scan and pick up contextual clues in English lessons have to 'unlearn' those skills when reading the wording of maths questions. If written maths problems are read quickly, important words might be skipped, resulting in a wrong interpretation of the question. Children often say that if a question is very long, often they forget the first part of the question by the time they reach the end. Children with directional difficulties who are reading from left to right sometimes do not see vertical tables if they are put into the middle of text, and express surprise when asked questions about the table.

There are several other points to consider about reading, especially when it is concerned with mathematics. Many people see reading ability as linked to levels of intelligence, so these people will assume that a poor reader will definitely be poor at mathematics.

Reid (1996) points out that:

> *Most children display some level of variance in their performances in school between different subject areas. Children with specific learning difficulties, however display extreme discrepancies .... Such children may have abilities at non-verbal problem solving ... although their performance may still be restricted by reading difficulties, since some reading is usually necessary in all curricular areas.*

Do mathematics teachers always know the reading level of a child?

Children who cannot read a multi-syllabic word easily will be breaking it down into phonic syllables to sound it out. However, this struggle with decoding means that they will find some written questions in mathematics almost impossible, because even when they eventually work out the sound of the word they may not remember its meaning. Their success depends on the level at which they are working and how much support they are receiving.

Do mathematics teachers always know the reading speed of a child?

Children who have difficulty with speed of reading, for whatever reason, will find their disability will affect their success in mathematics. For some reason school mathematics is often governed by speed, so children who read slowly will only be able to find answers later than the rest of their group, and will probably never finish their work unless they are given extra time to complete. If maths teachers are aware of class reading speeds, they will be able to give children sufficient time to finish their work.

Once out of the school system mathematicians are usually given enough time to reach the solution to problems without someone continually breathing down their neck and telling them to hurry up.

Do maths teachers always know the reading level of mathematics books?

It is difficult to ascertain the accurate reading level of mathematics books because most readability formulae have been developed to use with literary text. Mathematics text is different as there is not usually the amount of continuous text that readability formulae require. The flow of reading is not always right to left as questions often contain vertical tables, so these, as well as many non-alphabetical symbols, give false readings. In spite of these difficulties an informal study on some UK Year 2 maths books, for children aged 7 to 8, found that the average reading age required was 13.5 years. The reason for this high score is probably the multi-syllabic nature of mathematical terms such as isosceles, vertices and multiplication: the difficulty of these pushes up the reading age.

Is it any wonder that many children hate maths books?

Section B: Word problems

Basic word problems are difficult for both dyslexic and dyscalculic children, and complex word problems that require several stages to find an answer often overwhelm them, increase anxiety and may mean that they give up and mentally opt out of mathematics. If a word problem needs many steps before a solution is reached, children often forget where they are up to in the question, so are unable to complete it.

Non-mathematical words

Another difficulty with word problems are the non-mathematical words that are put into questions to make 'real life' situations. For example:

> *The centre part of the spinner (the arrow) is attached to the centre of the card, which is shaded as shown. The arrow is spun. What is the probability that when the arrow stops spinning its pointer will be on the black section?*

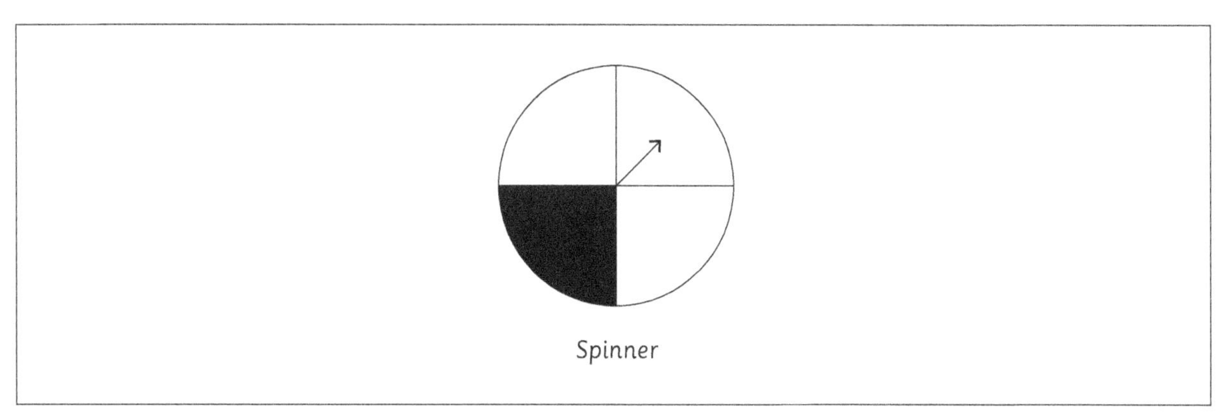

Figure 3.1 A spinner shown in a maths problems

In this question the words children stumbled over were 'centre', 'spinner', 'coloured' and 'pointer', emphasising the fact that the non-mathematical words hinder solutions. The word 'probability' and calculating the answer were not problems.

Difficult maths words and phrases

Often children read words and instructions that they cannot understand, so they are not able to comply with the demands of the question. Some words and phrases that might cause problems are:

> *fair, die, material, alongside, generalise*
>
> *at the edge of, about the same as, take a chance, point of symmetry, notice the digits*
>
> *use oral and written, prove and disprove theories, take a chance, devise and extend, investigate and predict*

Many words have several meanings which causes confusion in maths.

How to help

- Discuss difficult words. Make a memory card (number 2, see page 141) of them.
- Write the words down, and perhaps break them down into individual syllables.
- Encourage the pupils to make lists of words.
- Talk about phrases that pupils might encounter while studying a topic.
- Encourage pupils to read and analyse maths words until they become familiar with them.

Table 3.1 Words with differing meanings

Word	Possible meanings
scales	piano scales fish scales weighing scales thermometer scales capacity scales
right	opposite of wrong opposite of left meaning 'yes' meaning write meaning 'feeling fine' meaning accurate an angle of 90 degrees
degree	university degree measure of a geometrical angle measure of temperature

Maths words read incorrectly

Dyslexic children who have difficulty reading often see one word, but say another, just as, when they are reading a story, they might read 'rushed down the street' when in fact the actual words are 'ran down the road'. Sometimes the word they read is so near in meaning to the correct one that it does not affect the calculation, for instance when they read 'probability' as 'possibility'. However at other times the word that is 'read' is so different in meaning from the actual one (see Table 3.2) that it can make solving the question almost impossible. For example, a child might read 'diameter' as 'diagram'. Often children are too embarrassed to ask for help, and struggle to make sense out of the question, becoming more frustrated as they fail.

How to help

- Children having problems with reading from maths books might find it helpful to use a piece of card to follow the words across the page as they would do with a reading book.
- If there are too many questions on a page the child can either cut out a window in a piece of card to hide everything else or photocopy a question so that there are no other distractions.
- Difficult first names can be identified by one or two letters; in this way speed and not accuracy is affected.
- Put maths questions onto audio recorders. Children can then listen to the question as often as they want, and the lack of pressure will probably mean less errors.
- If older students use audio recorders in examinations they need to practise listening and working from audio.

Table 3.2 Words read incorrectly

Actual word	Word read	Actual word	Word read
continue	calculate	value	volume
correct	calculate	diameter	diagram
algebra	again	uniform cross-section	unit cross shape
circles	cities	approximate	appropriate
paperbacks	plastic books	recorded	record
whose	whole	category	calculate
lies	lives	frequency	frequently
volume	velocity	classify	calculate

Recognising relevant information in a question

Reading the correct word and understanding the way in which the question is presented can cause problems. For example:

> *Martha bought 48 packs of soup for her family holiday in the caravan with her three children. During the holiday they drank 24 packs and gave 6 packs to friends in nearby caravans. How many packs of soup did she take home?*

This is a simple maths calculation (48 – 24 – 6 = 18) but many children will not understand the question. They may not know which information is relevant or irrelevant, or where to start, or how to explain their thoughts, or how to ask or answer any questions about the maths involved.

How to help

There are no easy solutions, but if children become accustomed to word problems and begin to understand the way the questions are presented, they should become less anxious.

- Children with a poor 'number sense' are greatly disadvantaged in all areas of maths but helping them to develop mental images to manipulate numbers can enable them to become more confident to find answers.
- Even simple number patterns are hard for them to memorise, which results in an inability to generalise patterns to help with calculations. For example, instead of knowing that $3 + 6 = 9$ therefore $3 + 16 = 19$ many children will start to count on their fingers. Many lose their place in the calculation while they are counting.
- It can help if relevant patterns are practised on the computer, made into clear charts that are put on walls and onto memory cards (number 3, see page 141).
- When meaningful concrete apparatus (Numicon) is used to help children learn basic concepts in maths, children are able to understand the processes needed to problem solve. Manipulating the apparatus promotes confidence and allows children to begin to internalise patterns in the number system.

Develop a strategy

If children can work out a strategy for solving word problems, eventually there is a chance they will begin to pick out key facts for themselves. Dyscalculic and dyslexic children with organisational, visual, spatial or sequential difficulties find more complex word problems very challenging, and perhaps need more than a simple strategy to succeed.

How to help

- If children use coloured filters or lenses, encourage them to use them in mathematics.
- Read through a word problem, then re-read it.
- Highlight important information and key words.
- Underline important numbers.
- Break down information into manageable chunks.
- Discuss the problem and decide on a method.
- Decide which symbol $+$ $-$ $\times$ $\div$ to use (indicating an action).
- Estimate an answer (use easy numbers to help).
- Calculate an answer (use pictures or diagrams if necessary).
- Check against the estimate.
- Check against the original question.
- Make a wall chart showing the method that is easy to see.
- Put the method on a memory card (number 4, see page 141) with specific examples.

Section C: Spelling in mathematics

Mathematical words are often difficult to spell (for instance horizontal, perpendicular, eight or ate, forty or fourty).

Make a memory card (number 5, see below and page 141) to help with basic number spellings for the children with literacy difficulties.

Basic number spellings

Table 3.3 Basic number words

1	one	11	eleven	30	thirty
2	two	12	twelve	40	forty
3	three	13	thirteen	50	fifty
4	four	14	fourteen	60	sixty
5	five	15	fifteen	70	seventy
6	six	16	sixteen	80	eighty
7	seven	17	seventeen	90	ninety
8	eight	18	eighteen	100	hundred
9	nine	19	nineteen	1000	thousand
10	ten	20	twenty	1000000	million

Some ways that children spell isosceles triangle

issolise Trangle   I Cosalystryange   Sosileistryangle   Sausolees Hirangut

Other bizarre spellings

Children's version	Correct spelling
vendirams	Venn diagrams
horizonl and fertpal hoyt	horizontal and vertical height
graf to thekwashun	graph to the equation
exanpul ovpyitayeras	example of Pythagoras

As can be seen from these examples, children need help with spellings in mathematics. The words should be given in a systematic, structured way that would link into the method that they have been using to cope with difficulties in literacy. Teaching words in groups can be helpful: see Figure 3.2.

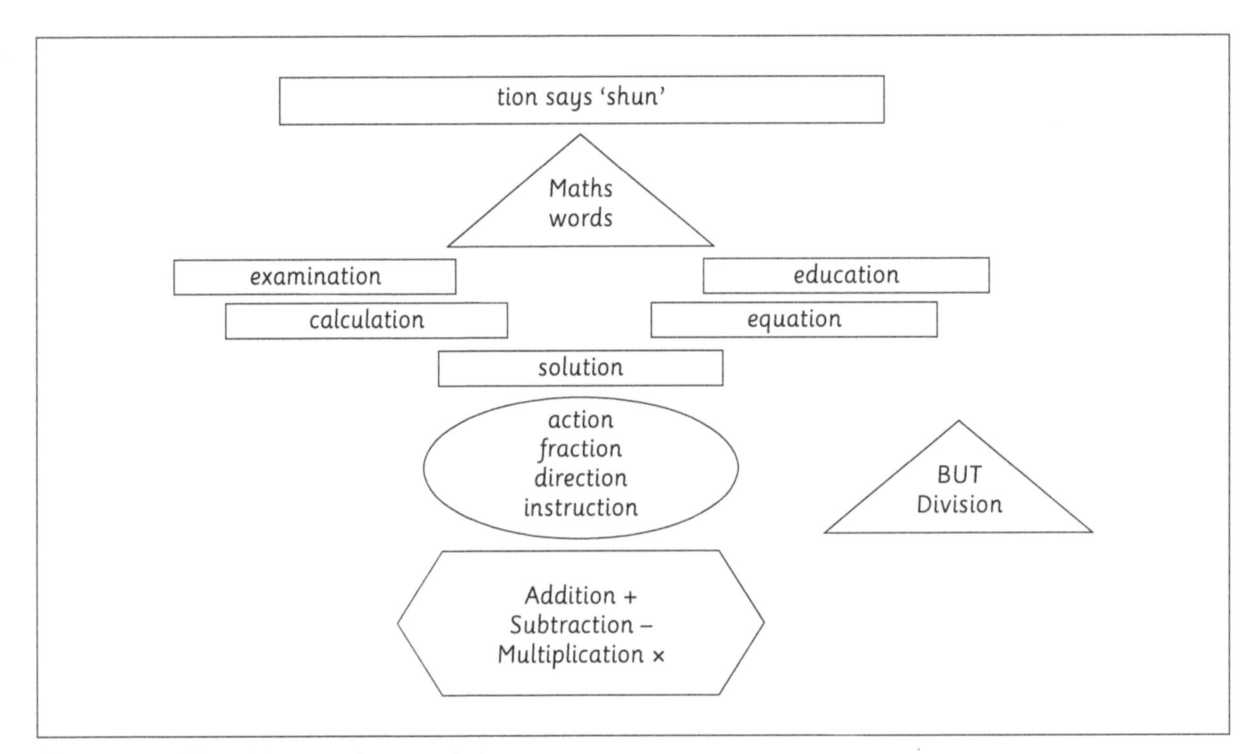

Figure 3.2 Teaching maths words in groups

A phonic approach can help some children with some of the difficult maths words, but others prefer a more analytical approach when the words are broken down into syllables. In this way the meaning of the words can be analysed and discussed just as they would do when studying the meaning of words in a comprehension exercise in an English language lesson.

Table 3.4 An analytical approach to maths vocabulary

Word	Syllable	Meaning
addition	ad di tion	to towards act of
subtraction	sub trac tion	under, below drawing act of
multiplication	multi plica tion	many folding in act of
division	di vi sion	apart seeing act of
fraction	frac tion	breaking act of
per cent	per cent	for hundred
perimeter	peri meter	around measure

Section D: Writing in mathematics

Although children seem to be rather reluctant to write in their maths books, they see benefits as soon as their attitude improves. When they begin to write down their own notes describing methods they can refer to them at any time. They are able to use their own words and phrases to describe a procedure which they can understand when they come back to the notes later. They are able to colour and mark as much as they like in order to assist their memory. Figure 3.3 shows the advantages of writing in mathematics.

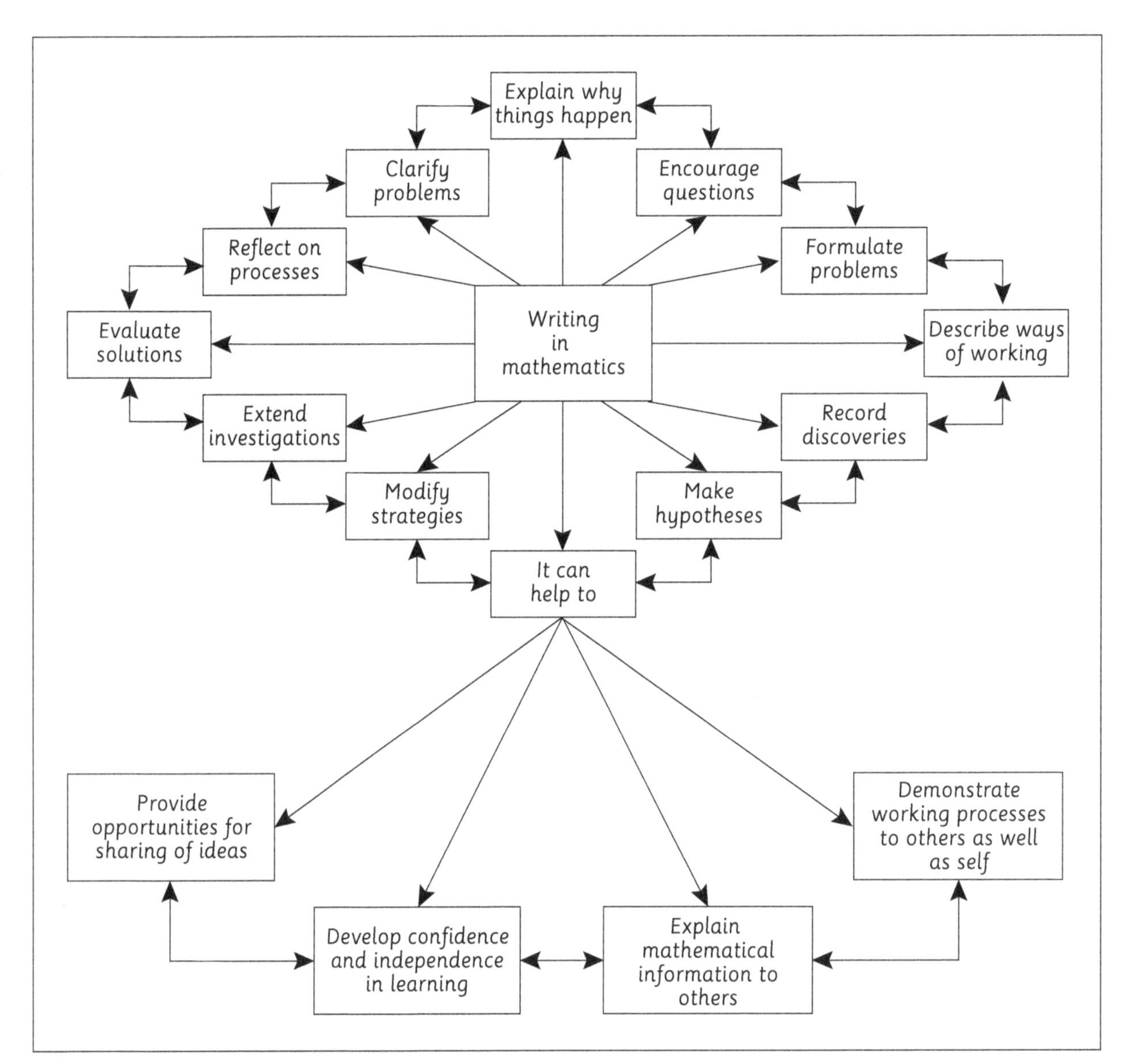

Figure 3.3 Writing in maths

Reading and writing numbers

Dyscalculic children with number difficulties often cannot read numbers, even though by the time they are receiving help they will have been in a school learning environment for some time. They may be picking up more visual information to do with pattern and shape, but basic numbers will be hard for them to remember. At this stage much practical work is essential – encouraging children to make visual connections and talk about what they discover and understand.

Reading and writing large numbers

Large numbers need practice. Practising writing cheques for large amounts of money improves the ability to write numbers using both digits and words. Bigger numbers need recognition from the right before they can be read from the left, which causes problems for dyslexic children struggling with directional difficulties.

How to help

For example, to read the number 23768054

From the right split 23768054 into groups of three digits. Put in commas, so the number can be read as follows.

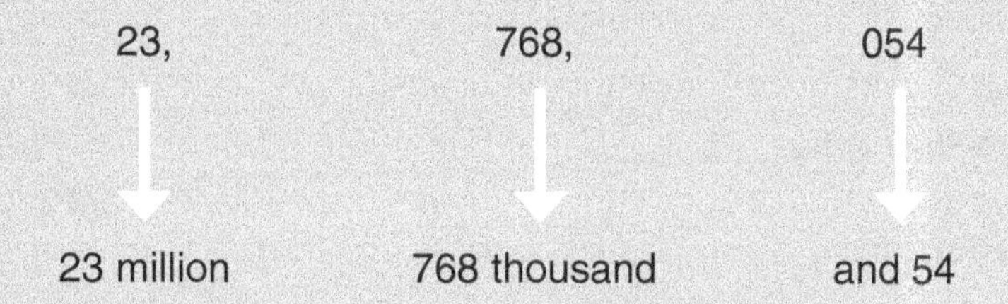

- It is worthwhile to spend time talking about this procedure.
- Make a big poster to go on the wall and a memory card (number 6, see page 141) to show the importance of the thousand and million positions.
- The 'look, say, cover, write, check' approach works equally well for numbers as it does for spellings.

Promote confidence and competence

When children can talk about methods in maths it usually indicates that they understand what they are doing. It is only when children are proficient with oral work that any attempt at formal written maths should be made. This step is very important for young children but also just as important for older children, many of whom will have often failed while shifting from concepts understood with apparatus to recording abstract concepts on paper. Sometimes teachers are not explicit enough when asking children to perform tasks; perhaps the language is too complex, or maybe the instructions do not describe clearly enough the outcome that is wanted. However, if the lesson objectives and success criteria are very clear, then the task should guarantee success.

Example

Lesson objective:	To recognise odd numbers up to 20
Success criteria:	If you colour in all odd numbers up to 20 on the table square your answer will be correct.
'I can' statement:	I can identify all odd numbers up to 20

Once children begin to understand basic numeracy, they can move on to simple concepts; then several concepts can be put together to make a topic. It is only when children acquire fluency within topics that the patterns in mathematics can be read and understood. So when asked to investigate a problem they will explore all possibilities with confidence and do it in a competent way as they begin to find solutions. They need to be treated gently and guided slowly through these steps if they are to be successful.

4 Assessment, intervention strategies and teaching

Section A: Assessment

Observational assessment

Mathematics probably more than any other subject is cumulative, with one concept building onto a previous one, so it is essential to recognise children's mathematical ability and also any difficulties. The Early Years Foundation Stage (EYFS) assessment of individual children enables teachers to see a clear profile of a child's problems. Early identification of difficulties may prevent confidence being lost or fear of mathematics developing. It is usually a parent or class teacher, or probably both, who spot specific learning difficulties in numeracy. A teacher is able to see by close observation where children at risk are struggling: perhaps when they are playing, using mathematical equipment, counting or taking part in informal discussions in maths lessons.

Written tests are not the only way in which children are assessed in mathematics. Oral and practical assessments, plus the correct type of questioning, allow children to show their understanding of both procedures and concepts. The teacher might find it useful to audio record a child's answer and play it back to them, saying, 'This is what you said,' before discussing it with them. The playback might not immediately cause the child to change their mind about what they want to say (if their answer is incorrect), but the discussion which ensues will probably stay with that child forever. Good assessment techniques enable specialist teachers to evaluate progress as well as to communicate this progress to the class teacher, parents and administrators. Children too like to know how they are progressing, so provided a test is non-threatening, it can be of benefit to all involved.

A teacher will begin to notice a child who:

- becomes anxious in a number lesson
- is always using fingers to count
- struggles to count accurately
- sees numbers as groups of 'ones' not whole numbers
- cannot remember the order of a number sequence
- cannot give a rough guess at an answer
- cannot remember 'what comes next'.

Parental involvement

The influence of parents on early and subsequent maths education cannot be overestimated. The *Review of Mathematics Teaching in Early Years Settings and Primary Schools* (Williams, 2008) states that 'the overwhelming majority of parents want to do their best for their children'.

Many parents who want to help do not understand the methods that are being used in schools to teach basic maths. This lack of understanding often leads to a lack of any incentive to help, and can also pass on a very negative attitude towards mathematics. Any training given to parents by schools is always greatly appreciated, especially if some computer materials can be recommended.

Different ways of assessment

Assessment that provides useful information enables teachers to identify specific difficulties. Methods often profile children's individual strengths and weaknesses. Some schools that are involved with the Every Child Counts, Numbers Count Programmes are using the Sandwell standardised test at the start and end of teaching interventions. The MaLT test (Mathematics assessment for Learning and Teaching), suitable for assessment from Reception to Year 9, is another test that can be used. BEAM mathematics offers a Diagnostic Interview and Numicon the Numicon Diagnostic Assessment, both of which provide the essential basis for planning intervention lessons for children struggling in maths. The Basic Number Screening Test by Gillham and Hesse and the Wrat Computation Math are diagnostic tests used in some centres.

Types of assessment

The main types of assessment used are:

- dyscalculia assessment;
- informal assessment;
- diagnostic assessment, carried out by observing a child to obtain information about any specific difficulties in mathematics;
- formative assessment: continual assessment by both the pupil and the teacher to observe, review and adjust objectives and targets;
- standardised assessment, which compares the performance of an individual pupil with others of similar age.

Dyscalculia assessment

Professor Brian Butterworth's *Dyscalculia Screener* (2003) is a computer test that can be administered individually or with a group to identify dyscalculic tendencies. The individual items are Simple Reaction Time, Test 1: (Capacity) Dot enumeration, Test 2: (Capacity) Number Comparison, and Test 3: Arithmetic Achievement. It takes approximately thirty minutes to complete, and provides a graphical read-out showing whether a child has dyscalculia, a learning/teaching difficulty, a problem with symbols or average maths ability. Dyscalculic children usually show low scores on all test items, particularly the two capacity tests. Intervention strategies are recommended, as is a further diagnostic test to identify specific mathematical problems.

Informal assessment

Informal assessment involving observation plus pertinent questioning produces vast amounts of information about the whole child. If linked with formal assessment, it allows for the diagnosis of difficulties and can provide a psychometric measure, which is often required for formal reports. Wechsler Objective Numerical Dimensions (WOND) is an assessment that looks at mathematical reasoning and numerical operations.

Diagnostic assessment

Observing children while they are working through a test enables tutors to see their methods, pose pertinent questions and view specific topics that are causing problems. By using the assessment time in a formative way tutors are able to give the best assistance. The National Curriculum provides guidance so that assessment can be specifically geared towards looking for difficulties within specific educational strands.

It is possible with observation to identify children who are struggling with:

- counting and understanding numbers
- knowing and using number facts
- calculating
- understanding shape
- measuring
- handling data.

In addition, various assignments and problem-solving questions show the child's skill in using and applying maths as correct links are made between symbols and language. As connections are made between problem solving, representing, enquiring, reasoning and communicating, the strengths and weaknesses of individual children become apparent. The gaps in a child's knowledge are often compared to missing bricks in a wall or to the missing strands in a spider's web: see Figure 4.1.

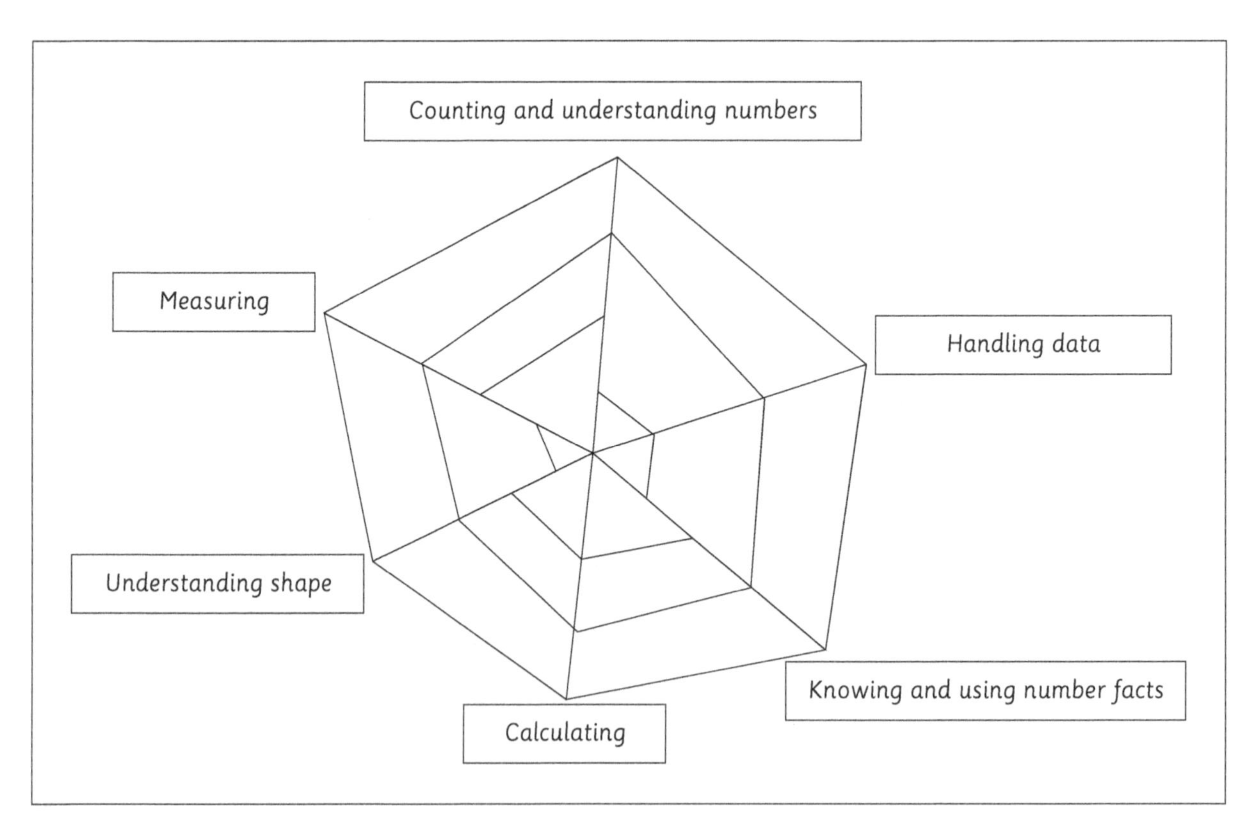

Figure 4.1 Missing links in a spider's web

A good teacher will spot the gaps in knowledge and provide support to make the child's understanding of a maths topic complete, just like a spider will aim to repair its web to make it strong and effective. In order to do these repairs to the strands, a teacher will need to appreciate that children require different kinds and different levels of support, depending on the severity and complexity of their needs.

Formative assessment

Continuous assessment is important to help ensure that children with difficulties receive the educational support they require. It is something the individual tutor should be doing at all times as they watch for recognition in the child's eyes and probably for some physical acknowledgement such as a shoulder shrug, a nod of the head, a more relaxed shape of the body or even a facial expression that says, 'OK. I'm with you!'

Teachers will always discuss aims and objectives at the start of a lesson, but children vary in how they begin to master a topic. Some children may like to be taught in small steps, gradually building up their knowledge, whilst others like to sit, listen and watch as a whole topic is discussed and worked through to a solution, possibly encompassing several varying, but interrelated, concepts. Catering for the individual needs of each child allows a teacher to demonstrate their skills to an interested and enthralled audience. What better environment for learning to take place?

Section B: Intervention strategies

Vygotsky is quoted in Feuerstein's *Revolution in the Teaching of Intelligence* (see Sharron, 1987) as saying:

> *Education must be orientated not towards the yesterday of child development but towards its tomorrow.*

The National Strategies/Primary (2009) state that:

> *So far there is no evidence that any one programme is best for most of our children .... Even when such research is done, it is likely that there will prove to be no single best intervention programme, and that different programmes would be suitable for different groups of children.*

Intervention techniques

Dyscalculia cannot be 'cured', but given appropriate help children should be able to acquire strategies that will support them in mathematics. Often this help will need to be consistent for long periods of their education, as short, sharp interventions are not always appropriate for many of these children. The report *Every Child Counts* (2008) states that even after specific intervention there are always children who would require further help: 'The remaining 5% of children continue to find reading and writing difficult and will require more intensive support and long-term assistance.' Possibly many dyscalculic and dyslexic children fall into this category.

The dyscalculic child is helped most when there is:

- early intervention in primary school;
- intervention during the transition to secondary school;
- additional support as the student is nearing GCSE examinations.

Two reports, from committees headed by William (2008) and Rose (2009), have addressed the difficulties referred to above and have put forward various courses of action to alleviate the problems.

The William report

This report made recommendations to inform development of an early intervention programme for children aged 5 to 7 who are failing to master the basics of numeracy. It made several recommendations that emphasised quality teaching for all children, excellent continuing professional development for teachers and more involvement for parents.

An important observation was made in the report:

> *It is of course commonly the case in education at all levels that the better teacher often teaches the more able students .... Yet there is a very compelling case that the reverse should be the case, because learners with difficulties present a considerably greater pedagogical challenge than those without. Nowhere is this truer than for the child in Year 1 or Year 2 with severe learning difficulties in mathematics. It therefore seems self-evident to us that for successful intervention in Every Child Counts there is a need for highly qualified specialist teachers .... Of course, they may well be assisted in certain respects by teaching assistants and others .... However, these are the adjuncts to high-quality teaching and not a substitute for it.*

The Rose Review

The Rose *Review of Mathematics in Early Years Setting* comments on the positive effect of the daily numeracy hour, which has been a key factor in raising standards. However, the review points out that instead of continually pushing forward with new mathematical concepts it is possible that:

> *learning could become more productively used, for example by delaying some of the learning for some children until they have a better grasp of more fundamental work, and by moving some children on a bit faster if they have already mastered the ideas .... It has led to the need for repeated teaching of the material over a longer timescale, and a lack of self esteem among children who learn more slowly and those whose results fell as a result of the Numeracy Strategy.*

National mathematics interventions

Almost all interventions at primary level include the following types of activity:

Counting activities:
- general practice in counting objects
- groups of ten
- finding individual numbers on a track
- building tracks using base 10 material- number lines
- counting to higher numbers – 100s.

Calculation activities:
- number bonds to 10
- use of patterns
- games including flash cards
- doubling (6 + 6) and deriving other facts (7 + 6)
- multiplication using multiples and step counting
- 'building' numbers with concrete material
- division accompanying multiplication using inverse.

Children should use the strategies that they find easiest

However, before any intervention takes place the points summarised in Figure 4.2 must have been discussed by all concerned with a child's education.

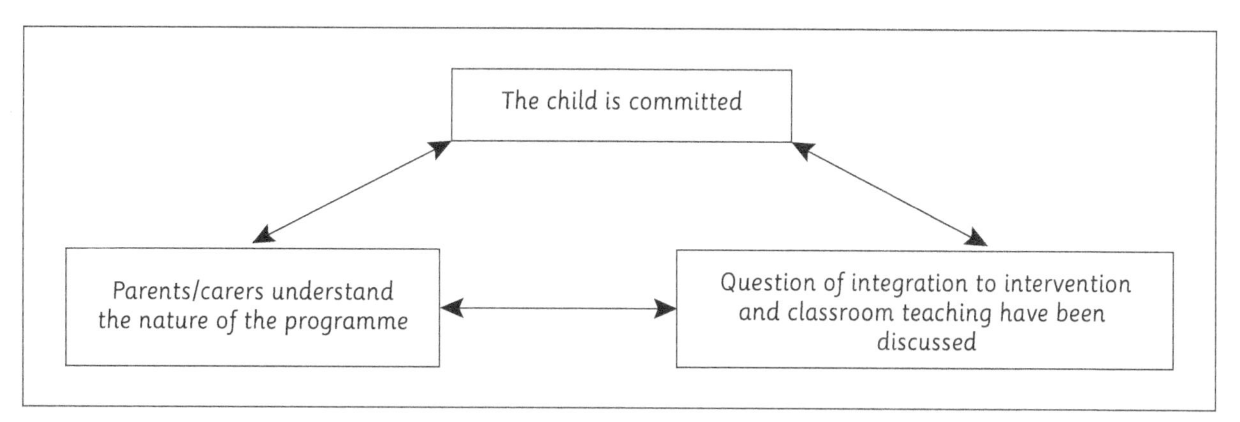

Figure 4.2 Important commitments before any intervention

The Primary National Strategy's 'Three waves of support' (see box) have been used nationally to good effect for some years.

Three waves of support

Wave 1
This is high-quality teaching in a whole-class environment, supported by effective policies meeting the needs of the children to move them from where they are in their education to where they need to be.

Wave 2
This type of provision usually takes the form of a tight, structured programme with regard to a small group, often within a class environment. The ideal outcome for Wave 2 is for learners to be back on track meeting national expectations by the end of the key stage.

Wave 3
This type of intervention is usually for the SEN pupils who need one-to-one support to help progress and minimise gaps in their learning.

Other interventions

There are many interventions in mathematics. Among the current and recent ones in the United Kingdom are Snap – on maths in Surrey; Moving on in Maths, Luton; Catch Up Numeracy; Numeracy Recovery; Mathematics Recovery; Making Maths Magic; Mind the Gap and Every Child Counts Numbers Count. (See Useful contacts and addresses, page 147.)

Information about Every Child Counts

The programme

Numbers Count is a mathematics intervention which was developed for Every Child Counts by Edge Hill University and Lancashire County Council. It provides intensive individual support for those children who are struggling in mathematics in Years 1 to 3. Children receive support for thirty minutes a day for twelve weeks. However, should a child require further help the upper limit for the intervention extension is twenty weeks. The results showed that the greatest gains were made by the lowest-attaining children. The average Number Age gain on exit is fourteen months. None of the children taught were predicted by their schools to reach the required levels, but in fact, after tuition, early results showed that over 72 per cent did achieve the expected level at age 7. While the majority of the teaching is on a one-to-one basis, teachers can also teach two or three children together.

Teacher training

Numbers Count teachers are highly trained specialists who have an excellent understanding of how young children learn mathematics. They understand the potential barriers to learning and know effective strategies to overcome them. All teachers are accredited by Edge Hill University, ensuring that all children in Numbers Count will receive high-quality support. Before being accepted onto the ten-day training course a teacher must have Qualified Teacher Status and two years of teaching experience. These highly trained teachers have a wider impact on both teaching and learning in their schools, and help to raise standards across the board.

Assessment

Children are observed on a one-to-one basis and assessed with the Sandwell Early Numeracy Test A, which enables accurate measurement of achievement and provides information teachers can use for diagnostic assessment. Initially up to two weeks is spent on assessment. At the end of the programme the children are reassessed with Sandwell Test B to check on progress. Follow-up tests are carried out three and six months after a child has exited the programme.

Teaching

All lessons are carefully planned, with specific resources always available to maximise learning opportunities. Lessons are videoed regularly, enabling teachers to review anything of interest that has occurred. The capacity to recall, review and reflect on lesson outcomes feeds information back into planning for the next lesson.

The concepts include:

- mathematical language
- development of mathematical thinking
- counting
- the number system
- number facts
- calculating.

Section C: Intervention teaching

Early intervention

Early intervention teaching

- Once children with maths difficulties are identified, it is essential that they are given help to overcome problems as soon as possible.
- If help is given before pupils become too anxious and before their confidence starts to ebb away, then there is a good chance that they will be keen to acquire the skills necessary to achieve their potential.
- Initially they may need one-to-one intensive teaching, possibly moving into a group situation once they have acquired basic skills.
- Later they should become confident enough to work in a class with support from a well-trained teaching assistant.
- An intervention teacher should know a child's strengths, weaknesses and cognitive problems, be able to adjust teaching to meet the needs of the child, use language to help them understand the concepts, and provide appropriate concrete materials to reinforce the concept.
- Above all the teachers should have a good working relationship with children that will enable these children to make progress confidently.

Individual help

Early intervention usually means that children will begin to succeed in mathematics, which can lead to success in other subjects. Once a specialist tutor begins teaching there will be careful diagnosis of individual difficulties, and appropriate strategies can be started. A child will begin to grow in confidence and furthermore start to make connections from one topic to another so that maths becomes a whole, not pieces of a jigsaw that they can never put together. After some tuition when basic skills have begun to make sense, the child may become confident enough to join in a class discussion. Some children who are given just a little help on a one-to-one basis make vast strides, while others need a great deal of individual help, and continual in-class support, right through their schooling.

Dyscalculic and dyslexic children in the classroom

As was stated earlier, speaking and listening are a vital part of any maths classroom. However, children who are not only struggling with the maths concepts but also have limited reading ability, poor memory and are generally failing will contribute little to a classroom discussion. If they are very brave they might make a stab at an answer, but what they say often sounds as if they have not listened to the question. Other children whose mastery of the basic concepts is poor will be struggling to understand the 'whole topic' and will probably never be confident enough to contribute to any oral maths sessions.

A considerable number of class teachers are able to give children feelings of self-worth and value their answers. Many, however, because of class size, overload of the curriculum and not least their own poor mathematical ability, are unable to consider the importance of obscure statements that children make, and 'bin' them without a thought for the unfortunate child, who will probably have thought deeply before making the comment.

Intervention at transition primary/secondary level

If a problem is only identified towards the end of primary school, other issues emerge. For some children reading maths words will prove hard, but for others it is understanding concepts that is the core of the problem. Frequently in maths we urge children to work quicker, not allowing children with difficulties enough time to complete their work. I always think that when you think you have allowed children enough time, you should try to allow them a little bit more (although I appreciate that is easier said than done for a busy teacher).

Many adults say that they were hopeless at maths and hated the subject: for some reason it seems that it is acceptable for someone to be no good at maths, although they would not expect others to find it acceptable if they were unable to read. Many parents do find mathematics very difficult: William's report (2008) found that '15–20% of adults do not have basic functional numeracy skills, many parents will be unable to support their child's learning'. Even so they still question the school assessment procedures and the quality of the teaching their child has received.

Teacher observation

A teacher should begin to notice a child who:

- becomes anxious in maths lessons;
- is slow to understand any numerical information;
- cannot give a quick answer in an oral session;
- claims to be 'thick and stupid';
- uses fingers to count, often still seeing numbers as groups of 'ones';
- struggles with place value and size value of numbers;
- is confused over ordering issues, so cannot clearly distinguish between for instance 13 and 31;
- cannot see the pattern in the number system;
- cannot remember the sequence of a calculation;
- cannot give an educated guess at an answer;
- shows a big discrepancy between what is said and what is written down.

Teachers can help by:

- providing vocabulary lists and discussing the meaning of newly introduced maths words;
- using voice recorders and recording maths questions and answers so that they can be replayed;
- using interactive whiteboards;
- using partitioning cards to help with place value and number reversals;
- providing highlighter pens to identify key words in questions;
- providing differentiated worksheets, preferably photocopied on cream-coloured paper;
- making triangular or easy grip pens and pencils available;
- displaying maths symbols clearly in the classroom;
- providing easy to hold rulers;
- having number lines, number squares and table squares readily available;
- providing worksheets to avoid pupils having to copy from a board;
- using computers;
- teaching in structured small steps to meet the child's needs;
- providing maths games.

How parents can help older children at home

Parents of older dyscalculic children frequently struggle to help them at home. Often children are tired, have forgotten the maths concepts and formulae they have been taught that day and probably cannot remember the exact work they are supposed to do. Parents should be encouraged to allow their child to rest after school to recharge their batteries and become destressed. They should try to understand their child's learning style, give support using their strengths, and try to stay calm.

Parents need to discuss with the teacher the importance of:

- making sure a homework diary is used, recording accurately the work that is to be done;
- ensuring the web page plus access codes and passwords are known for school websites where homework may be stored;
- making sure instructions are read slowly, clearly, and that they are understood;
- allowing their child to talk about the work they are doing;
- making sure the right books are taken home and back to school;
- using audio recorders if necessary;
- identifying a student's strengths and weaknesses and promoting strategies to help them learn more effectively;
- practising and reinforcing basic concepts to improve understanding and promote confidence.

As Ostler (1991) says, 'If none of this works, ensure that you have the telephone number of a classmate who will have all the necessary information.'

Intervention at the secondary level

Once a student has gone into secondary education, intervention can prove to be a little more difficult, as often the student has lost confidence and interest in the subject. A teacher will notice students who are always losing track of where they are in a calculation, who struggle with large numbers and who generally seem to be lost in a mist when asked anything to do with maths. A large number of older students have said how they dread and hate maths lessons. Some students value any help that is provided, because they appreciate that their teachers are trying to give them every opportunity to achieve the required grades in mathematics examinations.

Concepts in maths with older students

Many dyslexic and dyscalculic students have an erratic learning style, making leaps in learning when it is least expected. Some students are able to deal with complex concepts without being good with elementary processes, while others, who are unable to link new learning to something they have mastered previously, struggle right from the start.

When a student is receiving help there can be discussion about what has gone wrong. For example, a student might make an error with a decimal place. The supporting professional can discuss the error and if necessary, help the student to make an index card which tells them that each time they are dealing with amounts of money less than a pound, they must take great care with decimal places. This can be reinforced by taking the student through several calculations, making sure that the decimal points are put in correctly and that when the student writes, the points are lined up under each other. A student using a calculator must be sure to record that an amount under a pound is entered by always starting with the decimal point. For example 3p is entered as 0.03, 16p as 0.16 and 78p as 0.78.

Level checklist for understanding concepts in maths

1 I don't understand anything about this.
2 I think I can tell you what my teacher said about it.
3 I can tell you how I am thinking about this.
4 I think I am beginning to have a picture of this in my head.
5 I can show you what I know about this.
6 I can do my worksheet with confidence.
7 I can really understand this and apply it to other topics.
8 I can show the others in my group all about this.

This checklist is useful as a way of categorising just what students know about a topic with which they have asked for help. If they are working at levels 1, 2 or 3, they should go back to the beginning of the topic to start again. This time the topic should be reintroduced in a more appropriate way for their particular learning style, perhaps using different concrete apparatus, more motor movements, and colour and computer software. If they are working at levels 4 or 5 they probably have understood many of the basic concepts, but just a few details need to be discussed and worked through. If they are at the higher levels and have asked for help, it may simply be for reassurance or for some revision tips. Students who are regularly reaching the higher levels are demonstrating that no further help is required.

Some students decide that they cannot do maths so give up, not realising that in fact they are giving up on many other subjects, because as can be seen in Table 4.1, there is a mathematical element in almost every subject in the curriculum. These students will require a lot of emotional as well as cognitive support, if they are to try to overcome their anger and frustration at failing so often.

Classroom management

Classroom management is important at every level, but especially so with older students. Some students, when asked a question, do not give a measured reply, but go to the other extreme and into 'class clown' mode, shouting out silly answers to make the others laugh. That is how they cope with their specific difficulties. This situation makes class teaching very difficult because this kind of irrelevant distraction can spoil the lesson for all concerned. The teacher will feel angry and frustrated because their detailed preparation is wasted, while the majority of the class will lose valuable time when both teaching and learning are on hold. Yet the student causing the disruption knows that after the laughing is over, there is still yet another maths concept they have not grasped. Care must be taken so that the student does not make a habit of becoming MFM (missing for maths).

Many students have said that they like the following:

- looking at the board straight, not sideways;
- having enough space on their desk to work on;
- praise for good work;
- a teacher who gives them enough time;
- discussing maths problems with the others in class;
- being shown clearly what to do.

Table 4.1 How maths is used in other subjects

	Vocabulary	Fractions	Percentages	Basic rules	Equations	Pie charts	Place value	Data handling	Time and money
French	*	*	*	*			*	*	*
English	*	*	*	*		*	*	*	*
History	*	*				*			
Geography	*	*	*	*	*	*	*	*	*
Physics	*	*	*	*	*	*	*	*	
Chemistry	*	*	*	*	*		*	*	
PE	*	*	*	*	*		*		
Art		*	*	*					
Photography	*	*	*	*	*		*	*	*

Disorganised students

Some dyscalculic students seem to be very forgetful and disorganised: they are late for lessons, lose their books, misplace homework or miss appointments with staff.

How to help disorganised students

- Give clear instructions.
- Take small steps, making sure the students understand by careful discussion.
- Ensure students know how to use a calculator accurately.
- Provide study skill sessions.
- Provide a good model to copy or a sequence sheet.
- Give written homework instructions.
- Provide models of different ways of recording maths answers.
- Organise timetables around short and long-term goals (to help ensure that students see the big picture).
- Provide a colour-coded timetable (with different colours for different days/subjects).
- Set written homework.
- Encourage students to make plans to meet assignment deadlines.

It was reported by the BBC in May 2011 that students in Kenfig Comprehensive School did better in their GCSE examinations than had been predicted earlier in their education. In fact their results were the best in South Wales. The head teacher said the good results had been achieved because staff had provided extra intervention sessions from Year 8 in Maths, English and Science. This intervention proved to give enough help to enable students to achieve the required level.

Interaction between classroom and specialist teachers

If students know that their class and specialist teacher are working together, this gives them confidence. They know that should they find any particular difficulty in the mainstream class, they can quite openly bring along work to show to the specialist teacher. Then together they can find a way through the problem, so that the students will not only understand a concept, but also become confident enough to apply it generally throughout maths lessons.

Very often a specialist teacher has access to different resource material as well as different school situations. They provide an opportunity for students to acquire new and varying knowledge to which a classroom teacher might not have access. The classroom teacher on the other hand is an expert at working with a particular topic and indeed a particular group of students, so they have the opportunity to pass useful information to the special teacher. This interchange of ideas keeps doors open, linking different information.

Successful inclusion

For inclusion at any level to be a success, teachers and teaching assistants should have sessions built into their weekly timetables in order to prepare long-term goals and lesson objectives. However, if teaching assistants are timetabled to work with students from 8.30 am to 3.30 pm, it is almost impossible for the teacher to plan and discuss a shared vision with them. *Time for this exchange of information should be programmed into the school timetable.*

Any teacher should find helping children and seeing them make progress (if often slowly) rewarding. As more teachers cater for differing learning styles by using multi-sensory approaches, visual, audio and kinaesthetic techniques, they begin to see smiles in the classroom instead of worried frowns. When children start to enjoy maths lessons, they relax as they begin to make sense of the number words and number patterns they are learning.

Case study: Simon (aged 10)

When doing maths Simon often had panic attacks. His teacher discussed his problem with him, and they worked out a plan. When he began to feel panicky, Simon was to place his hands on the table and think of the three-times table. Doing this enabled him to calm down. The teacher spent much time in discussion with Simon, to explore his fears and also to boost his confidence and develop his understanding of how he learned. She drew up a memory card (number 1, see page 141) to show Simon's thinking style, and had him put it in his memory wallet. Throughout the sessions spent to support Simon, the teacher revisited and reinforced work from earlier lessons that he still did not fully comprehend. She used two assessments, the Dyscalculia Screener and the Basic Number Screening Test, to identify the precise nature of Simon's difficulties.

Dyscalculia Screener assessment

Simon's dyscalculia assessment identified that he had a low overall performance, and that his scores were particularly low across two capacity tests (dot enumeration and numerical stroop). This pattern of results is typical of a dyscalculic child. The assessment indicated that he did not understand numerosities, and recommended that:

- any intervention should focus on very basic aspects of arithmetic
- any attempt at rote learning would lead to frustration and avoidance
- intervention should focus on helping Simon to master use of a calculator
- further diagnostic assessment should be carried out.

Diagnostic assessment

Diagnosis showed that Simon had problems with:

- number work and bigger numbers (HTU: hundreds, tens, units)
- mental calculation strategies (× ÷ + −)
- doubling/halving
- fractions/decimals/percentages
- times tables/multiplication
- problem-solving word problems.

Number work and mental strategies

It was apparent that reading large numbers caused Simon problems, so a copy of memory card 6 (see page 141) was put into his memory wallet as a memory jogger. Later after discussion memory card 5, showing important numbers, was also put in the wallet. By the end of the session Simon could read numbers beyond a million with zeros in different places, but although he could now read the numbers he did not understand their size or value.

Initially Simon was helped with Dienes blocks to become familiar with HTU. He liked this apparatus, but still struggled to see connections and patterns that would help when adding three-digit numbers to two-digit numbers. Through all this work, the teacher supported Simon by encouraging him to use a place value line so that he could see the numbers clearly, improving his visualisation skills. Lots of practical work was used throughout to reinforce concepts.

Simon was shown quick ways to add up 9, 10 and 11, using Dienes blocks, which show that 10 – 1 is good for adding 9, and 10 + 1 is good for adding 11. Later he was helped to use this method to add 8 and then 12, and eventually when he had grasped this method, he went on to practise quick ways to add 99, 100 and 101. Once he had mastered the method the teacher showed him how to use it for subtraction, and by the end he was calculating answers quickly and accurately. This addition and subtraction work continued, with Simon being showed strategies for adding two digits to three digits, mentally bridging tens and hundreds using more mental strategies and less concrete materials.

Doubling/halving

The teacher started off the one-to-one lessons by having Simon count beans, to show him how to recognise patterns. Eventually Simon comprehended the concept, which was apparent when he said, 'It's your two-times table.' Then the teacher extended his range to doubling and halving larger numbers (up to 20) using Dienes blocks. Simon became more confident when halving even numbers, but was less so with numbers that included odd digits. The teacher showed him a technique to halve 78, by separating the odd number (70) into two units of 60 and 10. This worked with him. Eventually he was halving numbers such as 758 in the way shown in Figure 4.3.

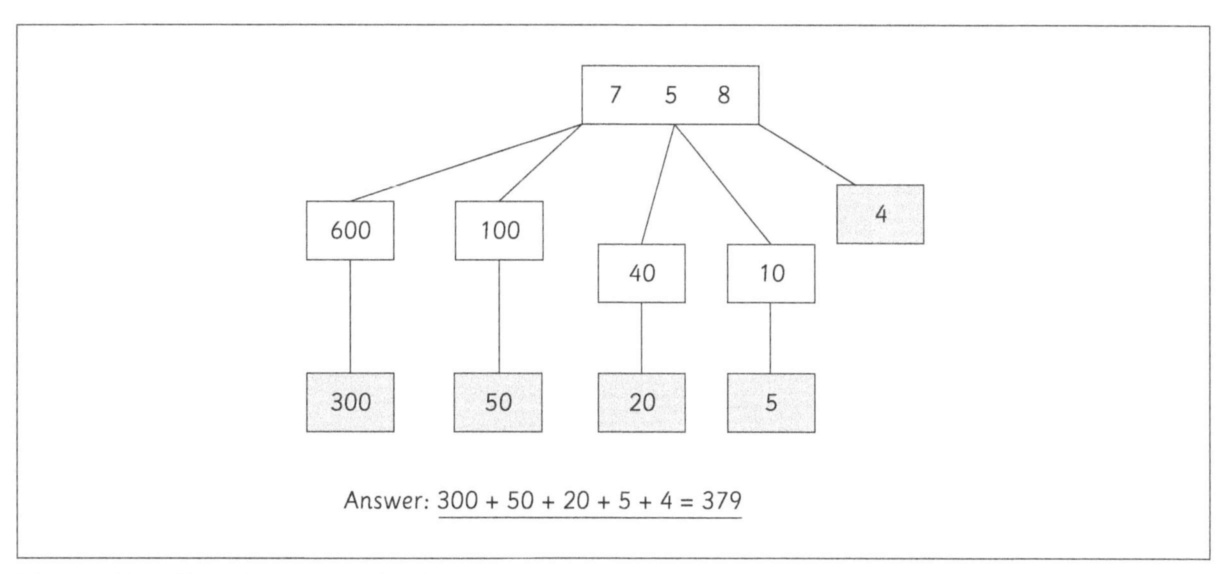

Figure 4.3 Simon's method for halving 758

Fractions

The teacher helped Simon to understand fractions by making an A5 copy of a fractions wall (see Figure 6.8, page 73) which shows how a unit can be divided up from a whole one down to tenths. She laminated the figure and referred to it constantly during these lessons. Simon did some work on percentages using concrete objects and number lines to demonstrate the relationship between fractions and percentages. The teacher made up and laminated fraction cards (see numbers 10 and 11, page 142) to help Simon with these connections.

Times tables

Simon liked to do some times table work using his fingers, but became more interested when dice and a table quiz were brought into the lesson. He set himself goals that were achievable, and continually improved his strategies.

Problem solving

Word problems like the following caused Simon problems:

> *Laura paid £175.49 for a CD player, which had been reduced from £216.50. How much did she save?*

He could not readily connect the question with the addition and subtraction techniques needed to answer it, so he could not work out what he had to do. The teacher tried to put the question in a context he could relate to (buying a present for a family member), and took him through the calculation using easier numbers. Finally Simon began to make sense of it. Later the teacher used a memory card (number 4, see page 141) to help him learn a strategy to help with written questions.

Summary

Simon made steady progress through the one-to-one support he was given. It enabled him to master many basic concepts, and with continued practice he slowly began to make important connections. It was recommended that support continued to boost his self-esteem, that access to suitable computer software would promote his use of strategies, and that his calculator skills should be reinforced to help maintain his confidence.

Intervention success

Nothing succeeds like success. That is an old adage that teachers of dyslexic and dyscalculic children should remember! (See the acronym in the box below.)

Success

Start from where the child is struggling with a maths concept, and allow plenty of time.
Understand the problem, use questions to evaluate, consolidate and monitor progress.
Concrete materials and good support worksheets are essential.
Communication is vital: allow children time to talk and discuss, and listen to them.
Easy to understand drawings, diagrams, procedures and numbers help with comprehension.
Structured lessons should build on knowledge mastered.
Small steps should be used, not long explanations.

5 Early numeracy skills

Section A: Early numeracy

Language

When children talk to others they become involved, motivated and more inclined to remember what they have been doing. Talking expresses thoughts, so when discussing maths ideas children make connections and begin to understand the words. A word only starts to have meaning when children try it out, experiment with its meaning and see how it fits in with their thinking. When teachers listen to group discussions they can identify misconceptions and recognise the concepts that children have grasped or not grasped.

How to help

- Encourage 'talk' about maths, as this promotes sharing of ideas.
- Encourage translating maths into a story they can relate to, for instance $3 + 2 = 5$ translated as 'Mum bought three apples then two more so altogether she had five apples.'
- Let children get used to new words easily.
- Make wall and ceiling charts of important numbers (use numbers specific to the child).
- Recite numbers in order.
- Use number lines showing the number sequence and words to help with the sequence of the number system.
- Sing songs and rhymes.

One, two, three, four, five
Once I caught a fish alive,
Six, seven, eight, nine, ten,
Then I let it go again,
Why did you let it go?
Because it bit my finger so,
Which finger did it bite?

This little finger on the right

Memory

How to help

- Present information in small 'chunks' so the short term memory is not overloaded.
- Use multi-sensory methods: practical apparatus, colour, music, large and small motor movements, stories, cheeky rhymes to make information 'stick'.
- Point out clearly specific points that need to be emphasised.

Visual-spatial difficulties

Visual-spatial difficulties may affect a child's ability to write and copy numbers correctly and may inhibit them from mastering the sequence of numbers.

How to help

- Use sand, clay, sandpaper and tracing on hand and backs to focus on numeral formation. The Early Years Foundation Stage framework encourages children to learn through play using these mediums.
- Use dotted shapes of numbers that can be written over to help with number shapes.
- Give lots of practice with looking at numbers, saying them aloud, writing them down then checking back to see that it has been done correctly.

Visualisation skills

Visualisation skills are helpful when basic maths skills are being taught as very little is written down. Encouraging children to 'Close your eyes and see in your mind's eye' can be a positive start in developing mental strategies.

How to help

Pupils need to:

- see numbers – the pattern and shape of numbers;
- see numbers as wholes not clusters of ones;
- see a number line, putting numbers in order;
- see number positions on a picture number line;
- see connections – such as between 'adding on' and 'taking away';
- see – 'one more' and 'one less';
- see an answer, maybe a guess or an estimate;
- see an empty number line and put the numbers 1 to 5 on it.

Visualisation game

Visualise the numbers 1 to 8.

Put them mentally into two rows with four in each (see Table 5.1).

Close your eyes.

What number is under 4?

Is the number 6 under the number 3?

What number is under 2?

Table 5.1

1	**2**	**3**	**4**
5	**6**	**7**	**8**

Extend the game by starting with the numbers 1 to 12 in three rows, visualising the number under the 8 and so on.

Counting

Counting is a most important skill, and counting accurately is just as important. Children need to understand that the counting order is always the same, that the sequence is always the same so the number words themselves are always constant. Often if children have fun, working in groups, when they practise counting skills the numbers become more automatic. When children understand the sequence of the numbers and feel happy with them, then counting forwards, backwards, stopping and starting again will be easy. Later on children need to recognise visually and orally that 15 fifteen is different from 50 fifty. Connecting that saying' teen' makes the mouth 'smile' can help them understand it is different from saying 'ty'.

How to help

- Have fun playing with counting apparatus to embed important number facts in memory.
- Say numbers in order.
- Count accurately a specific number of objects.
- Count exciting objects like dinosaurs, frogs, pretty coloured beads and flowers.
- Put a dinosaur on each space of an empty number line.
- Provide tactile numbers: wooden, plastic and magnetic.
- Large wall and floor number grids help with large motor movements while reinforcing the number system.

A Chinese proverb:

> *What I see – I forget.*
> *What I hear – I remember.*
> *What I do – I understand.*

Multi-sensory teaching

Multi-sensory teaching at all stages will help children to internalise each concept. This means using concrete apparatus, pictures, colours, singing, music, clapping, tambourine tapping, large motor movements (like jumping from numeral to numeral painted on the floor), sand and water. There should be lots of games and lots of repetition to reinforce each step. Technology provides interactive programmes that help children learn, so computer programs specially designed to meet the needs of children who struggle in maths like Dynamo Maths are very useful. Interactive white boards as well as individual white boards are a big help for teachers to reinforce certain topics. Specific applications on DS and iPad technology provide children with teaching games that can be very beneficial. It is important to remember that all children are different and have their own unique way of learning, so prefer apparatus and teaching that suit their learning style. Above all children should be taught at their own individual learning pace, and for those children who base all strategies on counting in ones, intervention may need to be slower and more intensive.

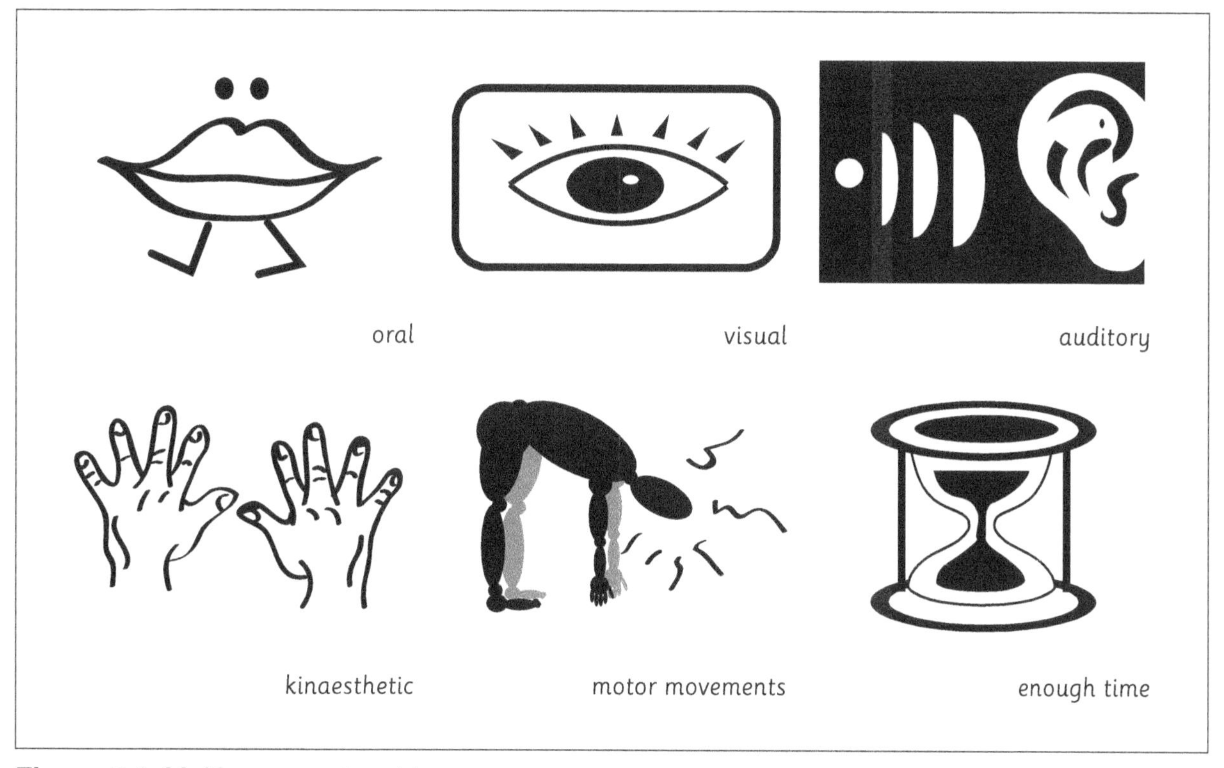

Figure 5.1 Multi-sensory teaching

Numicon

Numicon shapes are multi-sensory three-dimensional apparatus that provide structured imagery of the numerals. They are recommended in conjunction with other resources to help with numeracy skills.

Dealing with anxiety

The coloured shapes give children the 'big' picture of the value and sequence of numbers so they can grasp size and relationships between numbers. The shapes are easy to hold, helping the dyspraxic child, and fun to use. In this way lessons become enjoyable, which takes away the anxiety often associated with maths lessons. Once children have mastered the shapes, coloured number rods are used to move children further along with their mathematical thinking.

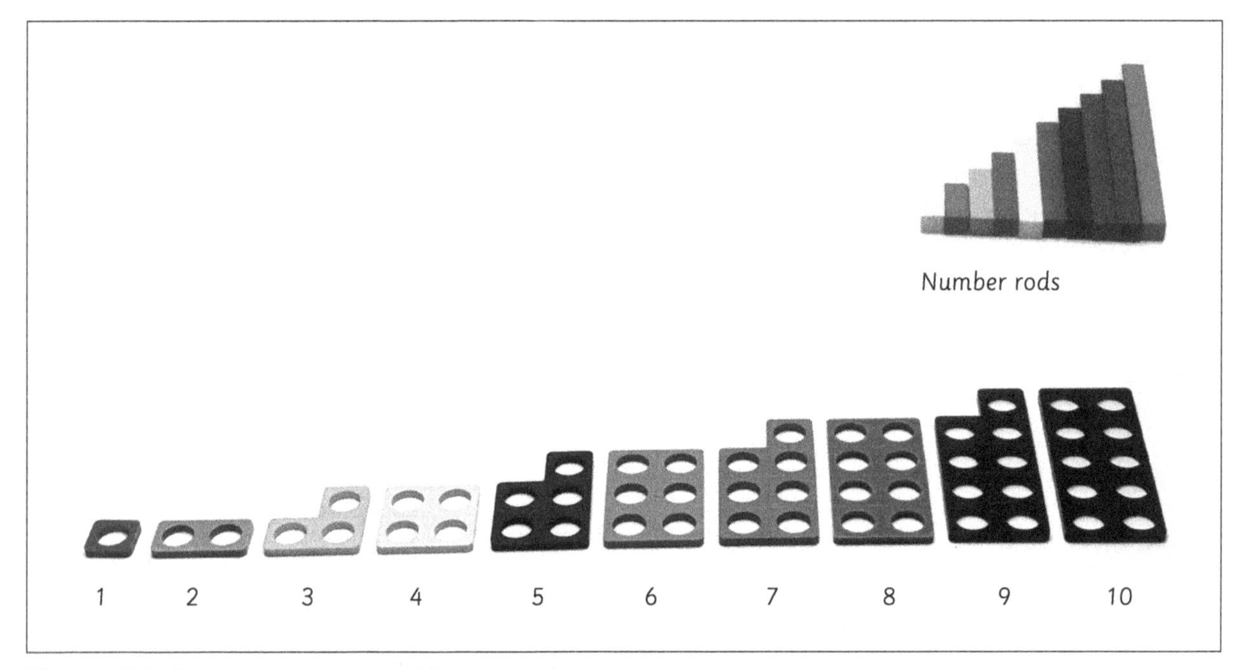

Figure 5.2 Numicon shapes with numerals

Seeing numbers as wholes

Children often find counting very difficult; it is often slow and done incorrectly, resulting in wrong answers. They need to practise reciting numbers, and this becomes easier with the help of a number line and numeral cards. Numicon provides a large-format book for introducing numeral recognition to young children (*Numicon at the Seaside, Big Book*). This Big Book is complemented by a CD with songs for each numeral plus small-sized books for group reading so all can sing together. One-to-one correspondence is so important for children to grasp, and this can be done with the shapes and counters filling in the holes.

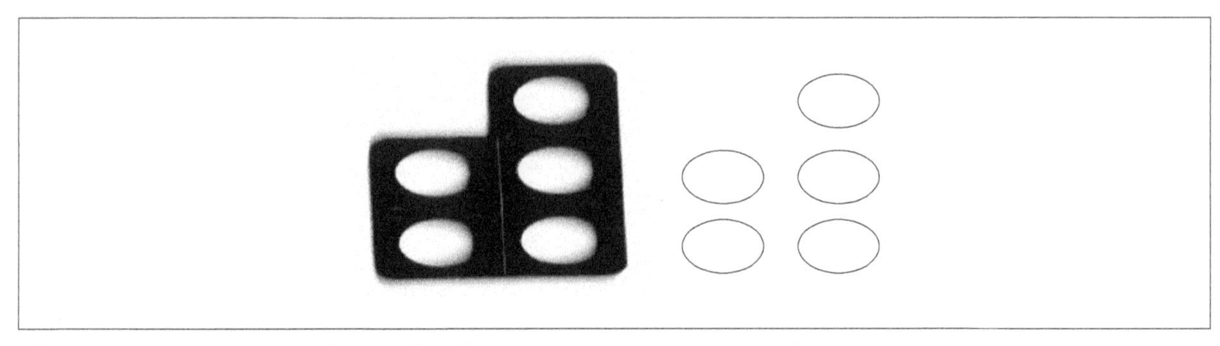

Figure 5.3 A Numicon shape showing one-to-one correspondence

Seeing numbers as wholes improves visualisation skills and can help dyscalculic children with their 'number sense' as they begin to appreciate the value of numbers. The structured images of the Numicon shapes have a pattern that they become familiar with by playing in sand and water and by exploring ideas with the shapes in the classroom.

Sequences

Wall charts and large number lines provide visual representation that helps children remember the order of the number sequence. Desk number lines allow for easy access to the sequences, and the children are able to make comparisons between the shapes and the number pictures.

The language of maths

The exciting and multisensory approach by Numicon to the five basic symbols is most helpful for all children as they are shown with physical actions.

It can make an original start to a maths lesson to have a whole class stand up and then call out the name of a maths symbol. The actions of the children will provide a way for the teacher to continually assess who really understands the differing names for the symbols. In this way the children start to put together – add – shapes and check their answer with another shape. Once again they are extending their own maths language.

The equals symbols = is clearly demonstrated with arm movements, and this is reinforced with the use of an easy-to-use weighing balance. The Numicon shapes weigh accurately so children can physically put a 3 and a 5 onto one of the scale pans, then by putting an 8 shape on the other pan will see that they are equal. The children are seeing equivalence: the shapes look different but are of equal value.

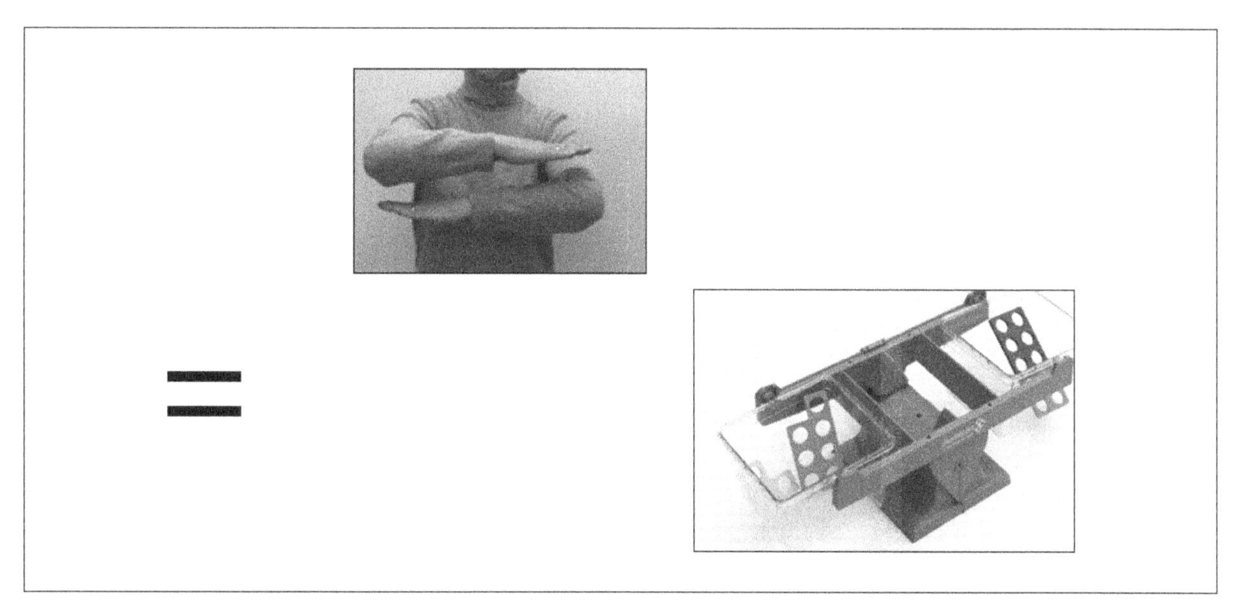

Figure 5.4 Equality, equivalence and action

Mathematical language is used constantly as the children play with the shapes in pairs and small groups, discussing their actions. Children are encouraged to make up arithmetic stories to fit in with their actions. Subtraction, multiplication and division all are clearly shown with the apparatus. A three-dimensional number line enables the coloured number rods to be incorporated into the activity, to show multiplication and its inverse, division, very well.

Confusion with the language of division, for instance how many 3s in 9; divide 3 into 9; share 9 into 3s and split 9 into 3 groups, can be shown with the apparatus.

Numicon helps with grouping in tens. This is supported with visual imagery, which is so important as children meet the teen numbers. Partitioning cards can also fit in with the Numicon apparatus to reinforce this. A number line with Numicon numbers up to 100 put along a corridor illustrates number and place values clearly. The easy-to-use interactive white board technology makes lessons vibrant and interesting.

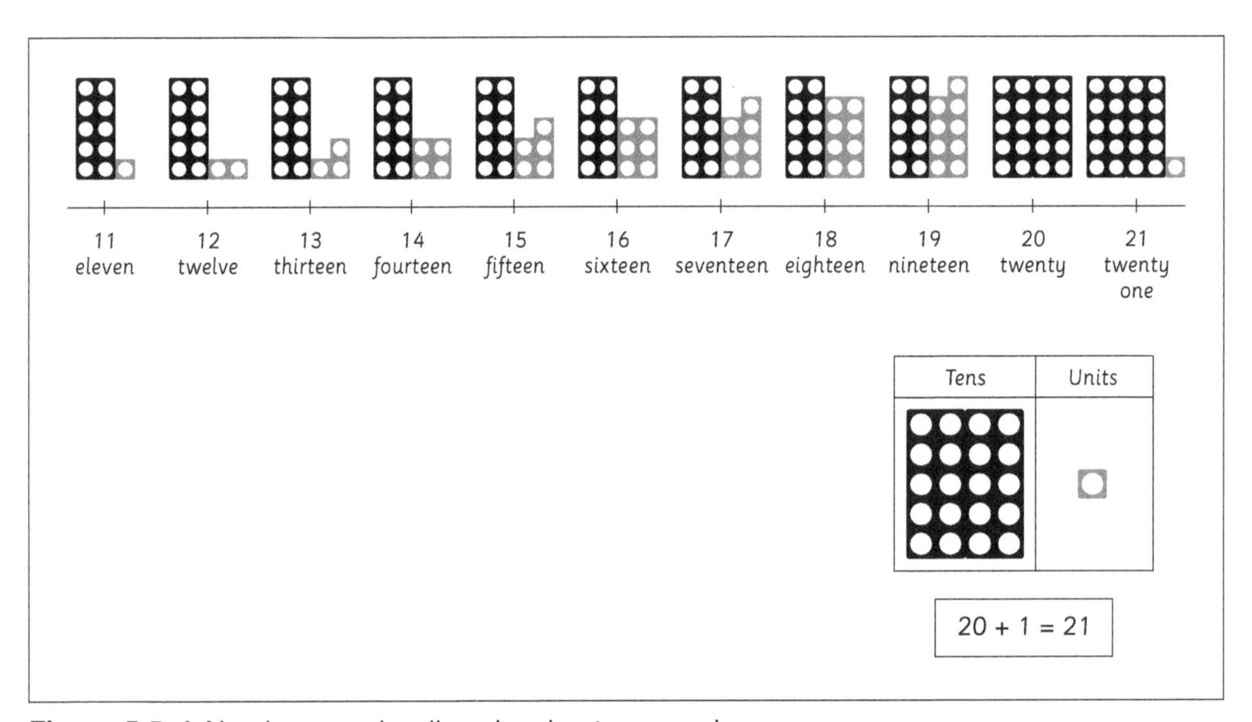

Figure 5.5 A Numicon number line showing teen numbers

Teacher training

Teachers need to be trained thoroughly in intervention techniques before they begin to use Numicon. The Diagnostic Assessment is closely linked to Planning Signposts, Teaching and Assessing Guidance. All Numicon Kits have photocopiable masters plus activity groups, all following the National Curriculum, and all have:

- a clear structure – the pupils follow numbered activities in order
- highlights to show the aim of each activity
- clear descriptions of each activity
- ways of making connections
- a language vocabulary box
- assessment questions to promote continuous assessment.

The Numicon Diagnostic Assessment Checklist includes the aspects shown in Table 5.2.

Table 5.2 The Numicon Diagnostic Assessment Checklist

Oral counting	Comparison of number
Counting object	Recognising and naming arithmetic symbols
Recognising and naming numerals	Addition and subtraction
Recognising and devising sequences	Rapid recall of addition and subtraction facts
Ordering structured apparatus and numerals	Inverse
Writing numerals	Addition and subtraction calculations
Recognising number patterns	Using and applying
Place value	Multiplication and division

Other influential factors that affect early numeracy skills

Other difficulties that affect learning should always be taken into consideration. Coordination problems linked to dyspraxia, lack of concentration and visual stress often impede a child's progress. A teacher always has to provide appropriate support so that a child's self-esteem and confidence remain high. Grauberg (1998) liked to work with quantity pictures before moving children onto number squares.

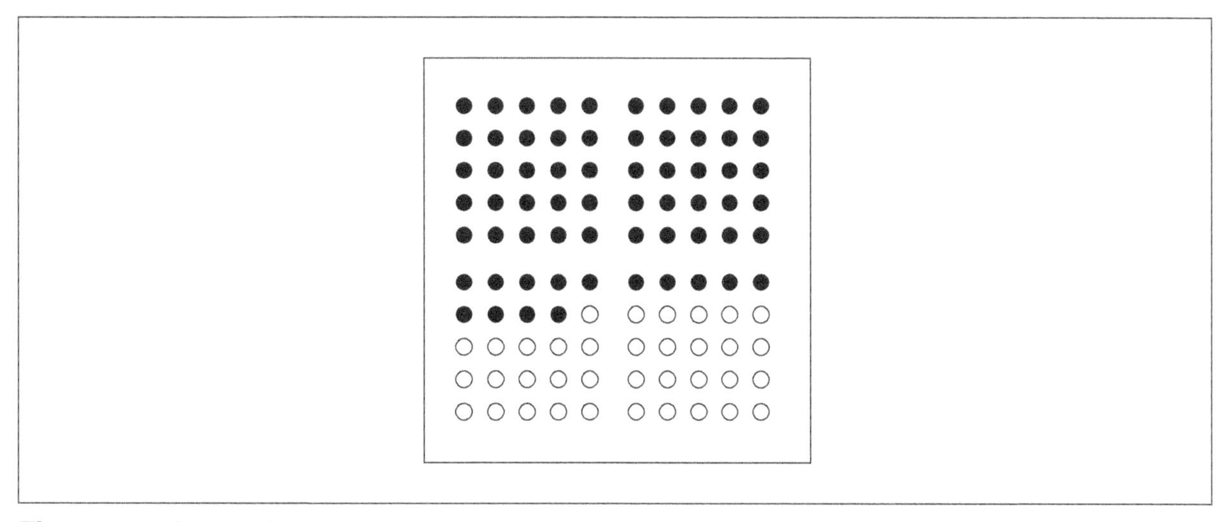

Figure 5.6 A quantity picture showing a value of 64

Children need to understand the value of numerals, so the teacher should help with practical apparatus, play and as many practical experiences as necessary.

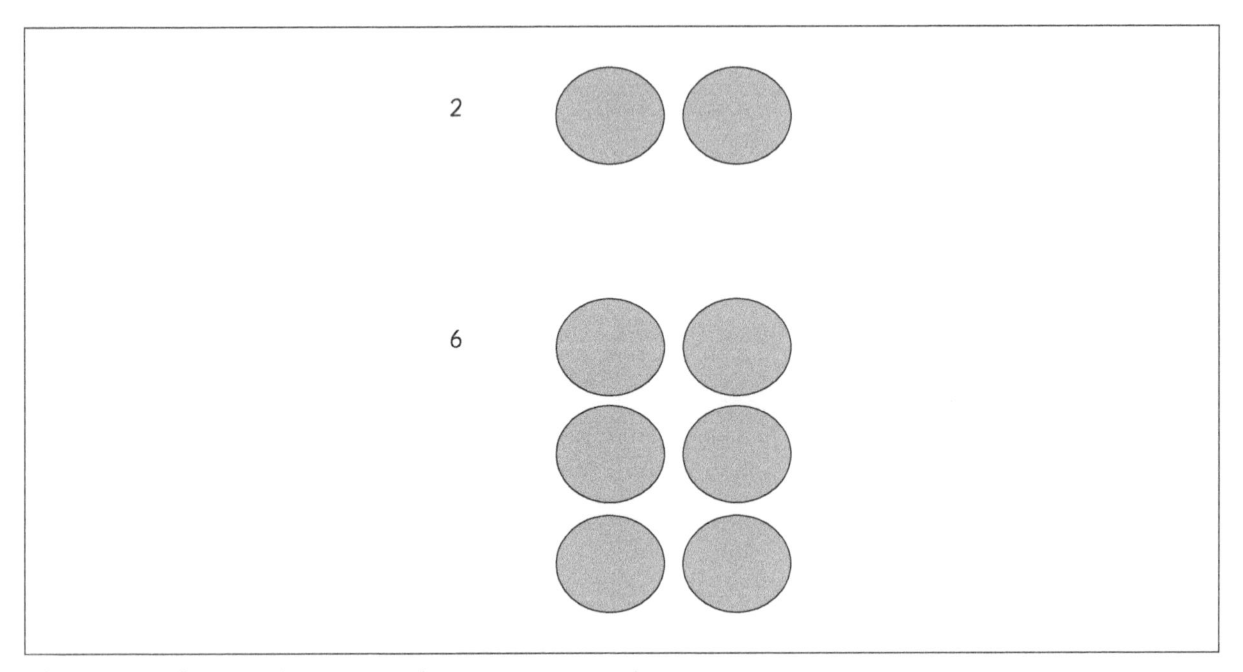

Figure 5.7 Connecting numerals to correct number patterns

Later this has to be connected to the number line, always accompanied with pictures, concrete apparatus and lots of fun.

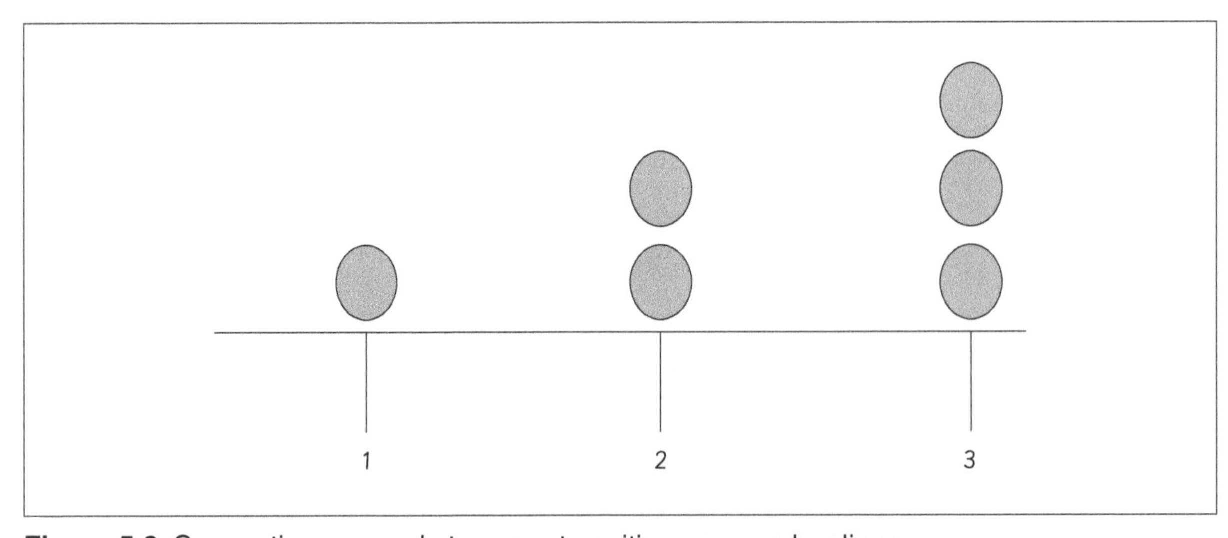

Figure 5.8 Connecting numerals to correct positions on number lines

Calculating

Once children know the sequence of the numerals on the number line, the number bonds to 10 are very important for them to remember. Children with learning problems may need intensive support at this stage to commit these early number concepts to long-term memory.

> *Dowker (2004) describes a 20-minute successful intervention strategy when children received two to three minutes practicing counting skills, two minutes revising individual known facts, ten to twelve minutes practicing derived fact strategies building on known facts, and two minutes playing with big numbers or working on a problem.*

Children begin to combine two groups of numbers and relate the action to addition, gradually understanding that the inverse subtraction means taking a number away. Taking time with this will benefit all children as these bonds are a vital part of the patterns throughout the number system. Children who have them in long-term memory have an advantage over other children because the knowledge will stand them in good stead throughout their lives.

The Helical Number Line

The Numdrum is a continuous number line wound round a cylinder with ten numbers for each turn. It is often described as a helical number line. It introduces children to a more structured number system following on from the number line. It forms number patterns as seen on the number square, but the direction is upwards starting with zero, so the larger numbers are higher up the Numdrum. Children find it fun to use because they can see number patterns easily as they turn it around, recognising the smaller numbers at the bottom and appreciating the bigger numbers at the top.

Number lines and squares

More advanced patterns of number bonds can be seen on number lines but become more effective when they are identified on a number square. Some children prefer number lines and squares with the zero shown (see Table 5.3).

Table 5.3

0	1	2	3	4	5	6	7	8	9
10	11	12	13	14	15	16	17	18	19

Others prefer number lines and squares without the zero (Table 5.4).

Table 5.4

1	2	3	4	5	6	7	8	9	10
11	12	13	14	15	16	17	18	19	20

Patterns of number bonds seen on part of the number square enable children to understand calculations, for instance:

$2 + 5 = 7$ $\qquad$ $2 + 15 = 17$

Some children prefer the number square starting with 1 (Table 5.5) on the bottom row with the bigger numbers ascending.

Table 5.5

91	92	93	94	95	96	97	98	99	100
81	82	83	84	85	86	87	88	89	90
71	72	73	74	75	76	77	78	79	80
61	62	63	64	65	66	67	68	69	70
51	52	53	54	55	56	57	58	59	60
41	42	43	44	45	46	47	48	49	50
31	32	33	34	35	36	37	38	39	40
21	22	23	24	25	26	27	28	29	30
11	12	13	14	15	16	17	18	19	20
1	2	3	4	5	6	7	8	9	10

Some children prefer number squares with the 0 at the top (Table 5.6) with bigger numbers descending.

Table 5.6

0	1	2	3	4	5	6	7	8	9
10	11	12	13	14	15	16	17	18	19
20	21	22	23	24	25	26	27	28	29
30	31	32	33	34	35	36	37	38	39
40	41	42	43	44	45	46	47	48	49
50	51	52	53	54	55	56	57	58	59
60	61	62	63	64	65	66	67	68	69
70	71	72	73	74	75	76	77	78	79
80	81	82	83	84	85	86	87	88	89
90	91	92	93	94	95	96	97	98	99

Patterns of columns ending in 2s and rows starting with 2s shown in number square

As children grasp the sequence, size, value, patterns and connections of these interrelated facts, counting in 2s, 5s and 10s using number lines and squares becomes easy to do.

Number squares can provide endless fun as children are asked to find, for instance:

- a row where all numbers start with 2 or 8 or 5;
- a column where all numbers end in 2 or 6 or 9;
- a number that is bigger than 30 less than 40, is even and is a multiple of 6.

Section B: Maths symbols

The five basic symbols

Connecting symbols and words in mathematics is difficult for children of all ages. Visual images that show the symbol and the words have proved to be most successful.

These symbols must be introduced one at a time with younger children. Older children, who are still struggling with word–symbol connections, can be shown all the symbols together on the same page. This is followed by discussion of each one individually, noting the similarity between the subtraction and division sign but not allowing 'Miss, can I take the dots off the division and do subtraction as I'm better at that?' To link multiplication/addition and subtraction/division, colour each pair in the same or a similar colour. You can discuss the similarity of the signs and then give a practical demonstration of how multiplication is a quick way of doing addition and how that sign also gives bigger answers.

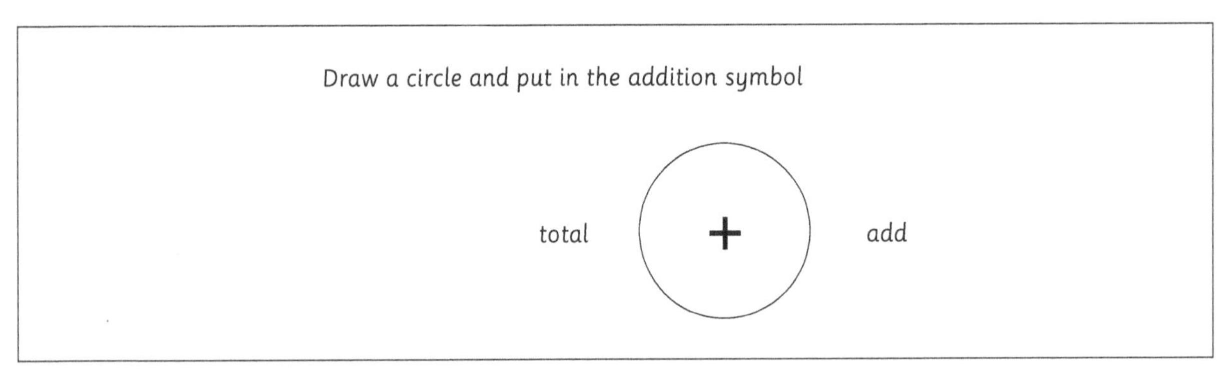

Figure 5.9 A method of introducing symbols

How to help

- Draw a circle and put in it the addition symbol.
- Add words that the child uses regularly to describe that symbol, such as 'add' and 'total'.
- Discuss what the symbol means and what sort of answer we shall find if we use the symbol.
- After much discussion use apparatus to work out a few calculations, and ensure the child notes that the answer is bigger than either of the two numbers they have added together.
- Continue in this way until all symbols have been written down and discussed. Then display the symbols as in Figure 5.10 which correspond with the way they are displayed on the calculator. Make a memory card (number 7, see page 142) showing the symbols with connecting words.

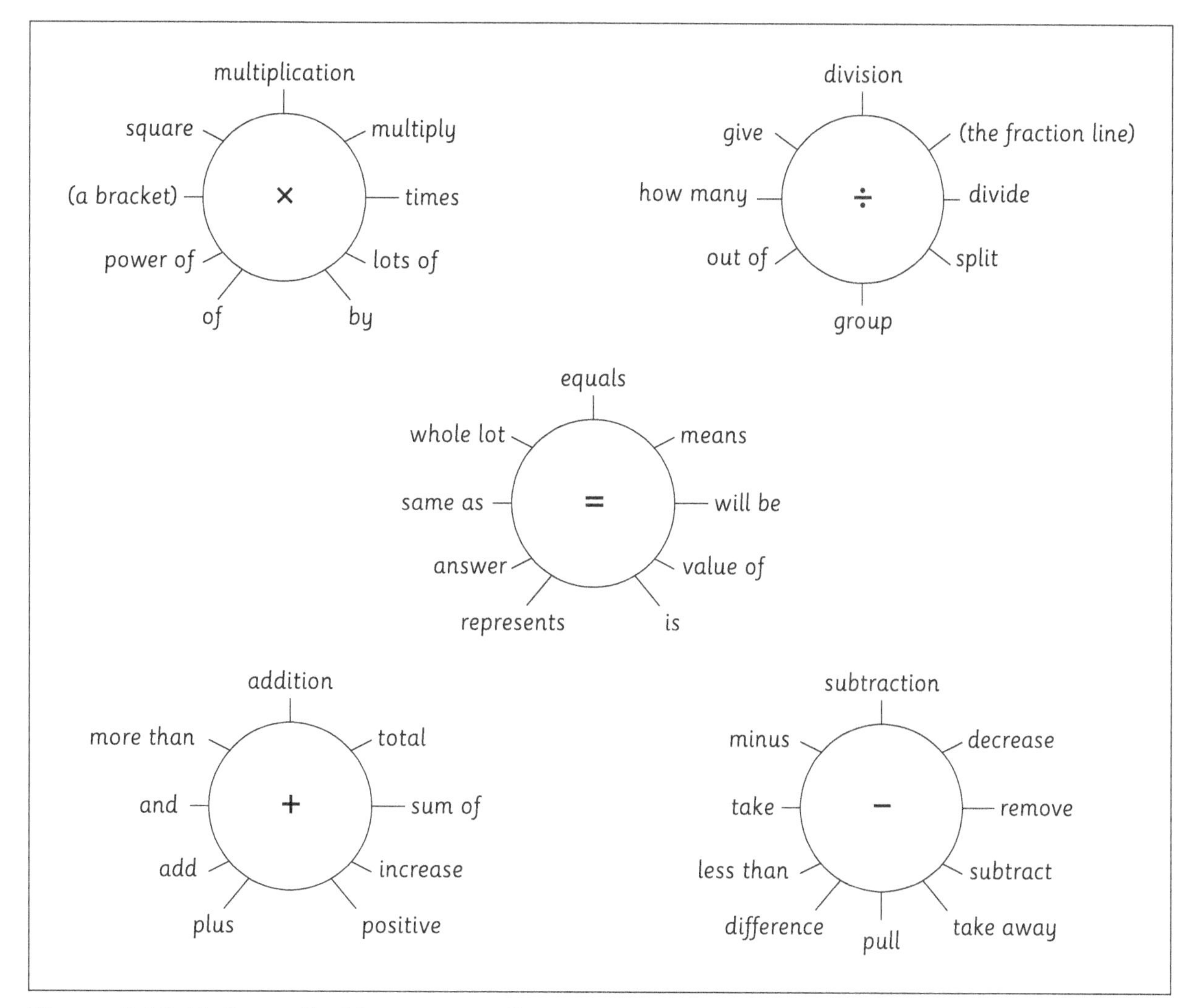

Figure 5.10 Mathematical language patterns

Word problems and symbols

When teaching the solving of written questions, procedures need to be discussed. After reading through a problem, highlight or underline (whatever method the child prefers) the important parts, just as you would do in a comprehension exercise, so that instead of children seeing a mass of words, certain sections become clearer and offer a 'way through' a problem. Once a problem has been discussed and a method chosen, encourage the children to write down the mathematical symbol in the place where they would normally use it, and highlight it.

How to help

- Ask 'Is your answer going to be bigger than the original number, or less?'
- If the answer is going to be bigger, decide whether + or × is the symbol to use (+ is a slower way of doing ×).
- If the answer is going to be smaller, decide whether – or ÷ is the symbol to use.

Dyslexic and dyscalculic children try to avoid both of these processes!

However, the decision between – and ÷ is usually easy, as children seem to recognise the subtraction computation quickly – perhaps seeing it as the 'easy' alternative to dividing.

If children are confident, encourage them to estimate an answer. If they are terrified of estimation (many of them are), practise a few estimations together to show how easy it is to use whole or easy numbers. Write the estimated answer down and then check answers on a calculator.

Begin to work through a problem, using pictures or diagrams only if the child finds that this method helps. Many children have said that they find drawings distract their mind from the mathematics. Encourage them to see the problem in their 'mind's eye'. Once children have become proficient with these symbols and more confident with mathematics, it is possible to tell them that when we multiply with a number less than one, the answer is in fact smaller than the original number, and likewise, when we divide with a number less than one, the answer is bigger. However, from experience it is essential to choose the moment with care when this is done or much confusion will ensue.

The equals symbol

The equals sign is very important so it needs a colour of its own. Children using calculators do not realise that the = sign on the calculator means equals. They simply press the button that gives them the answer. They need to talk about the equal balance that is on each side of an equation. For instance:

$3 + 5 = 8$ $\qquad$ $8 - 5 = 3$ $\qquad$ $8 - 3 = 5$

If children are taught this when they are young, it appears to help them later on when they have to deal with equations in all subjects across the curriculum.

'Greater than' and 'less than'

This topic is generally introduced early, but children only deal with its formal application later. Children need to be aware that sometimes instead of the equals sign indicating a balance of equal amounts on each side of an equation, the > or < signs are used. These signs indicate an inequality, showing that one side of the balance is bigger than the other.

The words 'greater than' are represented by the symbol >

'bigger than'

'more than'

The words 'smaller than' are represented by the symbol <

'less than'

The Greedy Robot (see Figure 5.11) is ideal for teaching children the importance of placing the symbol correctly. The robot only eats the biggest numbers, and that is why his open mouth is pointing towards them. Once children become used to this procedure, the robot's body can be missed out and only the symbol remains. Make a Memory Card (number 8, see page 142) of the robot.

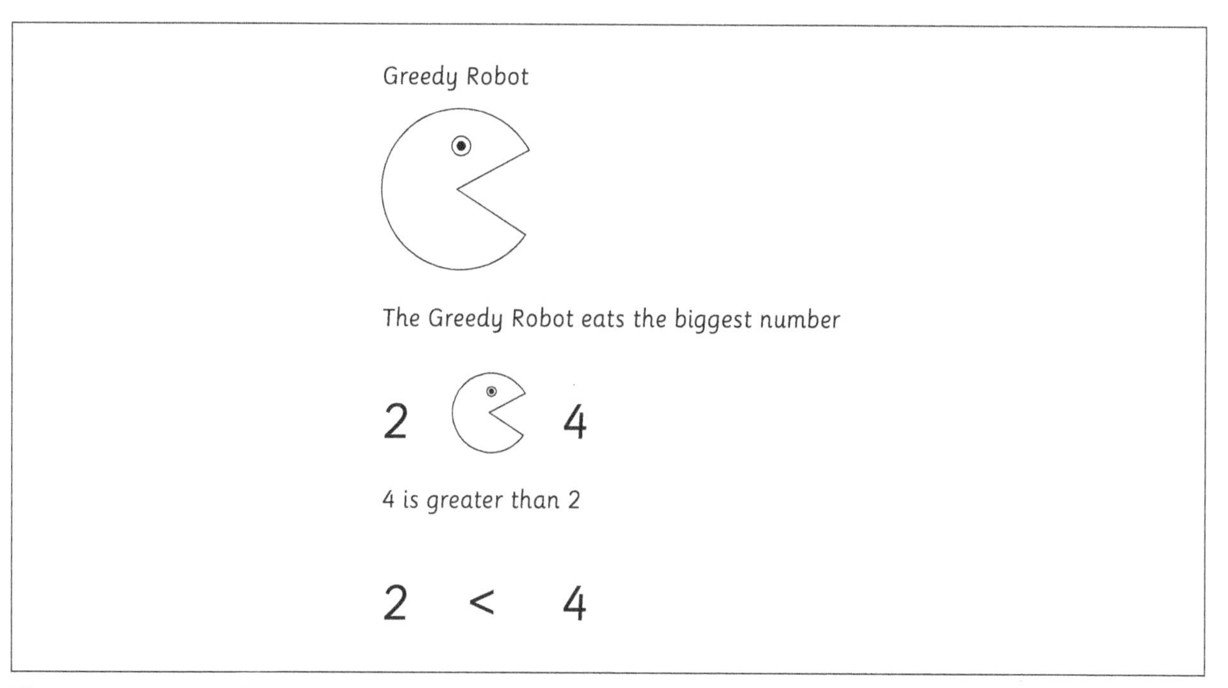

Figure 5.11 The Greedy Robot

Section C: Basic number skills

Odd and even numbers

Encourage discussion about odd and even numbers. (Numicon shapes are excellent to help with this.)

Colouring in patterns and constant referral to odd and even number patterns on a 1–100 square helps reinforce these number facts.

Make up rhymes that could help, like those below.

Try to remember the following thought:

Even numbers end 2, 4, 6, 8 or nought.

Remember, remember the following rhyme:

Odd numbers end 1, 3, 5, 7 or nine.

Point out that the last digit dictates whether a number is odd or even:

For example:

57	the 7 makes the number odd
132	the 2 makes the number even
17,846	the 6 makes the number even.

Factors

Numbers that divide exactly into another number without a remainder are factors. A factor 'creature' can help, especially if separate cards showing all the factors of one number are made using coloured sticky paper to make the creature exciting. Creatures with lots of legs enable children to write the relating factors on separate legs.

The 'Factorpus' with the factors on the ends of its legs can help to make the concept of factors 'stick'. Figure 5.12 shows the factors of 12 and Figure 5.13 the factors of 24.

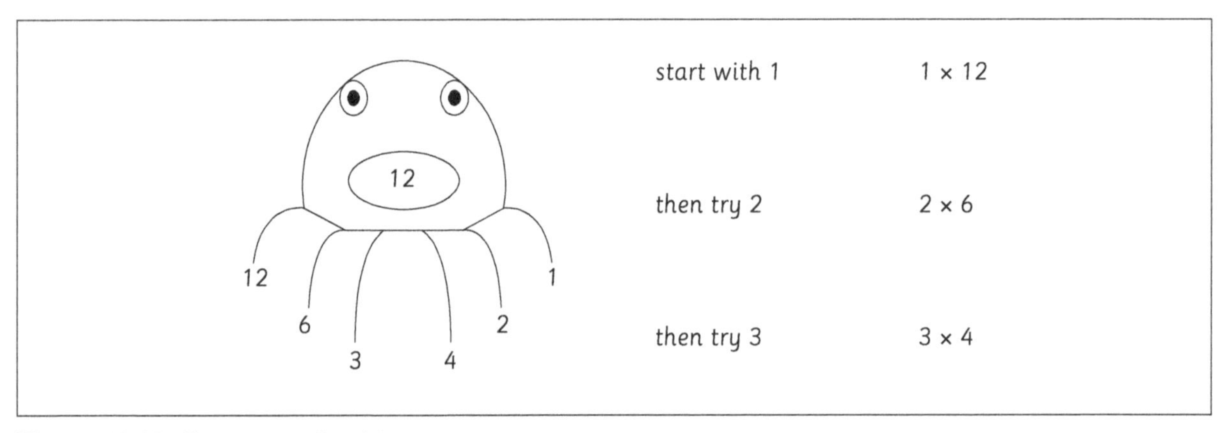

Figure 5.12 Factorpus for 12

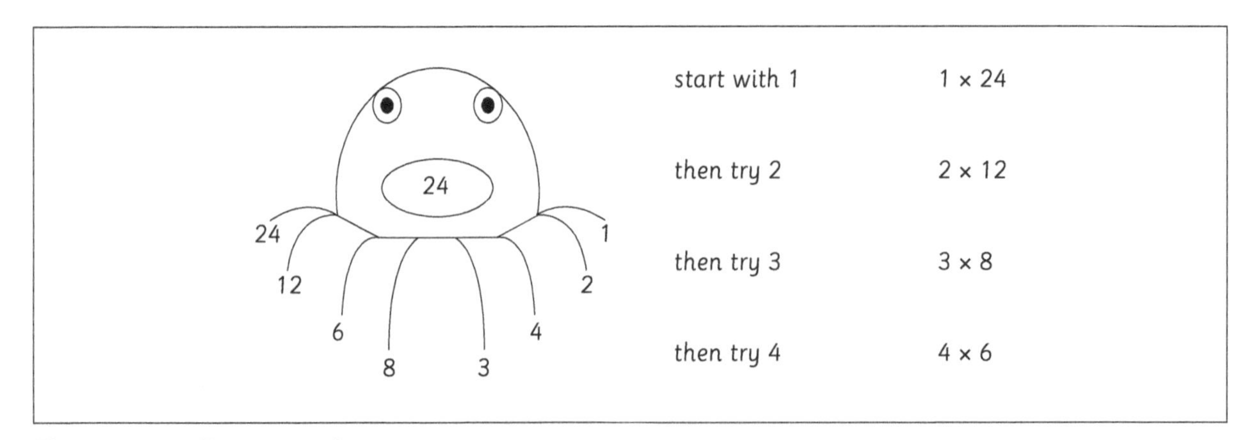

Figure 5.13 Factorpus for 24

Make a Factorpus for other numbers like 18, 20 and 40.

A table square can be useful in helping children to find factors as well as number facts as they search through the square to find answers. Once a child has made a pack of factor cards, games can be played to show how quick and accurate they have become.

Some hints for finding factors

- 2 is a factor of all even numbers
- 3 is a factor when the digits of a number add up to 3, 6 or 9
- 5 is a factor if a number ends in 5 or 0
- 9 is a factor if the digits add up to 9

Example: Is 9 a factor of 151?

Method (1) Add up digits 1 + 5 + 1 = 7 the answer is *not* 9 so 9 is not a factor of 151.

Method (2) Use a calculator
Enter 151 on the calculator
Divide it by 9 and press the equals sign
The answer is 16.7777.

This shows that 9 is not a factor of 151. If the answer had been a number without a decimal point, the number would have been a factor.

More factor practice using factor triangles

Practise multiplication and factors with the triangles shown in Figure 5.14.

Multiply numbers in the circles and put answers into squares.

Find the factors of the numbers in the squares put answers into the circles.

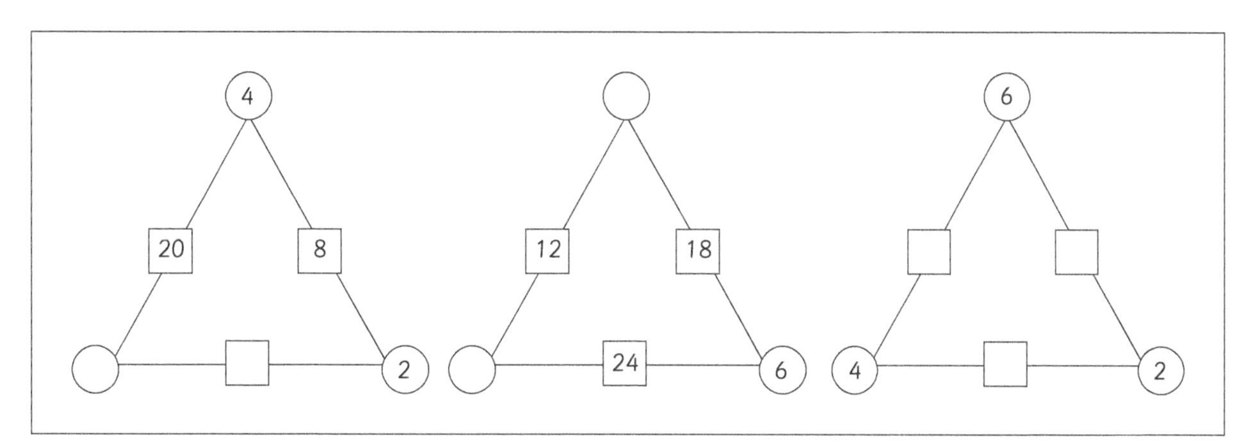

Figure 5.14 Factor triangles

Multiples

This is another word that dyscalculic children find difficult to understand. It identifies a group of numbers. Once again with the help of a table square we can discuss the word using easy numbers.

For example: Is 4 a multiple of 2?

4 is in the 2 times table so it is a multiple of 2.

Once children realise that multiples are the numbers in the times tables, there is no problem.

Prime numbers

A prime number is any integer which has only itself and 1 as a factor.

1 is NOT prime

2, 3, 5, 7, 11, 13, 17, 19 are important prime numbers up to 20: see Table 5.6.

Table 5.6 Prime numbers up to 20

1	2	3	4	5	6	7	8	9	10
11	12	13	14	15	16	17	18	19	20

You can also make a memory card (number 9, see page 142) of them and put them in a prominent place for children to see all the time.

It is helpful to use practical apparatus (such as Centicubes, Multilink and Numicon) to show that the prime numbers can only be put into groups of ones and themselves. They cannot be put into groups of twos, threes, fours and so on. Children will understand this better if you do this practically.

Place value

Place value is a vital skill that children need to acquire when working out calculations involving two-digit numbers. Understanding it also gives them confidence to develop calculation strategies that are efficient. Visualisation skills that allow children to see the 'ten-ness of 10' in their mind's eye help to reinforce place value. Some children are able to use money to develop their understanding of the decimal system, but, as was shown from the information on dyscalculic children, they rarely find our money system easy to understand.

Partitioning cards (see Figure 5.15) are readily available in a series of hundreds, tens, units, tenths and hundredths, each ranging from 0 to 9. They fit together cleverly to show place value. These cards show the decimal point position very well. If a child tries to put, for example, a hundred in the wrong place, then the cards will not fit together properly. It is like trying to push a piece of a jigsaw puzzle into the wrong place.

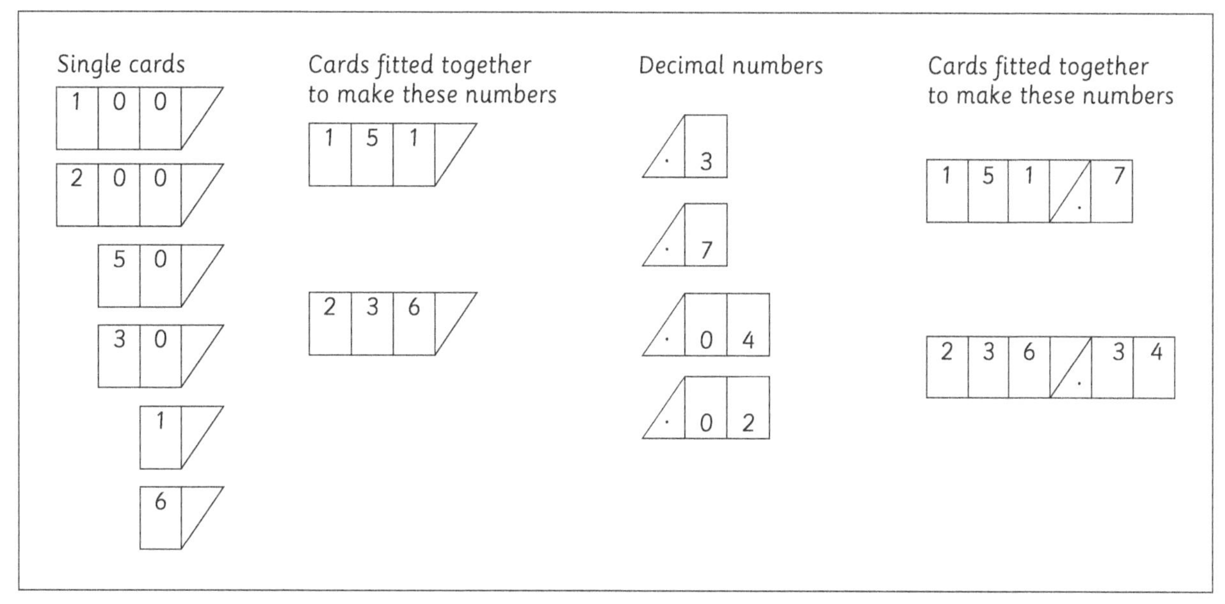

Figure 5.15 Partitioning cards

Children who fail to grasp place value find exercises like adding or subtracting 10 difficult, for example 10 more than 196 or 10 less than 521. It is also a big obstacle when they have to multiply or divide numbers by 10, 100 or 1000. Often teachers think this is an easy exercise but many children have been in tears because they could not grasp the mechanics of this computation. It is a good idea to practise a few of these problems as a start to a lesson using 1–100 squares, or if available an interactive white board that can take away the fear of these calculations.

How to help

- Use partitioning cards.
- Talk about the problem.
- Use colour to make hundreds, tens and units look different.
- Encourage practice in a friendly way.

6 Developing number skills

Section A: Times tables

Memory and times tables

'Once I knew all my tables but I can't remember any of them now!'

Many children find remembering multiplication tables hard, but for dyslexic and dyscalculic children it is extremely difficult. This has a knock-on effect because if they are struggling to connect a maths symbol to a maths procedure, struggling to remember a times table fact, then it is most unlikely that they will give enough attention to the actual problem they are trying to solve. Some children devise reliable strategies themselves but others can be taught strategies, such as building on to easy tables (like twos, fives and tens) to work out answers.

How to help

- Build up arrays. (see Figure 6.1).
- Make times table patterns and put them onto wall charts (see Figure 6.2).
- Make a table square (see Table 6.1) on the computer and print onto card.
- Make an L-shaped card to help with reading the table square (see Figure 6.5). This L-shape was devised by children to help them read a table square correctly.
- Make a pocket on the front cover of the maths book by sticking on a piece of card with sticky tape so the table square and L-shaped card can sit in it for easy access.
- Children will continue to use these tools to find multiplication answers until they are confident enough to work without them.
- Laminated table squares are useful as they can be put into wallets for easy, quick reference.

Arrays

- Using cardboard squares encourages the children to build up arrays (see Figure 6.1).
- The children can draw and colour the arrays on squared paper.
- They could also make shapes on the computer, colour and print them.
- Arrays help with learning and using times tables.

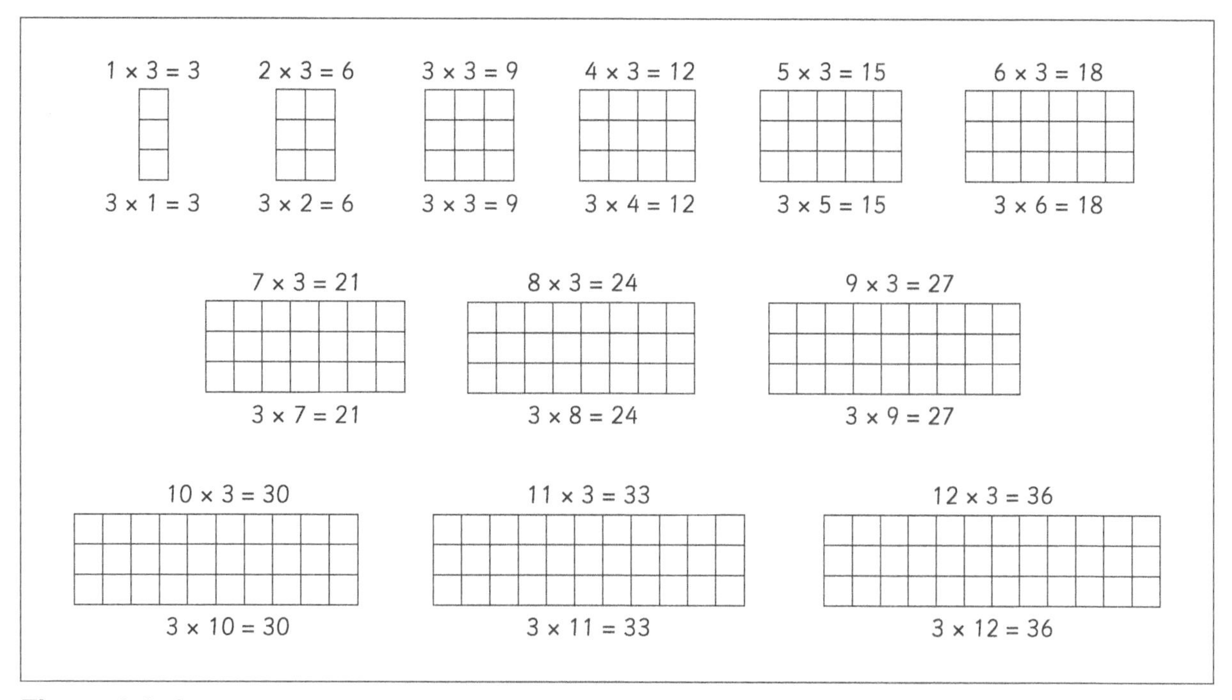

Figure 6.1 Arrays

odd	even	odd	even	odd	even	odd	even	odd	even
1	2	**3**	4	5	**6**	7	8	**9**	10
11	**12**	13	14	**15**	16	17	**18**	19	20
21	22	23	**24**	25	26	**27**	28	29	**30**
31	32	**33**	34	35	**36**	37	38	**39**	40
41	**42**	43	44	**45**	46	47	**48**	49	50
51	52	53	**54**	55	56	**57**	58	59	**60**
61	62	**63**	64	65	**66**	67	68	**69**	70
71	**72**	73	74	**75**	76	77	**78**	79	80
81	82	83	**84**	85	86	**87**	88	89	**90**
91	92	**93**	94	95	**96**	97	98	**99**	100

Figure 6.2 The three times table pattern

- Using a 1–100 number square, children can colour in the specific numbers of the times table being studied. For example, Figure 6.2 shows the three times table pattern. The pattern provides a visual representation to reinforce the learning process.

Finger tables

Finger tables help to do the times tables from 6 × 6 to 10 × 10. (See Figure 6.3.)

For example, to calculate 7 × 8:

- Each hand is numbered from 6 to 10 as in Figure 6.3.
- Make a bridge by putting the 7 from one hand to the 8 on the other hand.
- Counting the bridge as 2, add the remaining fingers nearest to the body from the bridge: that is three, so you are counting 5 altogether. These all represent 10s: 5 × 10 = 50.
- Multiply the number of fingers beyond the bridge on both hands: three on one, two on the other hand: 3 × 2 = 6
- Add the 50 to the 6: Answer 7 × 8 = 56.

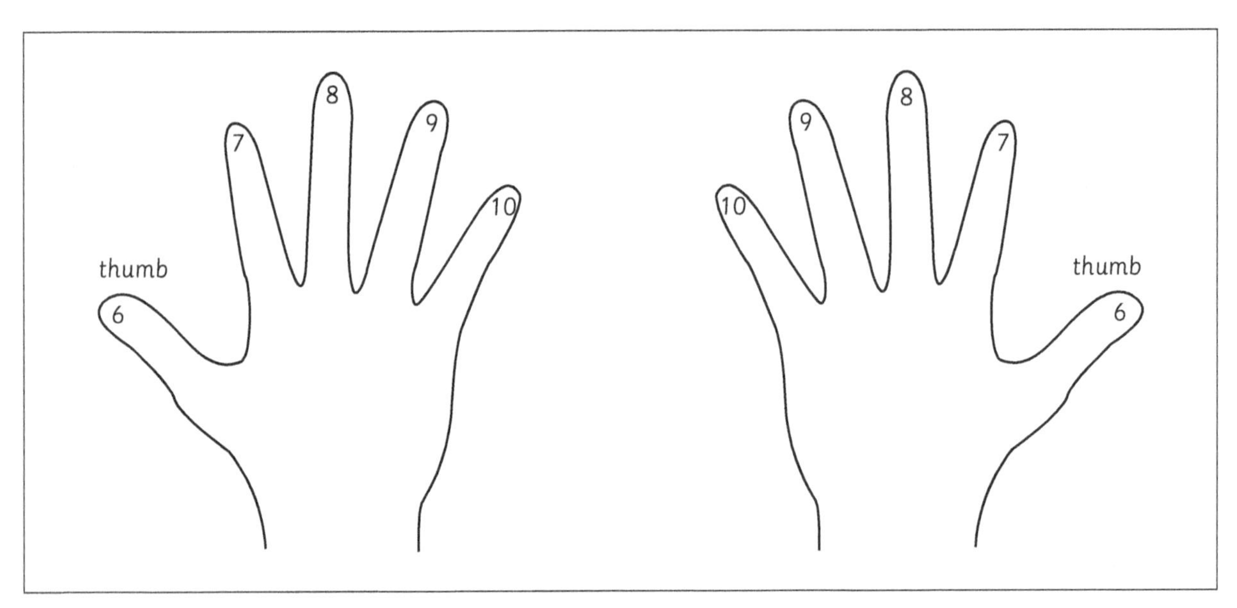

Figure 6.3 Finger tables

To calculate using the nine times table (see Figure 6.4), use this method:

- To do 1 × 9 put down the thumb on the left hand (marked 1×). There are nine fingers not bent which gives the answer, so 1 × 9 = 9.
- To do 2 × 9 put down the forefinger on the left hand (marked 2×), the thumb on the left hand now becomes a 10 and there are eight fingers not bent which gives the answer 2 × 9 = 18.
- To do 3 × 9 put down the middle finger on the left hand (marked 3×), the thumb and finger on the left hand now become two 10s and there are seven fingers not bent which gives the answer 3 × 9 = 27.
- To do 6 × 9 put down the finger on the right hand (marked 6×), the thumb and fingers on the left hand now become five 10s and there are four fingers not bent which gives the answer 6 × 9 = 54.

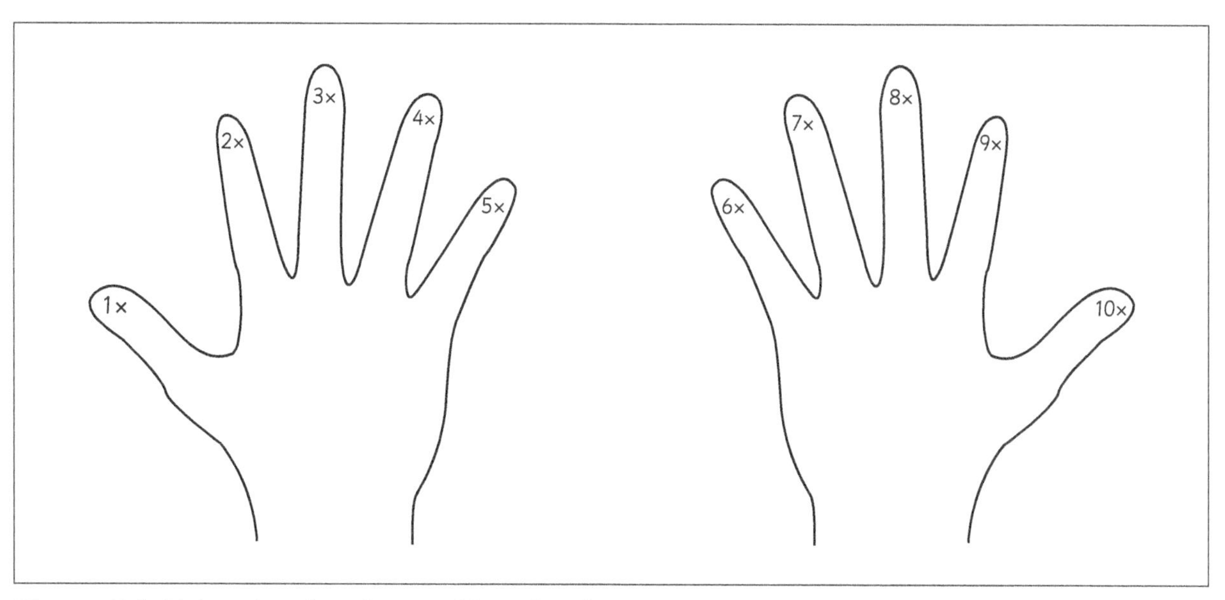

Figure 6.4 Using the nine times table using fingers to help

A number square and L-shaped card

Some children find that directional problems make reading numbers off a table square (Table 6.1) difficult. An L-shaped card (Figure 6.5) marked as shown has proved to be beneficial for such children.

Table 6.1 Table square

1	2	3	4	5	6	7	8	9	10
2	4	6	8	10	12	14	16	18	20
3	6	9	12	15	18	21	24	27	30
4	8	12	16	20	24	28	32	36	40
5	10	15	20	25	30	35	40	45	50
6	12	18	24	30	36	42	48	54	60
7	14	21	28	35	42	49	56	63	70
8	16	24	32	40	48	56	64	72	80
9	18	27	36	45	54	63	72	81	90
10	20	30	40	50	60	70	80	90	100

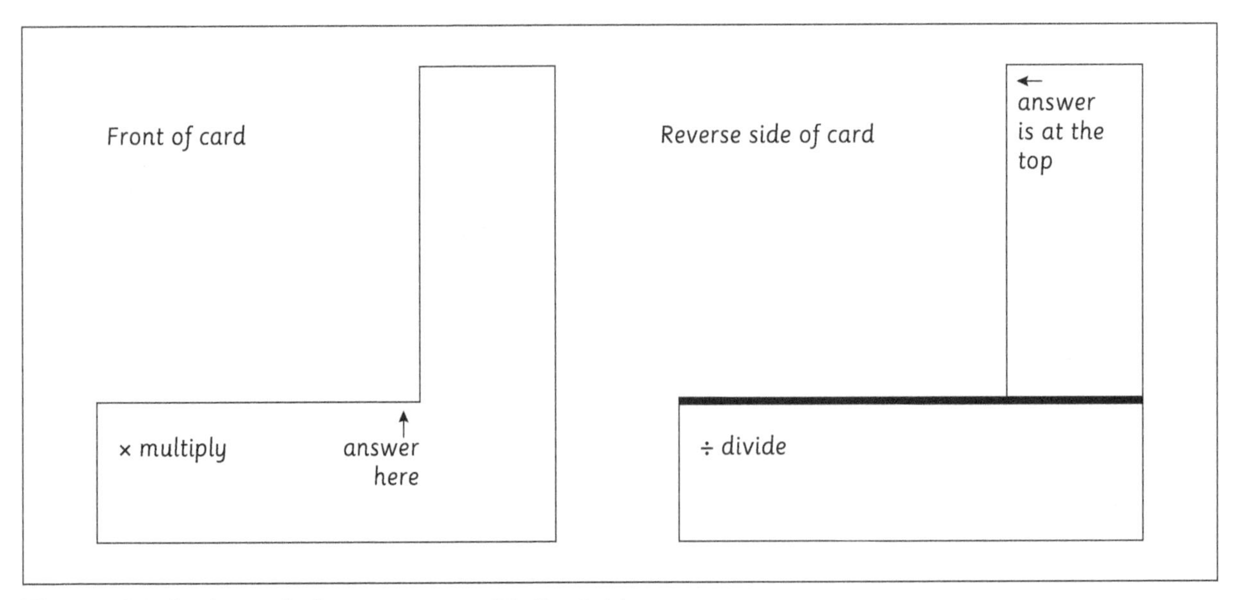

Figure 6.5 L-shaped pieces to use with the table square

A times table game

Table 6.2 shows a tables square to use with a times table game.

Table 6.2 A tables square to use with a times table game

	0	1	2	3	4	5
0	0	0	0	0	0	0
1	0	1	2	3	4	5
2	0	2	4	6	8	10
3	0	3	6	9	12	15
4	0	4	8	12	16	20
5	0	5	10	15	20	25

Make two of these table squares, one each for the pupil and teacher. Photocopy the larger cards shown on page 69 onto card and cut the squares into individual pieces. Use only the cards that match the specific table square you are using: for instance, if you are working with tables up to the five times table, you will use the cards shown in Table 6.3.

Table 6.3 Table cards to use for the times table game

0×0	0×1	0×2	0×3	0×4	0×5
1×0	2×0	3×0	4×0	5×0	1×1
1×2	1×3	1×4	1×5	2×1	3×1
4×1	5×1	2×2	2×3	2×4	2×5
3×2	4×2	5×2	3×3	3×4	3×5
4×3	5×3	4×4	4×5	5×4	5×5

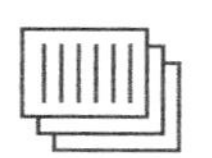

© 2012, *Dyslexia, Dyscalculia and Mathematics*, London: Routledge

Rules of the game

This can be played with one or more children, but the outline here is for a one-child game.

Shuffle the cards. Take one card off the top of the pack and show it to the child, e.g. 1 × 3. Ask the child if they know the answer. If they give the correct answer, give them the card, and let them colour in the 1 × 3 square on their copy of Table 6.2 in a favourite colour. (The teacher also marks their copy.) Repeat this procedure until you have used the entire pack of cards.

If the child cannot answer a question, for instance 4 × 3, they do not get that card and the square remains blank. At the end of the game you can discuss the questions for which this happened. Encourage the child to talk about how to find the answer, and maybe draw a memory jogger on the reverse side of the card.

Now show the card again, and if the child answers correctly put a tick on it. Show the card again in a different lesson and if the answer is known put another tick on the card. When three ticks are on the card the child is given the card and the corresponding square is highlighted. If the child still gives the wrong answer, encourage them to look at the reverse side of the card and use the memory jogger to rethink the answer.

Once the whole of the table square has been filled in, you can do the game again using the next line of the table square is added – see Table 6.4.

Table 6.4 A bigger tables square to use with the times table game

	0	1	2	3	4	5	6
0	0	0	0	0	0	0	0
1	0	1	2	3	4	5	6
2	0	2	4	6	8	10	12
3	0	3	6	9	12	15	18
4	0	4	8	12	16	20	24
5	0	5	10	15	20	25	30
6	0	6	12	18	24	30	36

Triangles to practise times tables

Triangles such as those shown in Figure 6.6 enable children to practise multiplication. In triangle A the pupil places their answer to 4 × 2 in the empty box. Then answers should be placed in the three empty boxes in triangle B (e.g. 2 × 10 = 20). In C, the pupil places their answers in the circles.

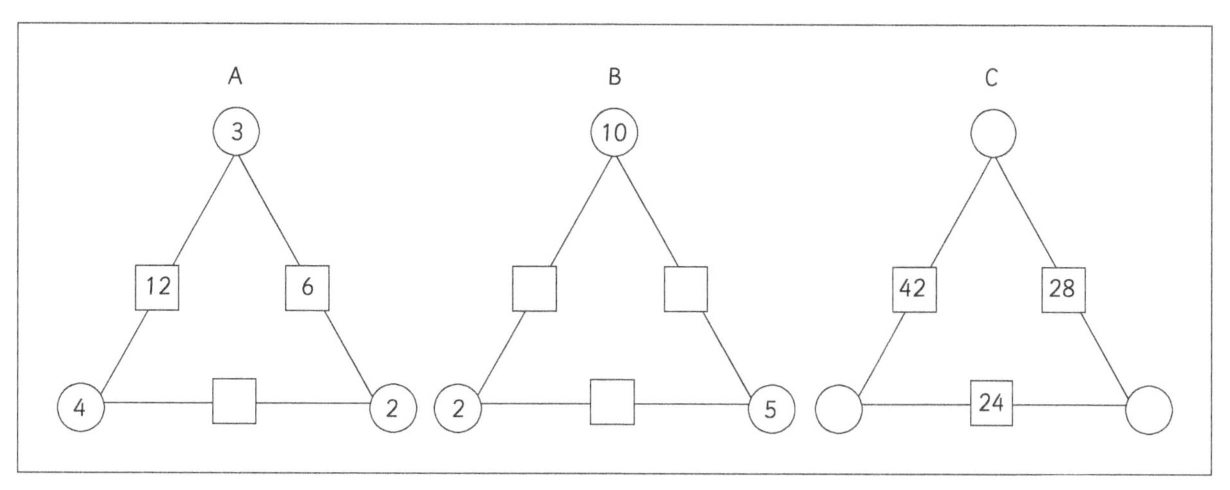

Figure 6.6 Triangles to help with multiplication

Section B: Fractions

A very high percentage of secondary children who struggle with mathematics feel threatened by fractions, and 'I've never understood them!' is the usual statement if the topic is mentioned. Children are introduced to fractions very early in their education but still find them a mystery when they are older. Possibly it would be more beneficial for some children if the first time they had to deal with fractions in a formal way was in secondary school. This could avoid the traumatic emotional frustration that is often seen because of the constant failure children experience with fractions in primary school.

Children need to be taught how to write fractions, how to read fractions, and need to understand that the bigger the number under the fraction line, the smaller the fraction.

In life we do very little with fractions apart from a half or a quarter. It is only for certain careers that children will need to use fractions, and then the mathematics will be quite specifically taught by specialists in that field. However children do have to deal with fractions in the mathematics syllabus, so strategies need to be used that will be helpful.

Words to know

cut	divide	split	equal	same	share
half	halves	quarter	third	whole	

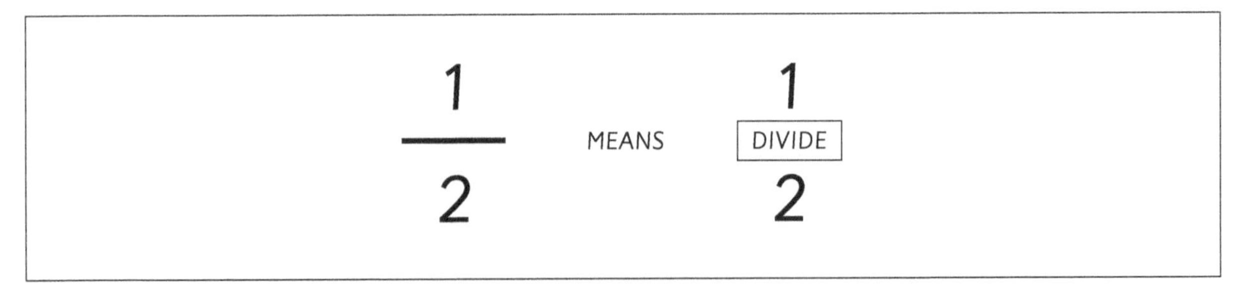

Figure 6.7 In a fraction the line between the top and bottom numbers means divide

- To find a half, written as ½, divide by 2.
- To find a quarter, written as ¼, divide by 4.
- To find a third, written as ⅓, divide by 3.

Strategies to help with fractions

1 Using A4 paper
  - Fold and cut up a sheet of paper so it makes two halves.
  - Colour both halves in, and write ½ and a 'half' on each one.
  - Stick them together again to show that two halves make a whole sheet of A4.
  - Discuss that 2/2 = 1 whole.

Use the same method to show ¼ (quarters, fourths), and ⅓ (thirds) making sure at the end of the lesson the children understands that 4/4 = 1 and 3/3 = 1.

2 Using string 24 cm long
  - Fold and cut into halves.
  - Fold and cut into quarters.
  - Fold and cut into thirds.

3 Using bars of chocolate or biscuits
  - Divide up and break into halves, quarters and thirds, as was done with the A4 paper.
  - The end results can be eaten, and sometimes children remember the eating part long after the cutting and sticking has gone!

4 Using 12 coloured marbles in a bag
  - Ask the children to give you half of them. How many in a half?
  - Do the same with a quarter and a third.
  - If this is done correctly start to write down the results.
  - Use different numbers of marbles.

5 Using a fraction strips or a fraction wall

1 whole											
1 half						1 half					
1 third				1 third				1 third			
1 quarter			1 quarter			1 quarter			1 quarter		
1 sixth		1 sixth		1 sixth		1 sixth		1 sixth		1 sixth	

Figure 6.8 Fraction wall

- Copy, enlarge, and laminate the fraction wall shown as Figure 6.8 to make it a useful resource.
- Cut out the fraction strips. Place them in front of the computer so they can be touched while a fraction wall is on the computer screen.
- Have the children draw a fraction wall and colour in the fractional parts with different colours to see the connection between them.

Euan's strategy

Euan, aged 13, was asked this question on fractions: 'Is 4/3 bigger than one whole?'

He said that a 1/4 was 15 but he was not sure about a third. When questioned further about these numbers it was discovered that for him a whole one was always 60. After discussing that to find a third of something you divide by three, he calculated that a third of 60 was 20, therefore 4/3 i.e. four-thirds were 80. He then saw clearly that 80 was bigger than 60. His answer to the original question was 'Yes, 4/3 was bigger than one whole.'

Euan had developed his own personal strategy to deal with fractions by basing the whole concept around the number 60. This example shows that some children are able to develop their own internal logic which could have the same validity in terms of arriving at the correct solution, as the accepted objective mode of logical thinking in mathematics.

Section C: Decimal fractions

As well as fractions to write numbers less than one, there are decimal fractions, which are numbers where the fractional part is written after a decimal point. This is not an easy topic, and time is needed for children to understand the concepts involved. Decimals need to be taught in chunks, and if after a week some children have not understood it completely it is preferable to revisit the topic at a later time. Revisiting topics is known as a spiral curriculum, which is a much more powerful approach than focusing week after week on the same topic.

Children need to know that noughts can be added after the decimal point without changing the size of the number.

1 = 1.0 = 1.00
2 = 2.0 = 2.00
3 = 3.0 = 3.00

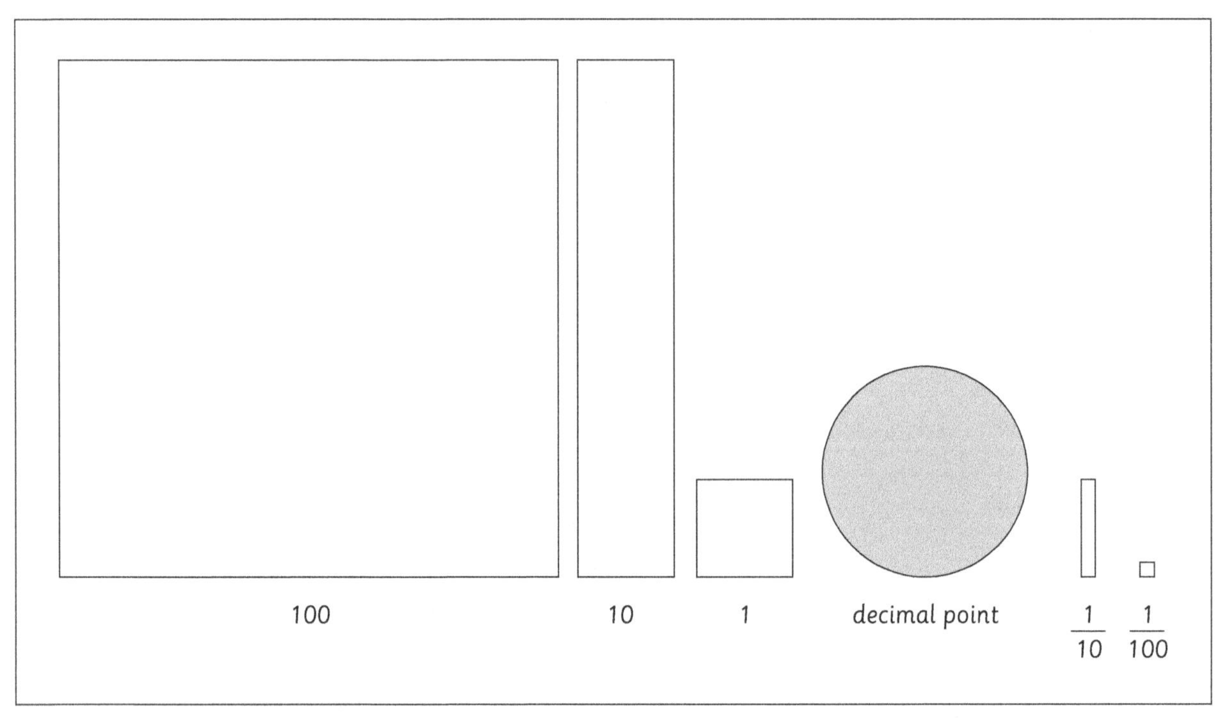

Figure 6.9 The decimal point divides the fractional part of the number from the whole numbers

Example 1

2.5 is read as two point five
which means 2 whole units and 5 tenths (5/10)
5/10 cancels down to ½ (a half), so 2.5 means two and a half.

Example 2

38.25 is read as thirty eight point two five
which means 38 whole units and 25 hundredths
25/100 cancels down to ¼ a quarter so 38.25 means 38 and a quarter

Decimal fractions and money

Working with money allows you to introduce decimal fractions easily, as the whole numbers are usually pounds written as £, the 1/10ths are 10p coins and the 1/100ths are 1p coins.
£42.36 is read as 42 pounds and thirty (3 × 10p) six (6 × 1p) pence

Section D: Percentages

Children should understand the following:

- Percent is shown with the symbol %.
- % looks like a divide symbol if slightly altered, and /00 looks like a hundred.
- Per cent means out of a hundred.
- Decrease means less (subtract).

- Increase means more (add).
- To find a percentage of something we divide by 100 somewhere in the calculation.

Useful facts

The information in Table 6.5 is also given on memory cards numbers 10 and 11 (see page 142).

Table 6.5 Useful facts about percentages

To find:	To find:
10% divide by 10	30% divide by 10 then multiply by 3
20% divide by 5	40% divide by 10 then multiply by 4
25% divide by 4	60% divide by 10 then multiply by 6
50% divide by 2	70% divide by 10 then multiply by 7
75% divide by 4 then multiply by 3	80% divide by 10 then multiply by 8
	90% divide by 10 then multiply by 9

Doing percentages on a calculator

The percentage button works differently on each calculator, making its usage complicated, so children tend to avoid it. Some children discover that percentages can be done quickly using a decimal fraction on the calculator.

Percentages as decimal fractions

The information in Table 6.6 is also given on memory cards numbers 12 and 13 (see pages 142 and 143).

Table 6.6 Useful facts about percentages as decimal fractions and about using a calculator to find a percentage

Percentages/decimal fractions	**Using a calculator to find a percentage**
2% = 0.02	When using a calculator the decimal fraction must
8% = 0.08	always be followed by the multiplication sign
16% = 0.16	(followed by ×)
35% = 0.35.	Colour 'followed by ×' in red
72% = 0.72	Example: Find 2% of 800
	Enter 0.02 × 800 = 16

Making connections

Children will usually have dealt with fractions and decimals by the time they meet percentages. Figure 6.10 shows the connections between fractions, decimal fractions and percentages.

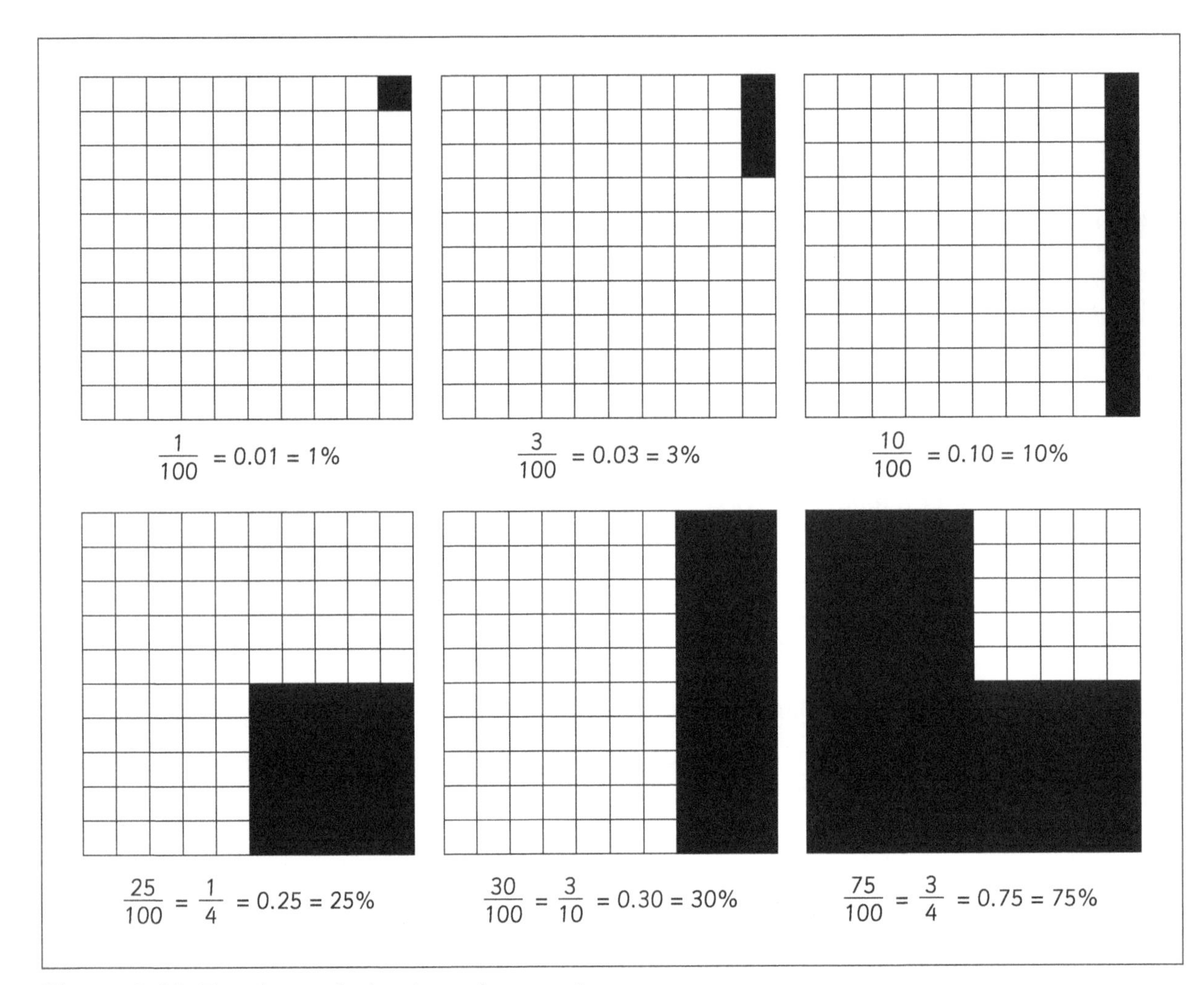

Figure 6.10 Fractions, decimals and percentages

Changing a fraction into a percentage

To change a fraction into a percentage multiply it by 100.

Example

- The marks you got in some of your school subjects were:
  - English 17/25
  - Maths 32/40
  - History 27/30
  - Geography 41/60
  - Music 11/15
  - Art 53/70.
- Which was your best subject?
- Which was your worst?
- Put them in order starting with the best.
- Then work out the percentage to check your average.

Table 6.7 shows how this is worked out.

Table 6.7 Changing fractions into percentages: an example

Subject marks into percentages	Subjects rearranged (average is 76%)
English 17/25 × 100 = 68%	History 27/30 × 100 = 90% best
Maths 32/40 × 100 = 80%	Maths 32/40 × 100 = 80%
History 27/30 × 100 = 90%	Art 53/70 × 100 = 76%
Geography 41/60 × 100 = 68%	Music 11/15 × 100 = 73%
Music 11/15 × 100 = 73%	English 17/25 × 100 = 68%
Art 53/70 × 100 = 76%	Geography 41/60 × 100 = 68% worst

To find a percentage using money

Example

What is 16% of £912?

$$\frac{16}{100} \times 912 = 0.16 \times 912$$

Answer = £145.92

Section E: Estimation and approximation

This is a skill that is useful not only in school but all through life.

Estimation is an exercise in which an approximate result is obtained by rounding off numbers and using them instead of exact ones to find a 'rough' answer. Dyscalculic children find this difficult to do, for if they have failed continually with correct values in problems they lack the confidence to use 'rounded off' numbers. Using a calculator accurately depends on a pupil's skill, and it is easy for a child with learning difficulties to 'read' a value that bears no resemblance to the size of answer required. For instance, 100052 might be read as 1.05.

Estimation is a most useful technique to acquire as it develops a sense of awareness of size and quantity, vital in achieving a good understanding of number concepts. Predicting the size of an answer is just as important as working out the answer accurately, for much of number use in life is estimation, so it is important children are encouraged from early years to develop this skill. It is good practice to divide a page into two, using one half to do the estimates and the other half for the accurate answer. Children then acquire the habit of doing a quick estimate each time they do a mathematical calculation.

Use easy numbers

18 + 34   20 + 30 = 50

Ignore decimal points

23.2 + 48.6   23 + 50 = 73

Later encourage a more precise estimate

24.5 + 102.3	25 + 102 = 127

Once children acquire estimation skills they can do 'advanced' estimation, finding answers for complicated calculations.

1.9 × 4.2	2 × 4 = 8	accurate answer 7.98
41.06 divide 3.6	40 ÷ 4 = 10	accurate answer 11.41

Using bigger numbers

Multiplying

238 × 591	200 × 600 count noughts	0000
Estimate	2 × 6 = 12 put 12 before the noughts	120000
Accurate	140658	

Dividing

923 ÷ 26 900 ÷ 30
Estimate cross off equal number of noughts 90 ÷ 3 = 30
Accurate 35.5

Practical applications of estimation

Using easy numbers

A typical question:

> *Isabelle is asked to estimate how much stock there is in the food shop where she works. She starts with cans of beans. She could begin to count but because that would take too long and only an approximation is required, she estimates. Tins are stacked 7 deep and 48 across on each shelf. There are nine shelves.*

7 shelves 48 across	(use 6 easier than 7) × 50
Estimate	Each shelf has 6 × 50 = 300 cans
9 shelves (use 10)	300 × 10 = 3000 cans
Accurate	3024

Rough estimates

A rough estimation of an answer is often needed quickly. Ask, 'Is the estimate higher or lower than the accurate answer?'

Question: To buy stereo equipment

The cash price is £600 or 104 weeks at £6.00
Is this more than £600 or less?

Using a rough estimate 100 × £6.00 = £600 so 104 × £6.00 must be more than £600

Making an educated guess

Often approximations are related to the context of the question. So to make an educated guess or work out a quick, fairly accurate estimate depends on the amount of money or quantity involved. Sometimes it is necessary to round off to the nearest penny, but at other times an estimate to the nearest thousand is good enough for the problem that is being considered. A larger amount usually means a more general estimate can be given. This can be seen in the following questions.

The cost of material to make a dress £36.38	estimate £36.50
The cost of materials to decorate a room £569.72	estimate £570
The estimated cost to build a garage £14,640	estimate £14,500
The price of a car (make, style, etc.?) £22,858	estimate £23,000
House prices are from £288,840	estimate £300,000

The list is endless. With much work done on this very important aspect of maths, children will improve their confidence as well as lose the fear of abandoning the exact number, and work happily with easy numbers.

Rounding off

Another way of giving an approximate size is by rounding off a number to a specific size, and a number line may be useful to do this.

For example:

1 Round off 2718 to the nearest 10

Figure 6.11 A number line for solving the problem (to the nearest 10)

Answer = 2720 rounded to the nearest 10

2 Round off 2718 to the nearest 100

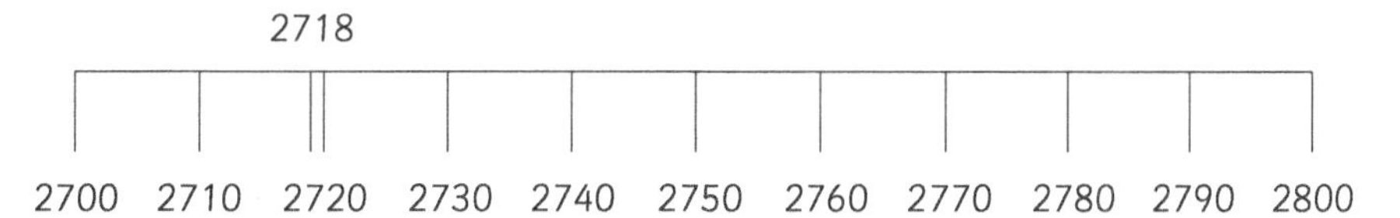

Figure 6.12 A number line for solving the problem (to the nearest 100)

Answer = 2700 rounded to the nearest 100

3 Round off 2718 to the nearest 1000

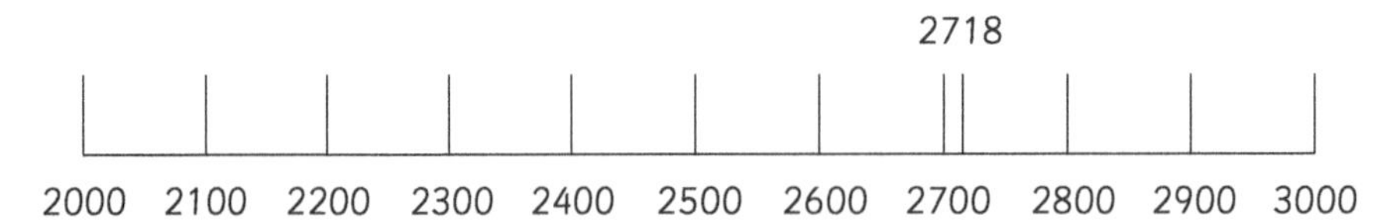

Figure 6.13 A number line for solving the problem (to the nearest 1000)

Answer = 3000 rounded to the nearest 1000

Correcting to a specific number of decimal places

It is necessary at times to read numbers which give an approximate size as opposed to an exact size, and this can be done by correcting it to a specific number of decimal places.

Abbreviations used within this topic

Correct – corr. Decimal places – dec.pl. or dp.

To correct a number to two decimal places emphasise:

- Only the numbers after the decimal point are involved.
- The numbers before the decimal point stay the same.

Method

To correct a number to two dp (see Figure 6.14):

- Count two numbers after the decimal point and draw a cut-off line.
- Look at the number to the right of the cut-off line (look right!).
- If it is 5 or more, add 1 to the number on the left of the cut-off line (look left!).
- If the number is less than 5 then the two numbers after the decimal point stay the same.

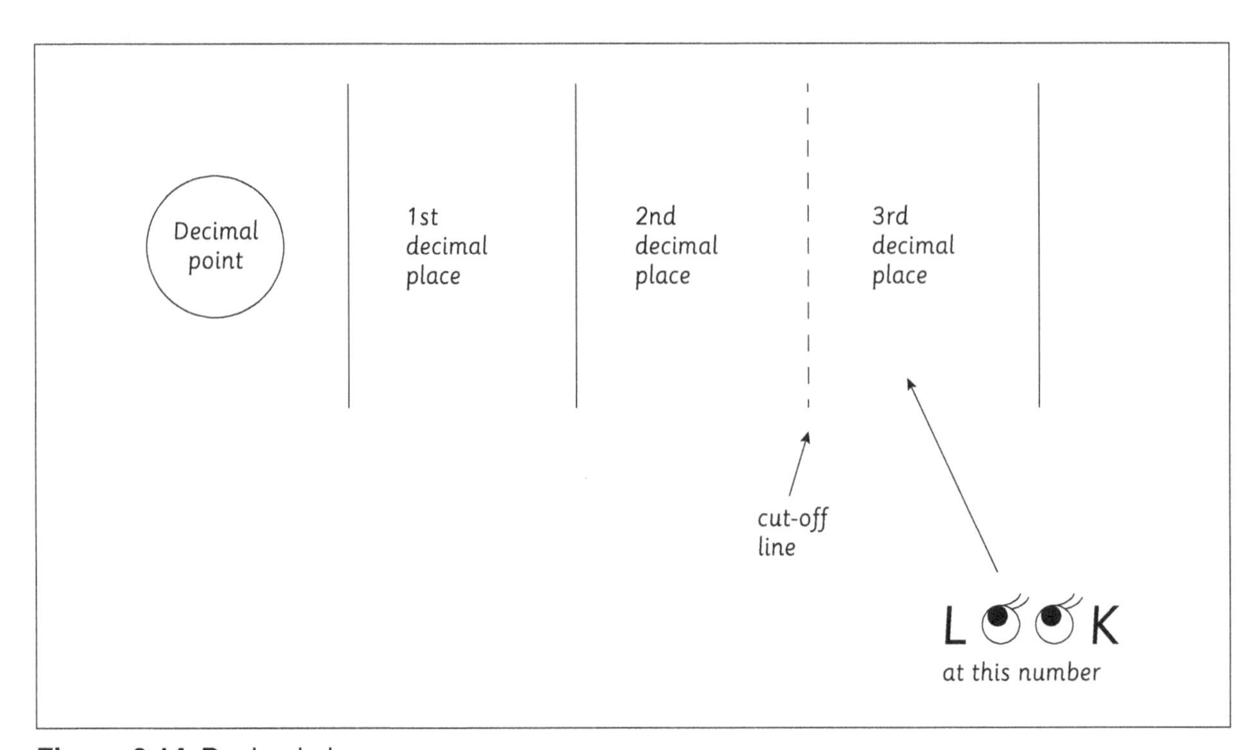

Figure 6.14 Decimal places

Example:

Correct 26.368 to two dp (see Figure 6.15):

Look at .368. The cut-off line is after 6, 8 is more than 5 so the answer = 26.37

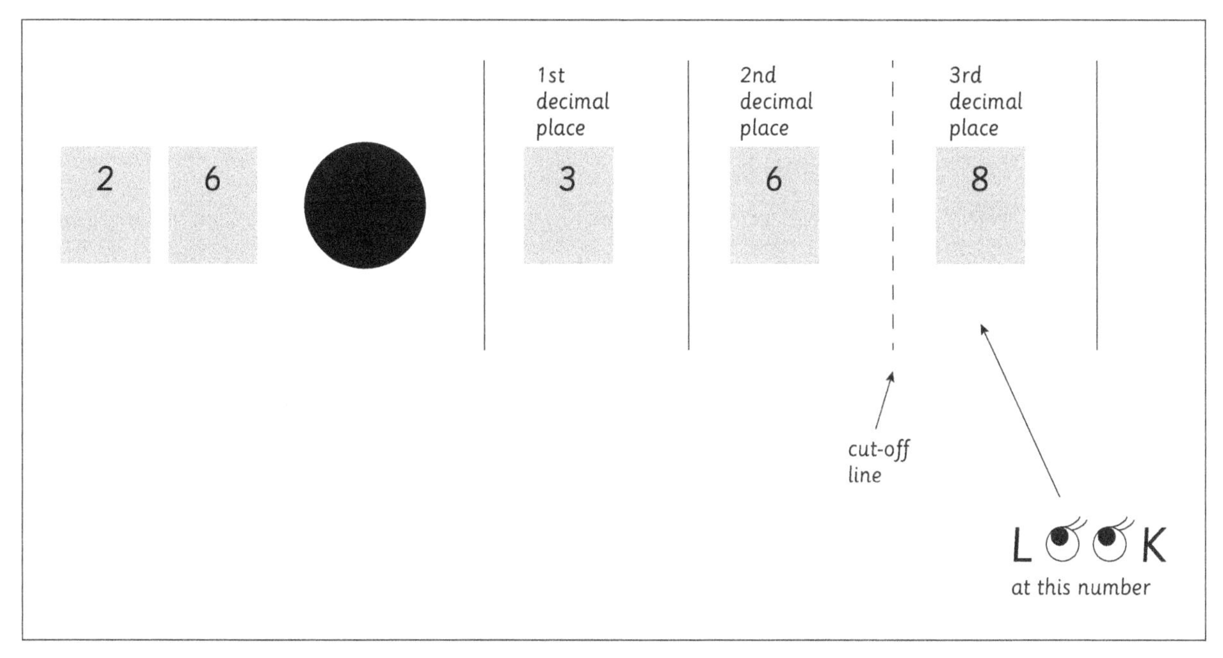

Figure 6.15 To correct 26.368 to two decimal places

Significant figures

Another way to read numbers to an approximate size is by giving them correct to a specific number of significant figures. When doing this children must remember that all numbers are important, not just the ones after the decimal point. To 'correct' a number to a particular number of significant figures, emphasise:

- Noughts at the beginning of a number can be ignored.
- Zeros inside a number must not be ignored.
- Every other digit in the number must not be ignored.

The following numbers are corrected to three significant figures (abbreviated 3 sig. fig. or 3SF):

Number	Number corrected to 3SF
3547	3550
32694	32700
2.481	2.48
3.598	3.60

Section F: Money

Money and shopping

Children need to practise giving and receiving change from 50p, £1, £5 and £10 using real, cardboard or plastic money. When shopping in real life the change received is usually 'added on' to the amount spent. However, to work out change on paper we have to do a subtraction calculation.

In the United Kingdom the following coins are used:

1p 2p 5p 10p 20p 50p £1 £2

- £1 is written as £1.00 in decimal form
- £1 + 10p in decimal form is £1.10
- £1 + 2p in decimal form is £1.02
- 50p in decimal form is £0.50

Rounding off using a money line

Here are some examples:

1 Round off 32p to the nearest 10p.

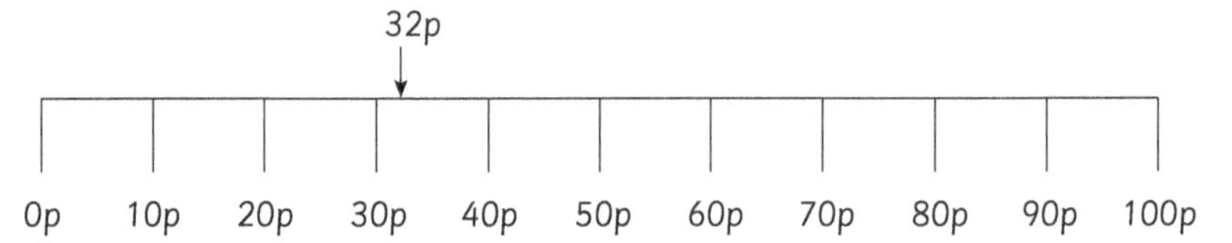

Figure 6.16 Money number line (to nearest 10p)

Answer is 30p to the nearest 10p

2 Round off £2.69 to the nearest £.

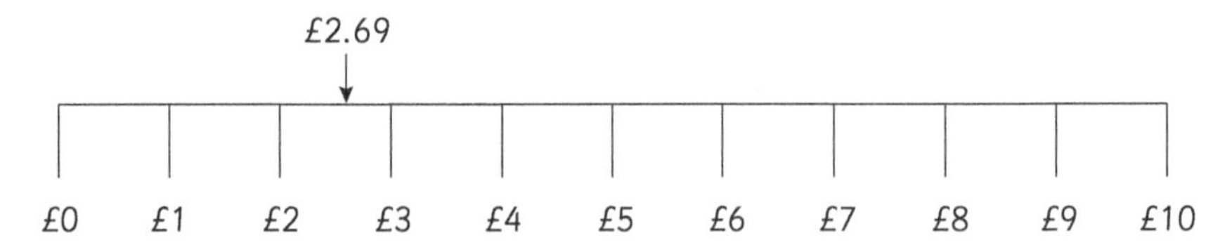

Figure 6.17 Money number line (to nearest £)

Answer is £3.00 to the nearest £

3 Round off £640 to the nearest £100.

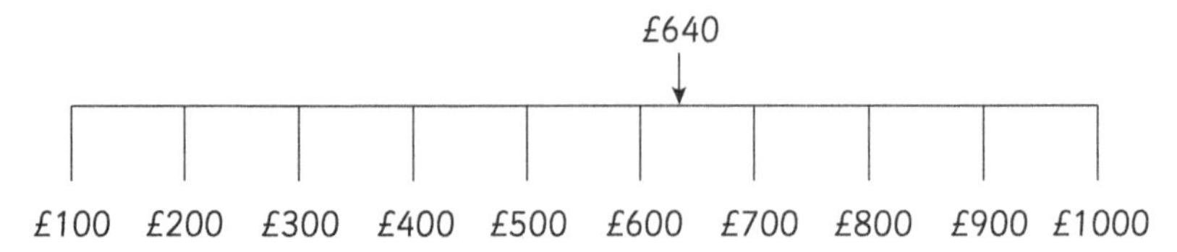

Figure 6.18 Money number line (to nearest £100)

Answer is £600 to the nearest £100

Section G: Time

Difficulties with time

This topic poses a serious problem for many dyscalculic children, for not only do they have to know twelve-hour time and twenty-four-hour time, they also have to recognise both digital and analogue times. They have difficulty with organisation of their own time because dates on paper can be meaningless. Often they do not know the sequence of months, so seasons and passage of time are confusing for them.

How to help

- Egg-timers and home-made pendulums are useful for comparing the time taken to do various activities.
- The use of stopwatches can be more meaningful to older children who come across them, often on the sports field.
- Try counting seconds to see how accurate a children is in estimation of time.
- Make a pendulum with a weight tied on to a piece of string and estimate the time taken for it to swing backwards and forwards.
- Egg-timers measuring different times can be used to measure the amount of time taken to walk across a room, count in twos up to fifty or count down in tens from 100.

Time words

Make clear wall charts, and give children an index card showing months, abbreviations, plus number names. At a later date children can write these into their books and onto an alphabet card for future reference.

These are core abbreviations and words to learn:

hour	hr	
minutes	mins	
seconds	secs	
a.m. means morning times	p.m. means afternoon and night	
lunch time	noon	midnight

Table 6.8 Number cards

First	1st	Seventh	7th
Second	2nd	Eighth	8th
Third	3rd	Ninth	9th
Fourth	4th	Tenth	10th
Fifth	5th	Eleventh	11th
Sixth	6th	Twelfth	12th

Annual/annually	once a year
Month/monthly	12 times a year
Quarter/quarterly	4 times a year
Day/daily	every day (7 days in a week)
Week/weekly	every week (52 weeks in a year)

Table 6.9 Months of the year and their abbreviations

1	January	Jan	7	July	Jul
2	February	Feb	8	August	Aug
3	March	Mar	9	September	Sep
4	April	Apr	10	October	Oct
5	May	May	11	November	Nov
6	June	Jun	12	December	Dec

Days in each month

Sing a song:

Thirty days has September
April June and November
All the rest have thirty-one
Except February alone
Which has 28 days clear
And 29 each leap year.

How to help

- Teach children the number of days in months by putting two hands together and looking at the knuckles of fingers not thumbs (see Figure 6.19).
- Starting with the left hand the knuckles are January, March, May, July.
- Now looking at the right hand the knuckles are August, October and December. These seven months have 31 days.
- The 'valleys' between the knuckles represent the other months.
- Starting with the left hand the first valley is February which has 28 days but 29 each leap year, i.e. every fourth year.
- The other valleys are April, June and then onto the right hand September and November. These four months have 30 days.

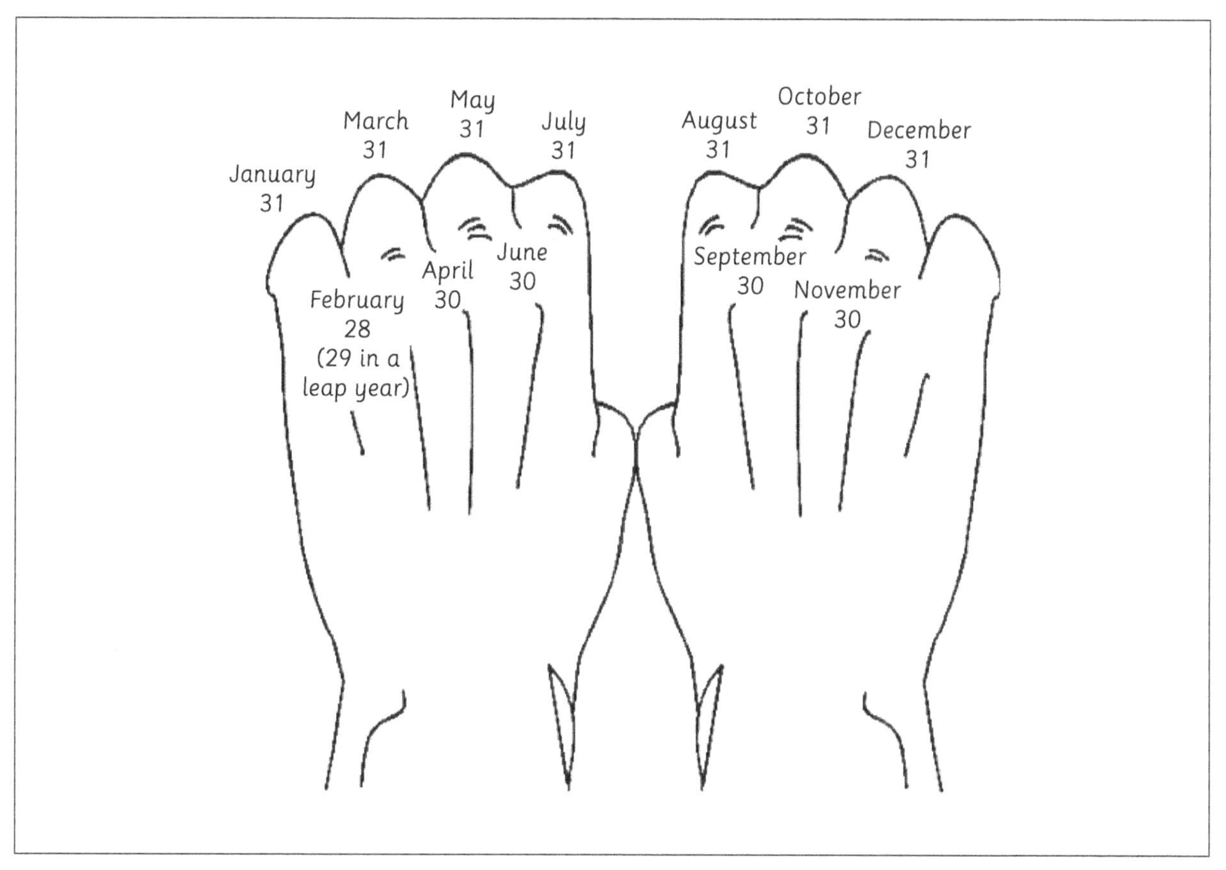

Figure 6.19 The knuckles on two hands showing the number of days in each month

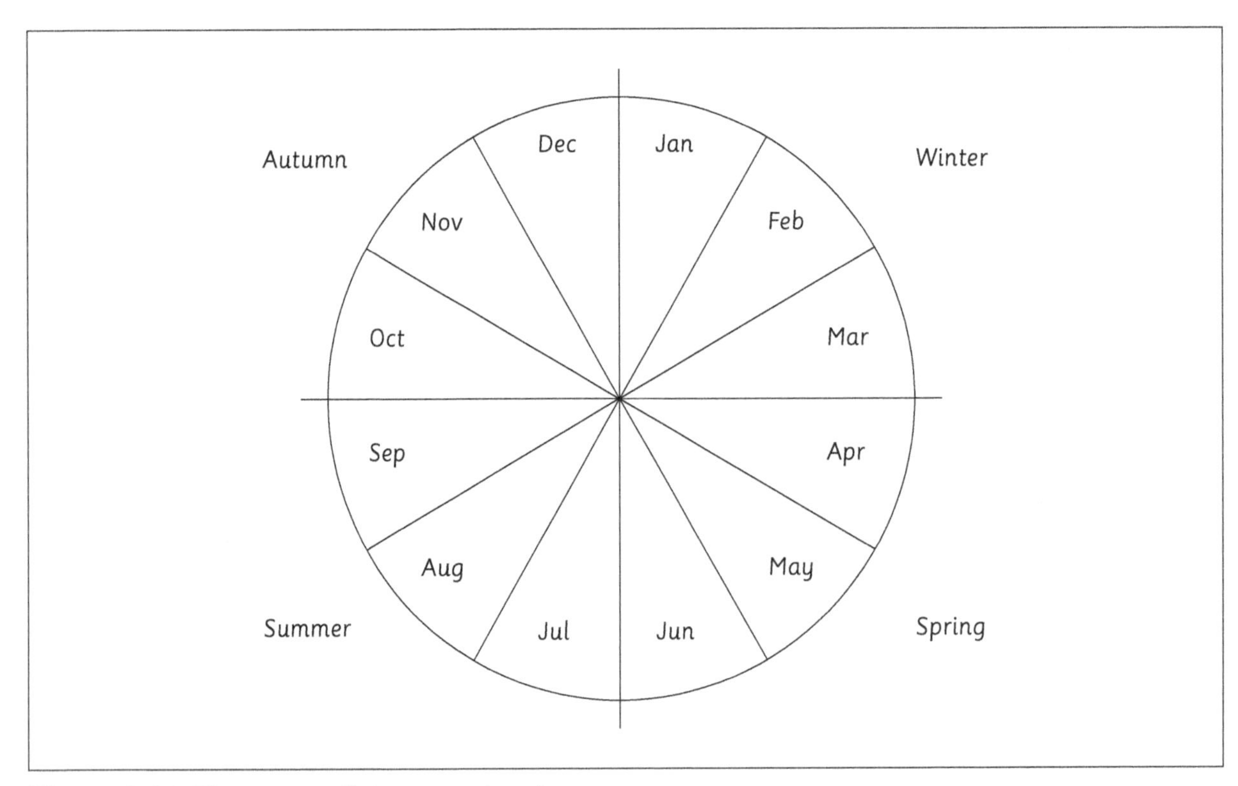

Figure 6.20 The year split into quarters/seasons

Splitting the year up into quarters can help, particularly if colour is used, or appropriate pictures, to illustrate the different seasons. See Figure 6.20.

Have the children look at a calendar of a month (Table 6.10) and discuss various questions.

- On what day of the week are the following dates? 6th 23rd 11th 19th.
- What day is the first (1st) of the month?
- What day is the last of the month?
- How many Saturdays/Thursdays, etc., are there in the month?
- How many days are there from Tuesday 15th to Thursday 31st?

Table 6.10 Calendar of a month

MAY						
M	T	W	T	F	S	S
	1	2	3	4	5	6
7	8	9	10	11	12	13
14	15	16	17	18	19	20
21	22	23	24	25	26	27
28	29	30	31			

Using the whole year calendar (Figure 6.21), have the children answer the following questions:

- The first (1st)/second (2nd)/fifth (5th), etc., month of the year is …?
- How many months are there in the year?
- On what day is Christmas Day?
- My birthday is on …?

January

S	M	T	W	T	F	S
			1	2	3	4
5	6	7	8	9	10	11
12	13	14	15	16	17	18
19	20	21	22	23	24	25
26	27	28	29	30	31	

February

S	M	T	W	T	F	S
						1
2	3	4	5	6	7	8
9	10	11	12	13	14	15
16	17	18	19	20	21	22
23	24	25	26	27	28	

March

S	M	T	W	T	F	S
						1
2	3	4	5	6	7	8
9	10	11	12	13	14	15
16	17	18	19	20	21	22
23	24	25	26	27	28	29
30	31					

April

S	M	T	W	T	F	S
		1	2	3	4	5
6	7	8	9	10	11	12
13	14	15	16	17	18	19
20	21	22	23	24	25	26
27	28	29	30			

May

S	M	T	W	T	F	S
				1	2	3
4	5	6	7	8	9	10
11	12	13	14	15	16	17
18	19	20	21	22	23	24
25	26	27	28	29	30	31

June

S	M	T	W	T	F	S
1	2	3	4	5	6	7
8	9	10	11	12	13	14
15	16	17	18	19	20	21
22	23	24	25	26	27	28
29	30					

July

S	M	T	W	T	F	S
		1	2	3	4	5
6	7	8	9	10	11	12
13	14	15	16	17	18	19
20	21	22	23	24	25	26
27	28	29	30	31		

August

S	M	T	W	T	F	S
					1	2
3	4	5	6	7	8	9
10	11	12	13	14	15	16
17	18	19	20	21	22	23
24	25	26	27	28	29	30
31						

September

S	M	T	W	T	F	S
	1	2	3	4	5	6
7	8	9	10	11	12	13
14	15	16	17	18	19	20
21	22	23	24	25	26	27
28	29	30				

October

S	M	T	W	T	F	S
			1	2	3	4
5	6	7	8	9	10	11
12	13	14	15	16	17	18
19	20	21	22	23	24	25
26	27	28	29	30	31	

November

S	M	T	W	T	F	S
						1
2	3	4	5	6	7	8
9	10	11	12	13	14	15
16	17	18	19	20	21	22
23	24	25	26	27	28	29
30						

December

S	M	T	W	T	F	S
	1	2	3	4	5	6
7	8	9	10	11	12	13
14	15	16	17	18	19	20
21	22	23	24	25	26	27
28	29	30	31			

Figure 6.21 Whole year calendar

Telling the time

Digital time

As digital time is used on all technology and watches are mostly digital it makes sense to begin telling the time by learning how to read digital time. A great deal of work should be done orally before anything is written down. All times are read as 'past times'.

Cards with digital time written on them with the words on the reverse side are helpful to children (see Table 6.11).

Table 6.11 Digital time cards

front	reverse
8.22	22 minutes past 8
2.26	26 minutes past 2
6.56	56 minutes past 6

- To change twelve-hour to twenty-four-hour time you add on 12, but to which number?

Show children that the 12 is added to the number they are saying last when they read digital time.
For example, if it is 22 minutes past 8, you add the 12 onto the 8.
Some children like to add on 12, but others prefer to add on 10 then 2.
For example, to change 6.51 to 24-hour time:

Read the number 51 minutes past 6
add 12 to the 6 $6 + 12 = 18$

or $6 + 10 = 16$ $16 + 2 = 18$

6.51 is 18.51 in 24 hour time

To reverse the procedure:

$18.51 - 12 = 6.51$

or $18.51 - 10 = 8.51$ $8.51 - 2 = 6.51$

Rules on how to change twelve-hour time to twenty-four-hour time

These are for children to write down:

Any a.m. time up to 9.59 always begins with a 0.

For example: 3.45 a.m. is 0345
8.57 a.m. is 0857
1.25 a.m. is 0125

10, 11 and 12 noon are just the same in 12 and 24-hour time

For example: 1015 a.m. is 1015
1108 a.m. is 1108
1238 p.m. is 1238

For p.m. times always add 12 to the first two numbers.

For example:

2.00 p.m. is 1400 in 24 hour time
6.30 p.m. is 1830 in 24 hour time

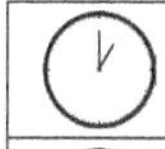	one o'clock	1.00 a.m.	0100	morning
	two o'clock	2.00 a.m.	0200	morning
	three o'clock	3.00 a.m.	0300	morning
	four o'clock	4.00 a.m.	0400	morning
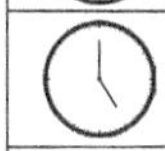	five o'clock	5.00 a.m.	0500	morning
	six o'clock	6.00 a.m.	0600	morning
	seven o'clock	7.00 a.m.	0700	morning
	eight o'clock	8.00 a.m.	0800	morning
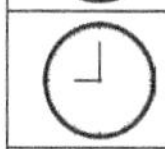	nine o'clock	9.00 a.m.	0900	morning
	ten o'clock	10.00 a.m.	1000	morning
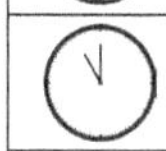	eleven o'clock	11.00 a.m.	1100	morning
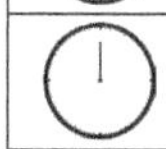	twelve o'clock	12.00 noon	1200	morning
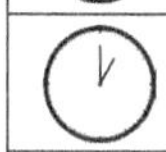	one o'clock	1.00 p.m.	1300	afternoon
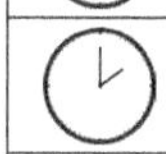	two o'clock	2.00 p.m.	1400	afternoon
	three o'clock	3.00 p.m.	1500	afternoon
	four o'clock	4.00 p.m.	1600	afternoon
	five o'clock	5.00 p.m.	1700	afternoon
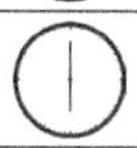	six o'clock	6.00 p.m.	1800	evening
	seven o'clock	7.00 p.m.	1900	evening
	eight o'clock	8.00 p.m.	2000	evening
	nine o'clock	9.00 p.m.	2100	night
	ten o'clock	10.00 p.m.	2200	night
	eleven o'clock	11.00 p.m.	2300	night
	twelve o'clock	12.00 midnight	0000	night

Figure 6.22 The twelve-hour and twenty-four-hour clock

A common error is to add 12 to the last two numbers so that 6.30 p.m. becomes 0642 in 24-hour time. It is useful to pre-empt this so it can be avoided.

Figure 6.22 linking up analogue, twelve and twenty-four-hour clock times is useful. Children can use different colours to identify different parts of the day or even do little drawings to remind them of what they do at a particular time: for example, 8.00 a.m. is breakfast time. This figure can be photocopied, cut out and pasted onto a cylindrical cardboard tube so that 1.00 a.m. is next to 12.00 midnight. Then as the tube is turned, children can see that day is following night.

Analogue time

There are excellent teaching clocks available showing twelve -hour time, twenty-four-hour time, minutes and Roman numerals. Show children that it is the small hand that points to the hour – perhaps by drawing a clock and colouring in the hand. Discuss the long hand and how to count around in fives. Initially try to avoid any 'to' times and use only 'past' times. A clock face rubber stamp enables lots of practice to take place.

Clocks that have digital displays are useful (see Figure 6.23), especially if they have a clock face with movable hands which can be used later.

'Half past' needs to be introduced fairly quickly, but try to connect as much as possible with the digital times with which children are familiar. Drawing a clock face, putting in the numerals and colouring half the clock can help to show half an hour.

Exercises in reading words, translating to digital time and then to analogue time are useful.

20 minutes past 8	8.20
45 minutes past 10	1045

This exercise can be used, with a further step added, when 24-hour time is involved, for example:

2020	8.20	twenty minutes past 8

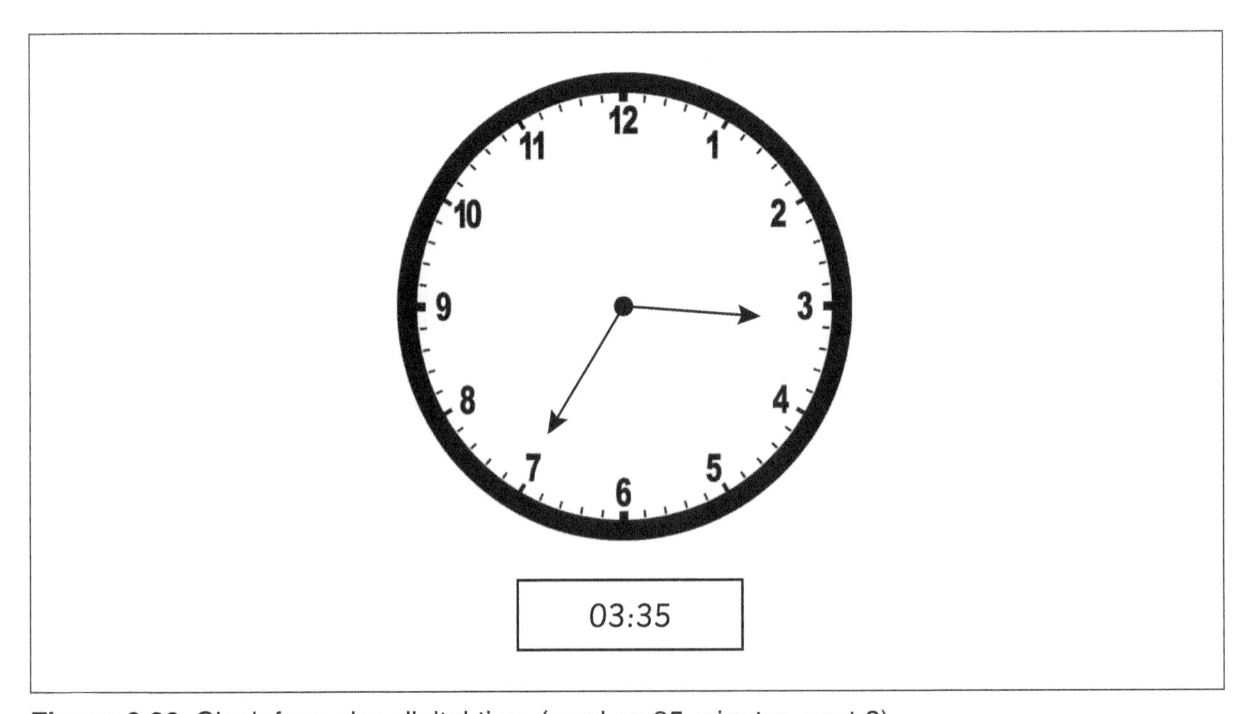

Figure 6.23 Clock face plus digital time (read as 35 minutes past 3)

When a child begins to master time, then more complicated times can be introduced. Children with confidence in this topic seem to grasp quarter past, twenty-five to, quarter to, if it is taught later, rather than pushing too much information at them too soon. Written problems do present more difficulties as initially the words have to be read, understood and then related to clock faces and digital time.

The fact that 60 minutes make an hour causes further problems, and the calculator procedure to do time calculations is rather complicated. It is important for a teacher to remember that a dyscalculic student will probably be using a different strategy to read a clock. An adult dyscalculic woman recently informed me that the first time a clock made sense to her was when her mother moved a mirror onto a wall opposite their clock:

> *'When Mum said that it was four o'clock, I heard the clock strike four and at the same time I saw the mirror image of the clock. Suddenly it all made sense! So that was what they meant by four o'clock. After that I could tell the time because I related it to the mirror image of the clock.'*

How to help

- Time is usually given in hours, so it is necessary to convert minutes into fractions.
- To change minutes into fractions of an hour divide by 60.
  30 minutes = ½ hour = 0.5
  15 minutes = ¼ hour = 0.25
  45 minutes = ¾ hour = 0.75
  5 minutes = $\frac{1}{12}$ hour = 0.08
  20 minutes = $\frac{20}{60}$ hour = 0.3

Time/distance graphs

Words and symbols to know are:

Speed (S), Time (T) and Distance (D)

Average speed (S) is measured in either:

Miles per hour abbreviated to mph or *kilometres per hour abbreviated to km/hr*

Students need to be shown exactly what graphs are, as they cannot easily interpret them because there are so many facts to be taken into consideration.

On a time/distance graph ask the following questions:

- What do the axes represent?
- What is the scale?
- How is the time shown?
- Is it in 12 or 24 hour time?
- What does a half represent?
- What does a horizontal line on the actual graph mean?

Formula using time

Distance = Speed × Time $D = S \times T$

Speed = Distance divided by Time $S = \frac{D}{T}$

Time = Distance divided by Speed $T = \frac{D}{S}$

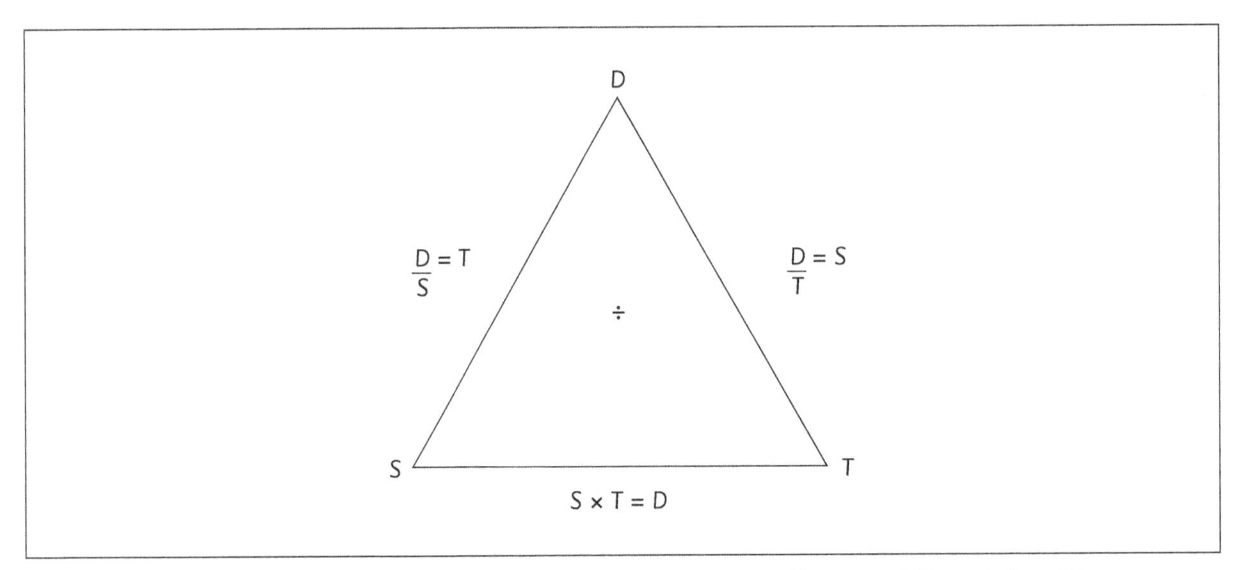

Figure 6.24 Triangle to show relationship between distance D, speed S and time T

Make a Memory Card (number 14, see page 143) of the triangle show in Figure 6.24 to use as a memory jogger.

Colour helps to sort out these relationships, as does making cards with the formulae written on them.

Make letters out of sandpaper and stick them on to wall charts to reinforce this concept.

For example

A driver can only drive for two and a half hours without stopping for a break. How far can he go on a motorway travelling at 52 miles per hour?

$S = 52$ $T = 2.5$
$D = S \times T$
$D = 52 \times 2.5$

Answer Distance = 130 miles

7 Calculating

Section A: New topics

Introducing a new topic

- Make it exciting and enjoyable.
- Talk about the topic; make it challenging; be interested in the children's views.
- If children use coloured filters or lenses, encourage them to continue to use them in mathematics.
- Discuss the new topic; write down words the children might meet.
- Allow children to speculate, hypothesise, search in other directions and make connections to other topics and subject areas.
- Encourage originality in discussions among children and with the teacher.

Organisation

General untidiness, badly spaced work, inky messy pages and illegible numbers seem to be the traits of most children with maths difficulties. Children will sometimes start their work half-way down a page, or in extreme cases at the bottom right-hand corner. Written answers are often numbered so messily that children will incorporate the number of the question into the main body of the work. For example: if calculation number 5 has the answer 12.6, the child might write '5 12.6' instead of '(5) 12.6'.

Sometimes children are unable to decipher their own work so will scribble over it, start again, have another stab at the question, cross that out and start yet again.

Organisational hints

- Explain why children should begin their work at the top of the page on the left-hand side.
- Some children may prefer to work on paper with horizontal or vertical lines, while others want blank paper. Another group might like squared paper, in which case they can use books with 0.7 cm squares. This is just the right size for both numbers and letters.
- If 1 cm squares are needed, use 1 cm squared paper, cut out the shapes and stick them into the maths book. This makes the procedure very multi-sensory.
- Encourage children to draw a margin down the left-hand side for the question/calculation number, and put a ring around it to divide it completely from the main computation.
- When doing long division children should draw a margin on the right side of the page to keep each piece of working out in the same part of the page.
- Encourage the use of rulers to keep work tidy.
- Encourage children to keep pencils, pencil sharpeners, pens and rubbers together for easy access.

Section B: Basic computation

Written computation should not be undertaken by dyscalculic children until they have worked with apparatus, talked a great deal about procedures and understood the concepts indicated by the four basic symbols in mathematics. If children start too soon with written formal maths, usually their progress is delayed rather than helped.

How to help with written computation

- Addition, subtraction and multiplication are all done from right to left, so teachers and children need to decide on a symbol which could show a child just where to begin. It could be a star, a green traffic light or simply an arrow indicating the direction of the calculation.
- Children need to be urged to make sure their figures are in the proper columns before they start the computation.
- The symbol they are using has to be highlighted so they will remember exactly which type of calculations they are doing.
- The carrying figure needs to be discussed, possibly with the class teacher, so that everyone is using the same type of notation and position to avoid confusion later.
- It is good practice to look at the errors children are making and ask them to explain exactly the procedure they are carrying out. In this way it is possible for a teacher to spot just where a child is going wrong.

A word of warning! If children are reaching correct answers, but using a long, tedious method, do not tell them that they need to change their method, as this may result in them losing all confidence in their ability and give up. It is preferable in following lessons, to show in small stages an easier way to reach the same solution. Sometimes after a teacher spends weeks trying to help children to problem solve, they will say that they have decided to change their method in favour of a shorter one.

Addition with magic squares

The idea of a magic square seems to have come from China. One was found on a document called 'Lo-Shu', dated 2200 BC. In India and Tibet the magic square is a charm.

A magic square is one in which the numbers, whether added upwards, downwards, across or diagonally, give the same answer, called the total.

Figure 7.1 shows a square partially completed, using only the numbers 4, 5 and 6. The total is 15. Can you finish the square?

4	6	5
6	5	4
	4	6

Figure 7.1 Magic square with a total of 15

- What is the total of the magic square in Figure 7.2?
- Complete the square using numbers 1, 2, 3, 7, 8 and 9 once only.

		4
	5	
6		

Figure 7.2 Magic square problem (1)

- Try to complete the magic square in Figure 7.3 (use a calculator if you wish).
- First find the total. (Clue – add the diagonal numbers.)

15		13
	12	
11		

Figure 7.3 Magic square problem (2)

Subtraction

Subtraction, take away or minus are just a few ways in mathematics that describes the action which is opposite to adding on, or in mathematical language is the inverse of addition. It is usual to introduce subtracting as the inverse of adding in the early days of teaching these processes. When only small numbers are being used, this works really well.

Example:

If 3 + 4 = 7 then 7 – 4 = 3 or 7 – 3 = 4

However as numbers become more complex, suitable strategies need to be taught. Many children who are using number lines are able to count on and count back with the help of the visual prompt of the line. However, some children struggle to count back even if the number line is there. So for this group of children it is better to teach a 'counting on' strategy to subtract or find the difference between numbers, instead of struggling to teach them to count back.

Example: 352 – 183

This has to be thought out carefully before using a number line because the numbering of the line has to reflect the values within the problem. Also it has to be decided if the counting on to the next whole ten, followed by counting on to the next hundred, will be done at the beginning or the end.

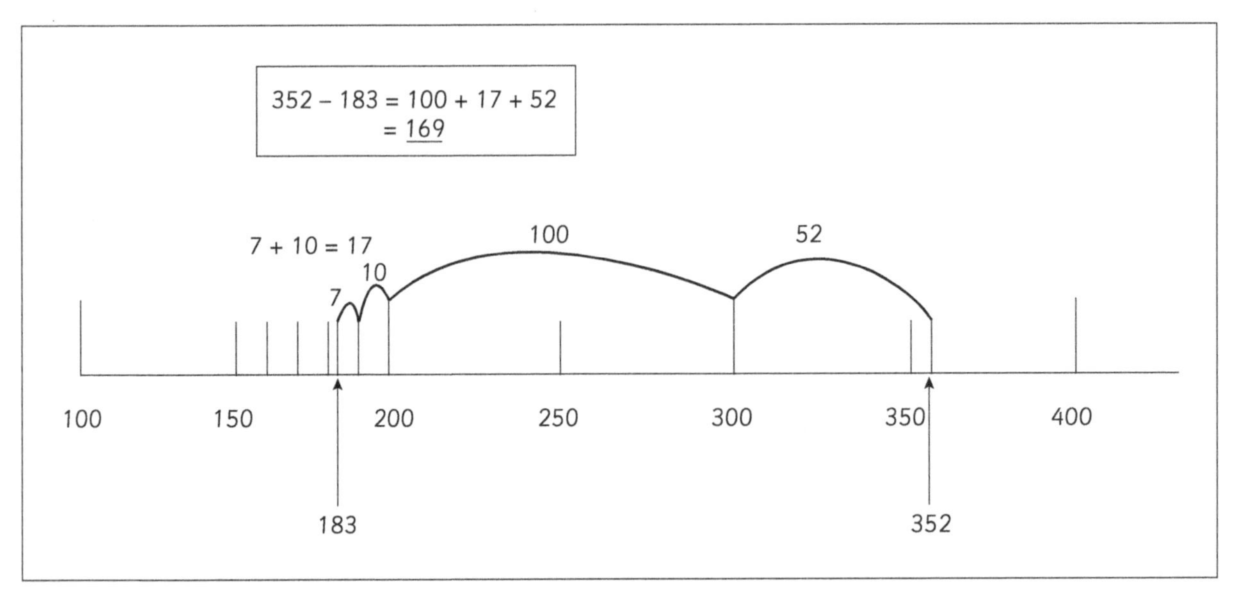

Figure 7.4 A subtraction strategy

Figure 7.4 shows the calculation with counting on done at the beginning.

- Start with 183 and count on up to 190 = 7
- Count on from 190 to 200 = 10
- Count on from 200 to 300 = 100
- Count on from 300 to 352 = 52

Add together 7 + 10 + 100 + 52 = 169

In their research asking children in Year 5 in twenty-two schools to calculate to '317 – 180', Borthwick and Harcourt-Heath (2010) found that almost half of the sample population were unable to complete the calculation. The remaining group who did answer could be divided into two categories, those who solved the calculation using decomposition and those who used number lines. A third of those who chose the decomposition strategy answered incorrectly, while the most correct were the ones who used the number line. Counting back on the number line seemed to give the most correct answers, but majority of children still chose a counting-on method.

Subtraction with a calculator

When using calculators to do subtraction, children are often confused by the words used, because they do not know which number they should enter first. Examples of wording that can be confusing are:

- Find the difference between 322 and 876
- Subtract 19 from 85
- Take away 37 from 91
- How much is 73 less than 142?

The bigger number should always be entered first, but dyscalculic and dyslexic children are not always sure which number is the biggest. Class discussion about this usually will focus on the problem so that errors may be pre-empted.

Multiplication

If children have successful strategies for knowing times table facts, then provided the correct starting place is used, short multiplication calculations should be easy to do. However, long multiplication can cause serious problems. The Chinese lattice method proves to be helpful for many children. Some children like to use colour for the diagonal lines as it seems to help them to know where they are.

Lattice method

See Figure 7.5.

Example (1): Multiply 64 by 58

- Do a quick estimation:

  60 × 60 count the noughts is 00
  6 × 6 = 36 add the noughts

  Estimate = 3600

Method (see Figure 7.5)

- Start in any square and multiply the top number by the side number, i.e.
  4 × 5 = 20 6 × 5 = 30 4 × 8 = 32 6 × 8 = 48
- Write the tens number above the diagonal line and the units figure underneath it.
- The diagonal lines can be identified as 1, 2, 3, etc., starting from the bottom right-hand corner.
- Put a piece of card across the first diagonal line and copy down the number underneath that line (in this example 2) and put in the first square.
- Then put the card across the second diagonal line and add together the numbers underneath that line (in this example 8 + 3 = 11), so 1 is put into the second square and 1 is carried forward.
- Then put the card across the third diagonal line and add together the numbers underneath that line (in this example 6 + 1 = 7), so 7 is put into the third square.
- Then put the card across the fourth diagonal line and add together the numbers underneath that line (in this example 3), so 3 is put into the fourth square.

Correct answer = 3712

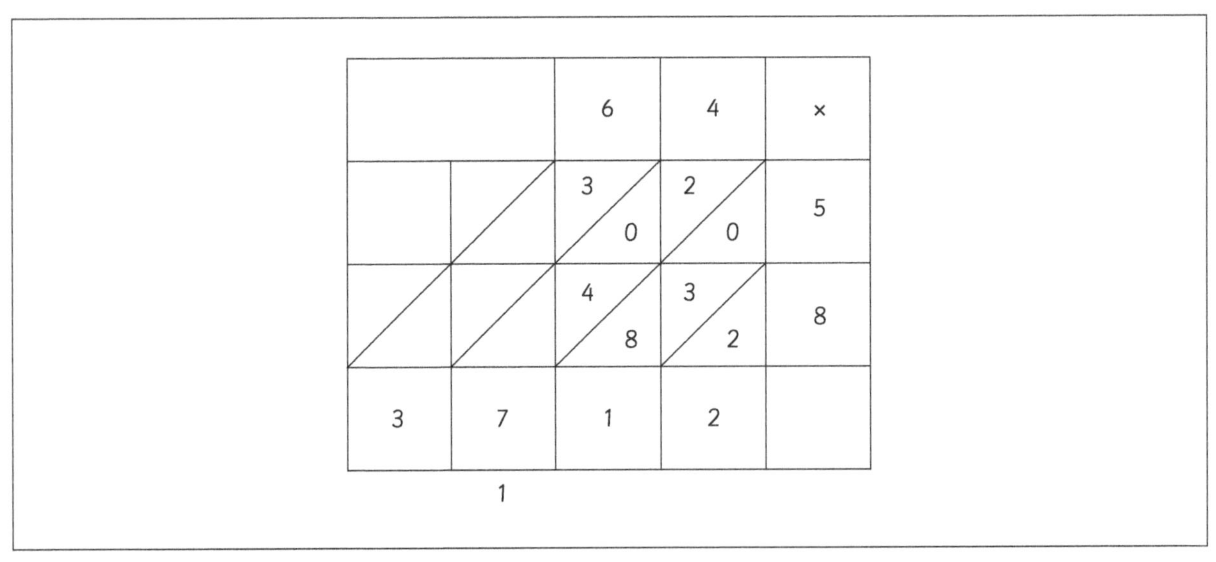

Figure 7.5 The lattice method

Method

- Estimate 400 × 90 = 36,000.
- Start in any square and multiply the top number by the side number, i.e.
  6 × 9 = 54 1 × 9 = 9 4 × 9 = 36 6 × 2 = 12 1 × 2 = 2 4 × 2 = 8
- Starting with the first diagonal, add up all numbers underneath and put them into the answer.

Correct answer is 38,272

Example (2): Multiply 416 × 92

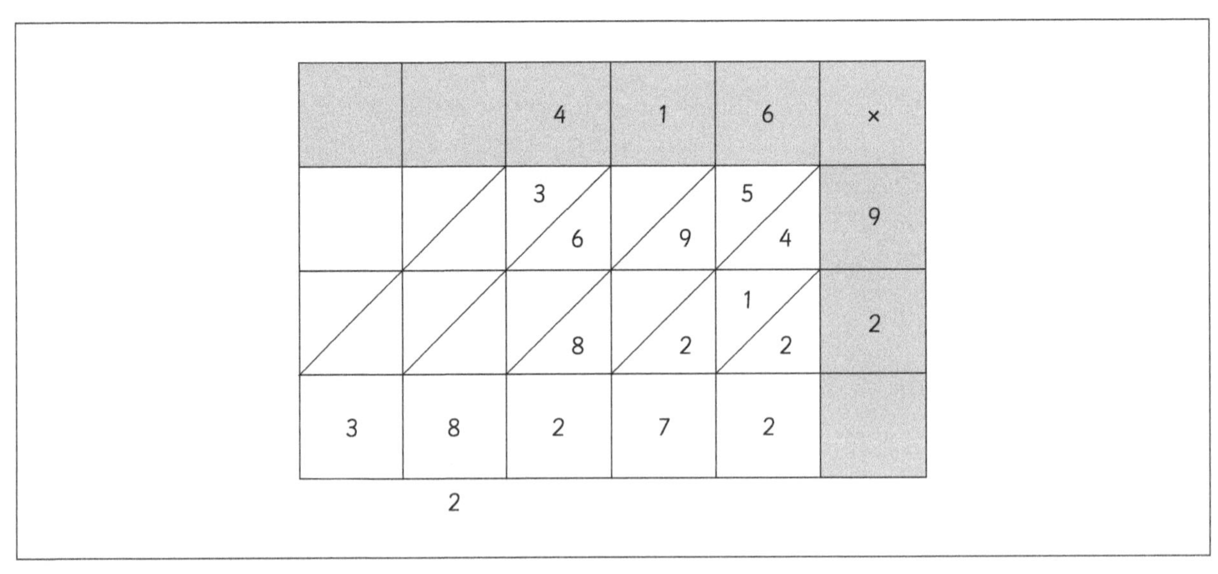

Figure 7.6 The lattice method: example 2

Multiplying using groups of tens

Another way that can be quite successful is for children to do small multiplications and then add the answers together.

Example: multiply 397 by 34

Estimate:	400×30	count the noughts 000 put them in to the answer
	$4 \times 3 = 12$	put 12 in the answer
	Estimate = 12,000	

Method

$397 \times 10 = 3970$
$397 \times 10 = 3970$
$397 \times 10 = 3970$

$397 \times 30 = \underline{11,910}$

397×4

$1200 + 360 + 28 = \underline{1588}$

$397 \times 34 = 11,910 + 1588$

Correct answer = 13,498

Division

Division can be written in three ways, and children should become familiar with them all:

a) $387 \div 9$

b) $9\overline{)387}$

c) $\frac{387}{9}$

Division without a calculator

Short division without a calculator can be complicated. For example: $387 \div 9$

- Translate the division sign ÷ into $9\overline{)387}$ (as from (a) to (b))
- Starting from the left:
- How many nines in 3? = none;
- Carry the three forward making 38;
- How many nines in 38? = 4. Write this on top over the 8;
- There are 2 left over, so carry this two forward making 27;
- How many nines in 27? = 3. Write this on top over the 7.

Answer = 43

Here is a more complex example: Divide 16.5 by 0.75:

Estimate: 17 ÷ 0.8
Make it easy!

- Multiply both numbers by 10.
- Calculation is now 170 ÷ 8 = 20 approximately.

Accurate: 16.5 ÷ 0.75

- *Make it easy!* Multiply both numbers by 100, so the calculation is now 1650 ÷ 75.
- Both numbers end in 5 or 0, so 5 is a factor of each. Divide each by 5.
  165 ÷ 5 = 330 75 ÷ 5 = 15.
- Both numbers these end in 5 or 0, so 5 is a factor of each. Divide each by 5.
  330 ÷ 5 = 66 15 ÷ 5 = 3.
- Digits of both numbers add up to 3 so 3 is a factor. Divide each by 3.
  66 ÷ 3 = 22 3 ÷ 3 = 1.

Correct answer is 22.

Division with a calculator is complex because children have to translate the question properly or they will reach the wrong answer.

Example: 387 ÷ 9

- Enter the numbers starting on the left and move towards the right entering each number and symbol as it appears. Using the second format of division:
- $9\overline{)387}$;
- Enter the numbers inside the division shape first (387);
- Enter the division sign;
- Enter the number on the left (9).

This particular operation is carried out incorrectly so often it is a good idea to have a 'nudge' policy. If the child enters the digits in the wrong order, nudge them, and they should realise the error and re-enter the numbers correctly.

Using the third form of notation:

$$\frac{387}{9}$$

- Enter the numbers on the top followed by the numbers under the line.

A fun way of checking answers: casting out nines

To cast out nines add up each digit in a number. For example: 567

5 + 6 + 7 = 18
1 + 8 = 9 9 is the 'magic answer'

If a calculation is correct the magic numbers of both the calculation and the answer will be the same.

To check if

$$64 \times 58 = 3712$$
$$6 + 4 \times 5 + 8 = 3 + 7 + 1 + 2$$
$$10 \times 13 = 13$$
$$1 + 0 \times 1 + 3 = 1 + 3$$
$$1 \times 4 = 4$$
$$\underline{4 = 4}$$ (the magic numbers are the same)

Using a calculator

A calculator has the advantages that it:

- allows children to reach solutions;
- promotes mathematical discussion;
- requires the early development of estimating and approximating skills;
- eases the transfer from concrete to symbolic thinking;
- allows real-life numbers to be used;
- allows mathematical exploration;
- helps to focus on the problem rather than on the computation;
- allows concentration on methods and concepts;
- takes away some of the fear of mathematics.

Many children have to be persuaded to use a calculator because they feel it is 'cheating' in some way. At other times it is necessary to suggest that it would be better to write down exactly what they intend to do on the calculator before they do it. This is because some children use the calculator, get an answer, then forget what they have done. This last point is particularly relevant to 'grasshopper' thinkers.

How to help

- Help children to understand the functions of the keys and recognise the ones they will use most.
- Encourage children to practise pressing the right keys because after reading a number they need to be able to reproduce it accurately in order to achieve a correct answer.
- Pre-empt reversal of numbers by encouraging children to read the number aloud, then check again aloud that this is the number that is displayed on the calculator.
- To avoid children pressing the addition key instead of the multiply key, encourage them to write the symbol down in a different colour so that it is a visual reminder of which key they should be pressing.
- Encourage children to place calculators on top of their desk, then they will see the decimal point more easily.

It is important that children with specific learning difficulties in mathematics are actively encouraged to use calculators in appropriate situations. They need to be given clear guidance on the procedures needed to obtain maximum benefit from their use. A curriculum that is investigational as well as practical encourages this, allowing children the chance to explore new horizons. Children who find using a calculator difficult need the opportunity to practise until they are confident in their own expertise.

8 Algebra

Section A: Overview of the topic

Algebra allows generalisations to be made in maths by using letters to represent numbers, and for this reason understanding the topic is important. However, it is one of the most difficult aspects of abstract mathematics, which is often found irrelevant by many students and hated by many others. Indeed, their intense dislike may colour their attitude towards everything connected to maths. The fact that numbers and letters are used together creates a huge learning step to climb, exacerbating difficulties for both dyslexic and dyscalculic students experiencing problems with symbols.

Students struggle to know the difference between 'bs' and 'ds' as well as 'qs', 'ps' and '9s'. A hurried 4 and an untidy continental 7 can easily be confused with an A if they are put together in a question. To help students understand the basic principles of algebra they need to be taught the following facts slowly using flash cards, colour and much patience. Explanations that show it is a magical way of looking at patterns, and finding solutions can help. Stick algebraic letters onto building blocks to demonstrate the meaning of $3x$.

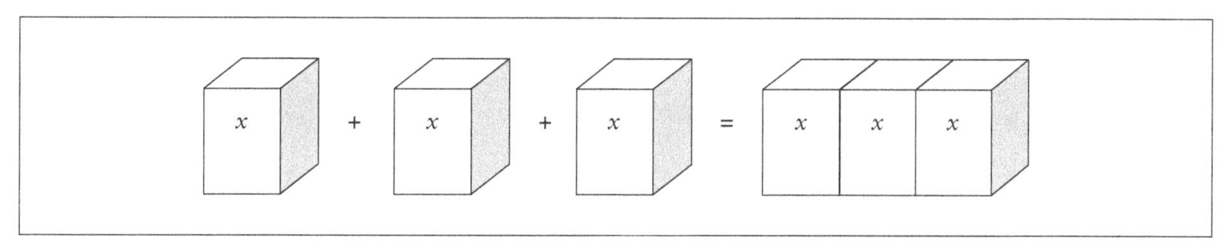

Figure 8.1 Building blocks showing that x plus x plus x equals $3x$

How to help with basic algebra

- The + or – is connected to the letter or number on the right (students often confuse left and right, so connect up the symbol with the letter or number that follows it.)
  For example:
  a in algebra means $+1a$
  x in algebra means $+1x$
  $2 - x$ means $+2$ and $-x$
  $a - b$ means $+a$ and $-b$

- The multiplication × symbol is not used in algebra to avoid confusion with the algebraic letter x. Letters or symbols close together, brackets and indices mean multiply.

- Letters or symbols put close together mean multiply:
  $2x$ means 2 multiplied by x $\quad 2 \times x$
  $3a$ means 3 multiplied by a $\quad 3 \times a$
  $4y$ means 4 multiplied by y $\quad 4 \times y$

- A bracket means multiply:
  $3(a)$ means 3 multiplied by a $\quad 3 \times a$

- Indices mean multiply:
  3^2 means 3 multiplied by 3 $\quad 3 \times 3 = 9$
  b^2 means b multiplied by b
  6^3 means $6 \times 6 \times 6 = 216$
  x^3 means $x \times x \times x$

- $4x$ take away x is not 4
  For example $4x - x = 3x$ $(x + x + x + x) - x = 3x$

The = sign

Students meet the equals sign early in their education and the language associated with it starts at this stage. Eventually students meet the sign formally in algebra and need to understand that equals sign = is used as a balance to show that one side of an equation, even though it may look different, is equivalent or the same size as the other.

Section B: Directed numbers (positive and negative numbers)

Dealing with negative and positive numbers can be a hard task for many students. Making a memory card (number 15, see page 143) has proved helpful.

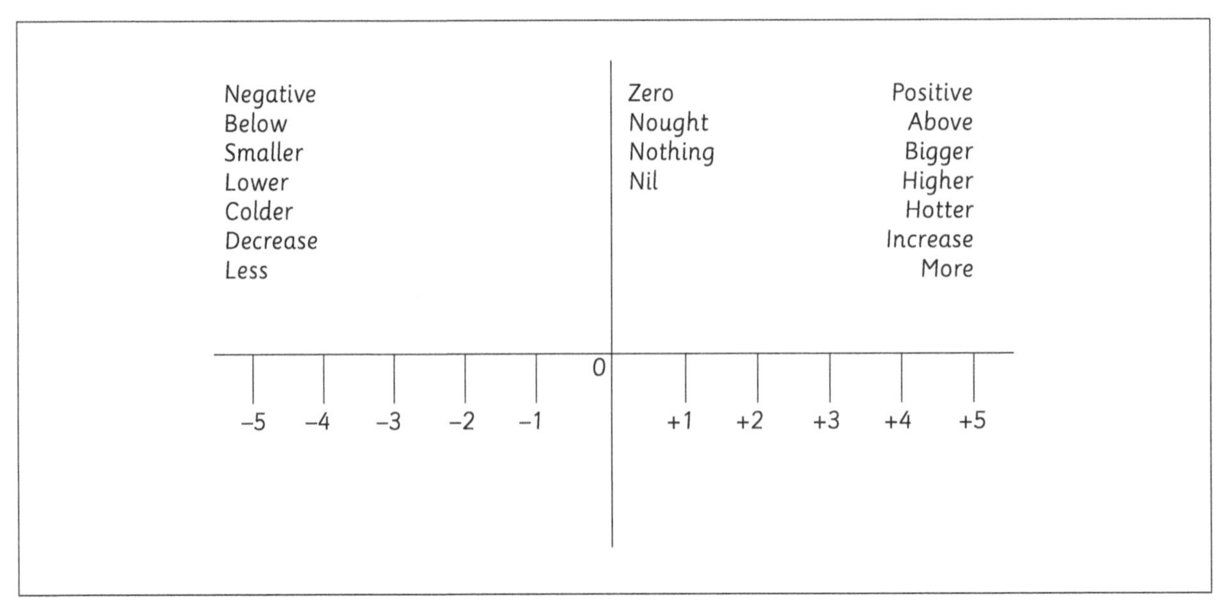

Figure 8.2 Positive and negative number line

How to help with directed numbers

- Negative numbers are:
  - less than 0.
  - shown in mathematics with a – (minus) sign placed on the left of the number (–3 is read as minus 3 and means negative 3).
- Make a number line on cardboard to show both positive and negative numbers: see memory card 15 (see page 143). Use colour to separate the positive side from the negative side.
- Put a drawing pin through the zero and turn the card through 90 degrees in an anticlockwise direction. Students can then see that the scale is the same whether it is vertical or horizontal.
- Temperature scales and reading thermometers are starting points to assist students with this concept.

Multiplying and dividing negative numbers

Students are often confused when they have to calculate with negative signs in algebra. The following simple tips may help.

- BEWARE if removing a bracket: a minus sign outside a bracket changes every sign inside the bracket.
  For example:
  $-3(b + 2)$ becomes $-3b - 6$
  $-a(6 - c)$ becomes $-6a + ac$

When multiplying negative numbers always remember that:

minus	×	minus	=	plus	minus	×	plus	= minus
plus	×	plus	=	plus	plus	×	minus	= minus

When dividing negative numbers always remember that:

minus	÷	minus	=	plus	plus	÷	minus	= minus
plus	÷	plus	=	plus	minus	÷	plus	= minus

This short rhyme can help:

Signs the same, play the game, make it plus.

Signs are different, not the same, make it minus.

Students can make a table square showing all four quadrants (see Figure 8.3) which may help when they begin to work with coordinates and other related topics.

–25	–20	–15	–10	–5		5	10	15	20	25
–20	–16	–12	–8	–4		4	8	12	16	20
–15	–12	–9	–6	–3		3	6	9	12	15
–10	–8	–6	–4	–2		2	4	6	8	10
–5	–4	–3	–2	–1		1	2	3	4	5
					0					
5	4	3	2	1		–1	–2	–3	–4	–5
10	8	6	4	2		–2	–4	–6	–8	–10
15	12	9	6	3		–3	–6	–9	–12	–15
20	16	12	8	4		–4	–8	–12	–16	–20
25	20	15	10	5		–5	–10	–15	–20	–25

Figure 8.3 Table square showing the four quadrants

Section C: A practical approach

- Use cubes of two colours, e.g. black and white, to make a pattern (see Figure 8.4).
- Substitute b for black and w for white into the pattern.

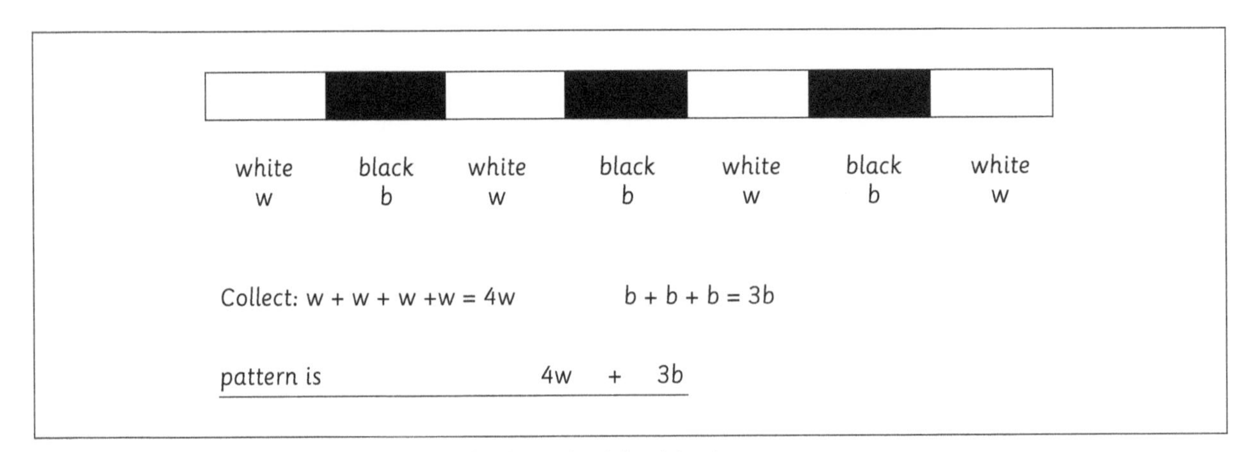

Figure 8.4 A simple pattern with black and white blocks

- Allow students to make up many easy different patterns, and write down their patterns in letters.
- When the students are confident, encourage them to make more complex patterns (see Figure 8.5).

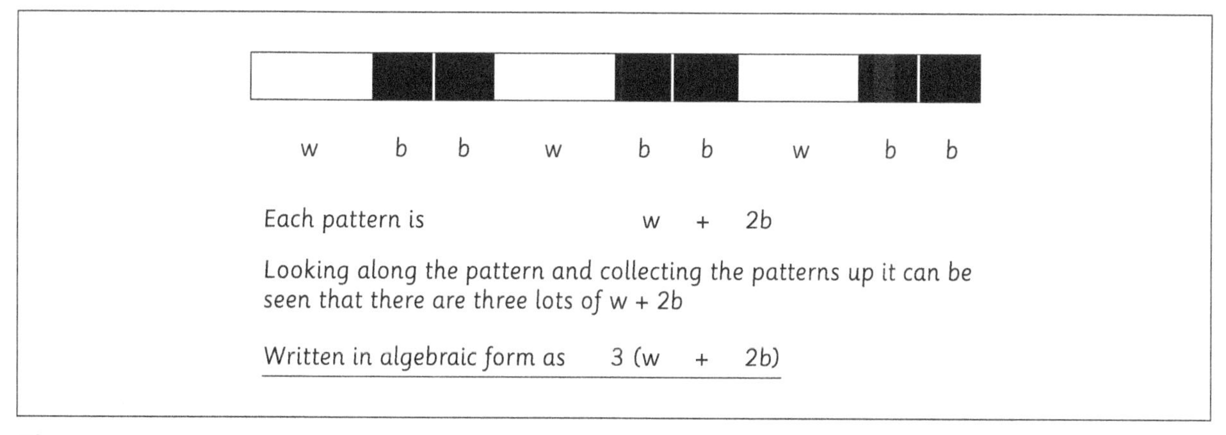

Figure 8.5 More complex pattern with black and white blocks

In this way students begin to see patterns, pattern repetition and practical use of brackets, as well as picking up general algebraic expressions.

Expansion of expressions

- To multiply one bracket by a value, for example: $5(2y - 3)$:
  multiply 5 by the $2y = 10y$ then multiply 5 by $-3 = -15$
  answer = $10y - 15$

- Always beware a minus sign outside a bracket; it changes every sign inside the bracket. For example:
  $-2\ (x + 3) = -2x - 6$

When faced with two brackets to multiply together students can be helped by using the following procedure and mnemonic (see Figure 8.6). A memory card (number 16, see page 143) helps as a memory prompt.

Eyebrow, eyebrow nose then mouth

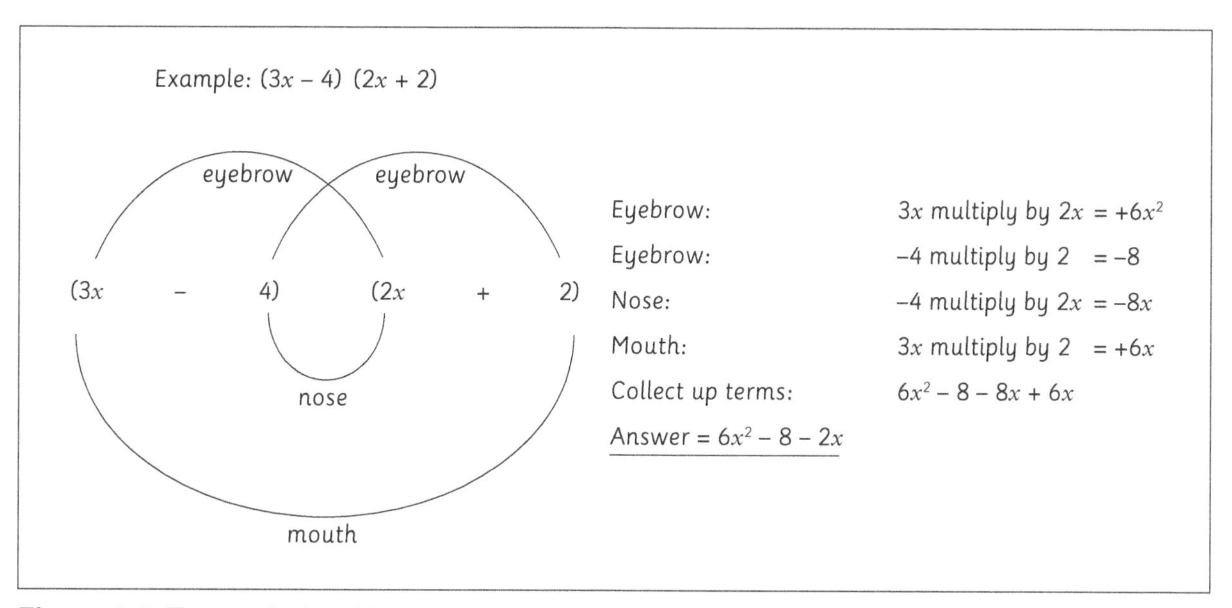

Figure 8.6 Face to help with algebra

Section D: Equations

Most dyscalculic and dyslexic students struggle with equations regardless of how many different methods they are shown. The only way to enable students to succeed is to repeat, revise and reinforce strategies using colour and practical materials where possible. Another big problem with finding solutions to equations is that students with 'grasshopper' learning styles will do simple equations easily in their heads without writing down a single piece of working out. The 'inchworm' will quickly grasp the idea of treating each side the same, which works well for equations.

For example:

Find the value of x in the following equation.

$$3x - 2 = x + 12$$

Do this to each side

$$3x - 2 + \mathbf{2} = x + 12 + \mathbf{2} \qquad \mathbf{+\,2}$$

$$3x = x + 14$$

$$3x - x = x + 14 - x \qquad -\,x$$

$$2x = 14$$

$$\frac{2x}{\mathbf{2}} = \frac{14}{\mathbf{2}} \qquad \mathbf{\div\,2}$$

$$\underline{x = 7}$$

Section E: Investigations

Investigations into various pattern formations lead students to describing them in an algebraic way, but often the students can spot the pattern but are unable to connect it to a formula. Many teachers have a favourite way of teaching the connection, and as long as it is in slow, easy steps which the students understand, such methods help. As patterns are such an important part of mathematics, it is hoped that pupils can enjoy identifying them and so lessen their fear of this subject.

Some practical examples

(Answers are at the end of the chapter.)

Complete the rows shown in Figure 8.7 by using the total number stated above each row and filling in the blanks so that the numbers either side of the circles add up to the numbers in the circles. You can use cubes as concrete apparatus to help students work out the answers. The first one has been completed as an example. If 5 is in the circle, the number patterns to be considered are 4 + 1, 5 + 0 and 3 + 2. In this case choose 3 and 2 using five cubes, so obviously if 2 is in the middle box, and the number in the second circle is 3, then the number in the last box must be 1.

Try to find a quick way of finding answers.

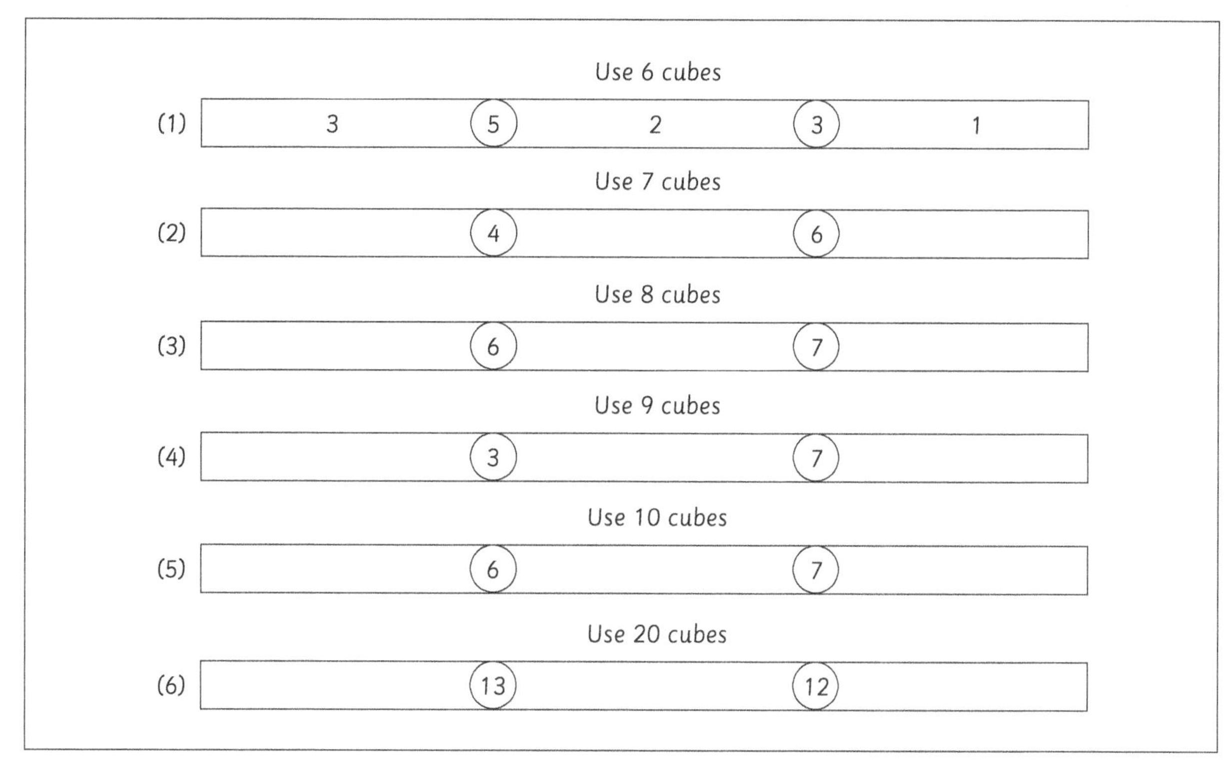

Figure 8.7 Cube exercises

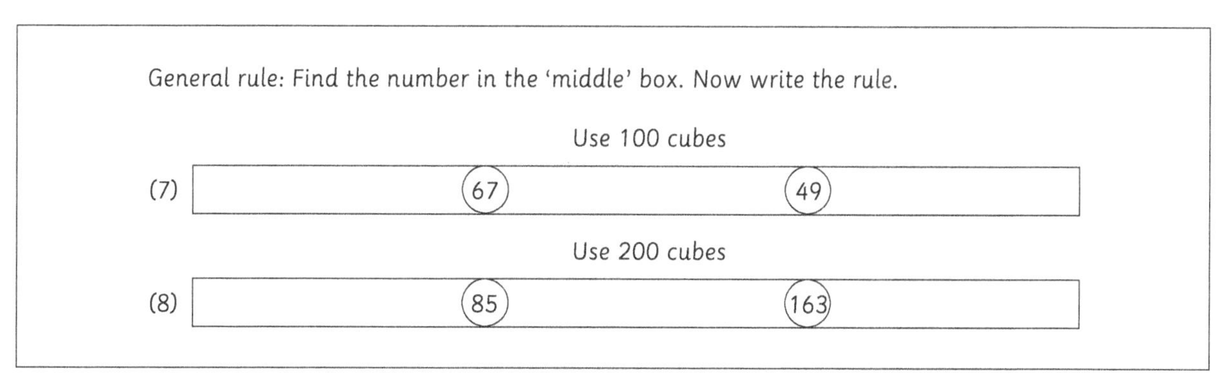

Figure 8.8 More cube exercises

Hints to help with investigations

- Choose an uncluttered method.
- Try to be systematic.
- Look for patterns. (Are you able to predict the next answer? If so, can you check it by drawing?)
- Record results in a table.
- Are you able to make more predictions and extend the table?
- If you have found a rule can you write it out in words?
- Are you able to write the rule using algebra?
- Check the rule.

For example, Figure 8.9 shows three patterns of white squares surrounding black squares. Draw the fourth pattern.

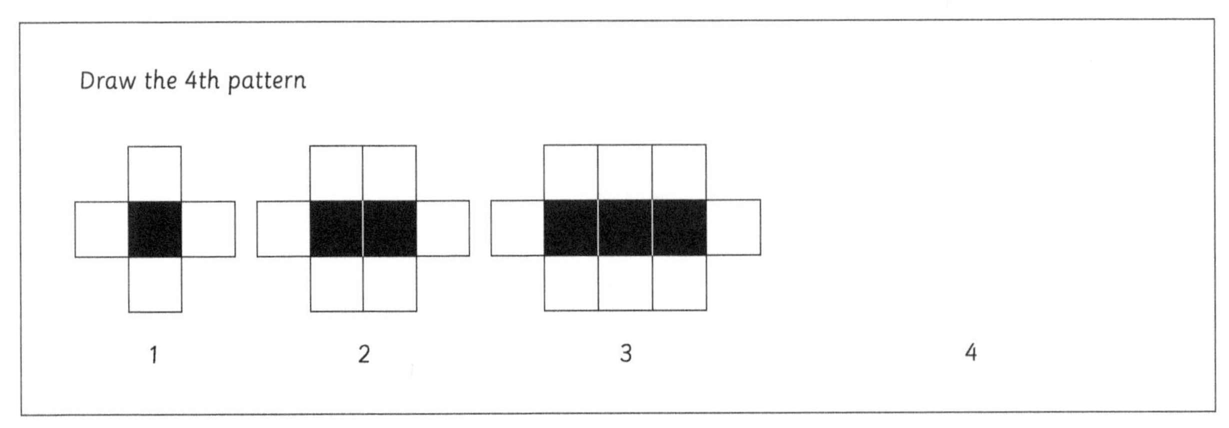

Figure 8.9 An investigation problem

- Complete the table shown in Figure 8.10.

Black	White	Black	White
1	4	1	4
2	6	2	6
3	8	3	8
		Prediction 4	10
		Prediction 5	12
		Prediction 20	Algebra check
		Prediction 100	Algebra check

Figure 8.10 A table to complete during the investigation

Algebra check

The rule seems to be that each time a black square is added the white squares increase by 2. Look at the first pattern:

1 black 4 white
$(1 \times 2) + 2 = 4$ $(1 \times 2) = 2$ which means 2 must be added to make the 4 as in the pattern

Second pattern:

2 black 6 white
$(2 \times 2) + 2 = 6$

Third pattern:

3 black 8 white
$(3 \times 2) + 2 = 8$ (this seems to be working 8 is correct)

Investigate 10th pattern

10 black		? white	
$(10 \times 2) + 2$	=	22	(check this by drawing pattern)

Investigate 100th pattern

100 black		? white	
$(100 \times 2) + 2$	=	202	(check this by drawing pattern)

Formula is $(2 \times b) + 2 = w$

Section F: Straight-line graphs

Students need to have each part of the equation explained clearly, then they are usually able to complete this topic with relative ease.

The gradient of a line

The gradient is the slope of a line in relation to the (positive) direction of the x axis (which tells us how steep the line is). It is easily calculated by finding the change in upward distance and dividing it by the change in horizontal distance.

> The gradient of a line is shown clearly in an equation because it is the number attached to the x value.
>
> If there is no number shown next to the x then it is understood that the value of the x is $+1x$.

Hints to help with graphs

- If the x number is positive + then the line will slope upwards towards the right.
- If the x number is negative – then the line will slope upwards towards the left.

Examples

In the equation $y = x + 3$

x means $\frac{+1 \text{ up}}{1 \text{ across}}$ positive sloping towards the right

In the equation $y = -3x + 4$

$-3x$ means $\frac{-3 \text{ up}}{1 \text{ across}}$ negative sloping towards the left

Method to draw the line whose equation is $y = 2x + 3$

Colour the $2x$ and the +3 in different colours.

The gradient +2 tells us that the line will slope towards the right moving upwards 2 units for each unit across.

The number +3 tells us where the line crosses the y axis.

We can sketch the line now by starting at +3 on the y axis and marking consecutive points in either direction by moving across one unit and either up or down by two units.

The coordinates will be (–2, –1) (–1, 1) (0, 3) (+1, 5).

Value of x	-2	-1	0	+1	+2
Value of y	-1	+1	+3	+5	+7

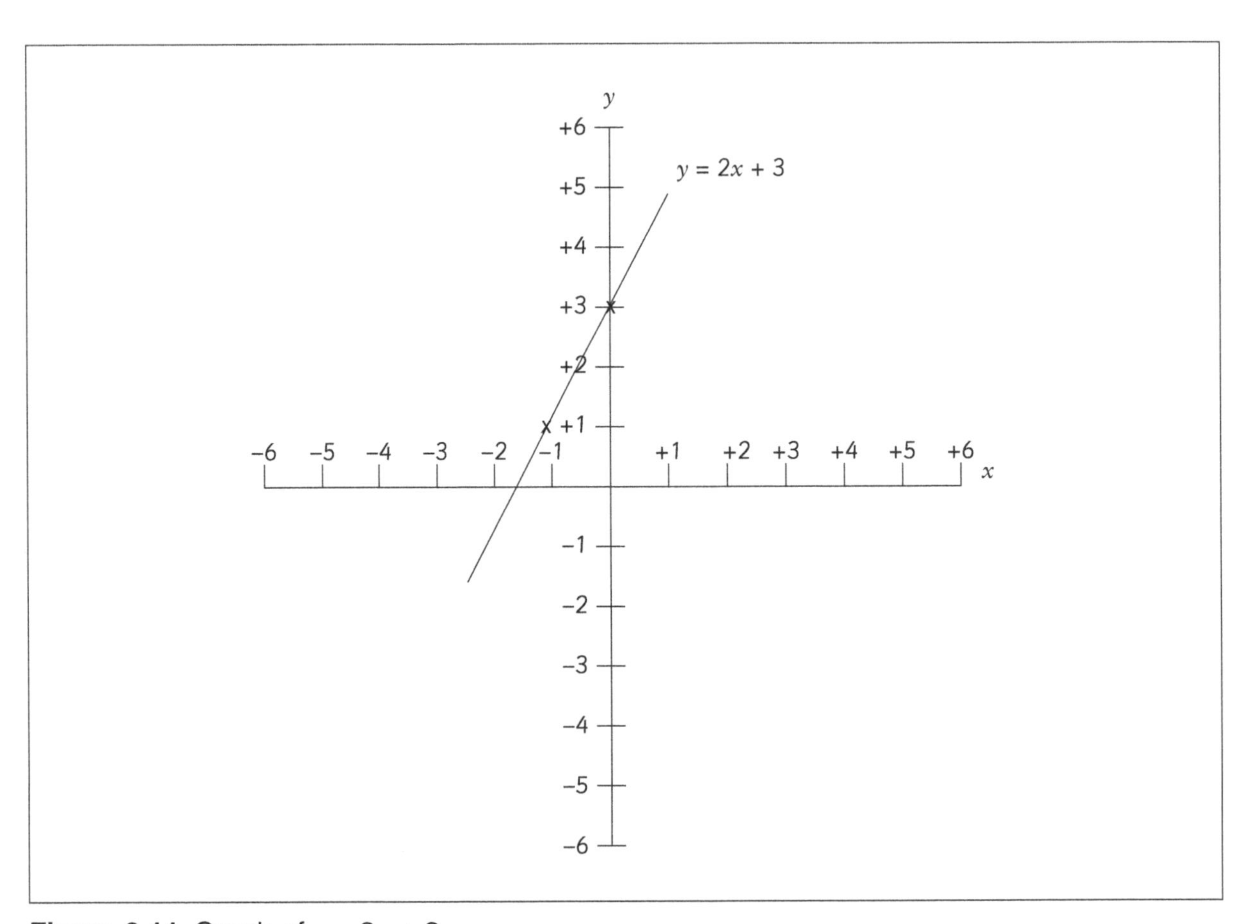

Figure 8.11 Graph of $y = 2x + 3$

Answers to investigations

(2) Use 7 cubes	1	(4)	3	(6)	3
(3) Use 8 cubes	1	(6)	5	(7)	2
(4) Use 9 cubes	2	(3)	1	(7)	6
(5) Use 10 cubes	3	(6)	3	(7)	4
(6) Use 20 cubes	8	(13)	5	(12)	7
(7) Use 100 cubes	51	(67)	16	(49)	33
(8) Use 200 cubes	37	(85)	48	(163)	115

(7): 100 – 67 = 33
49 – 33 = 16
67 – 16 = 51

(8): 200 – 85 = 115
163 – 115 = 48
85 – 48 = 37

Figure 8.12 Answers to problems in Figures 8.7 and 8.8

To help with cube problem (7)

100 – 49 = 51 is in the first box
67 – 51 = 16 is in the middle box
49 – 16 = 33 is in the last box

The rule

Number in first box: total number of cubes minus number in second circle.
Number in middle box: number in first circle minus number in first box.
Number in third box: number in second circle minus number in middle box.

9 Shape, space and measures

Section A: Overview

These topics are ones that most students seem to enjoy because, on the whole, they can understand them. The shapes are concrete, often three-dimensional and visually pleasing, which are the necessary ingredients to give success to students with specific learning difficulties. The main difficulty is with the complex mathematical words used to describe the shapes, their properties, and the connections and similarities between them. Occasionally students struggle with identifying specific lines within a shape, so they may need to use colour filters to cut out the glare in order to isolate the particular figures they need to study.

Section B: Use of practical equipment

Pencils and pens

If a student is writing badly in mathematics it may be because their pen or pencil is a poor shape for their grip. It is possible to buy rubber or plastic grips which help, from most educational suppliers. Badly written '4s' can be confused with 'As'. In addition, pencils should be sharp so the child can produce precise letters and numbers, and draw lines with exact measurements.

Richard was so afraid of mathematics that he wrote with his elbow touching his side at all times. To move across the page he had to move his whole body – so you can imagine the state of his book! As he was left-handed I was suggested that he pressed very hard on the desk with his right arm to see if that would help. He found that by doing this the tension went out of his left arm and his writing improved. I have recommended this technique ever since, and it has resulted in much improved writing for many students.

The ruler

It is important to ensure that students are able to use a ruler correctly. If they are anxious about maths their hands may be sweaty which will make the ruler slide about, so it is essential to talk to them to relieve the anxiety. You should convey the point that the ruler must be held firmly in the centre if a line is to be drawn straight. Also point out the end of the ruler. This enables students to realise that they must decide where to begin by looking for the first line from the end of the ruler (see Figure 9.1), which is usually marked with 0, and begin measuring from there.

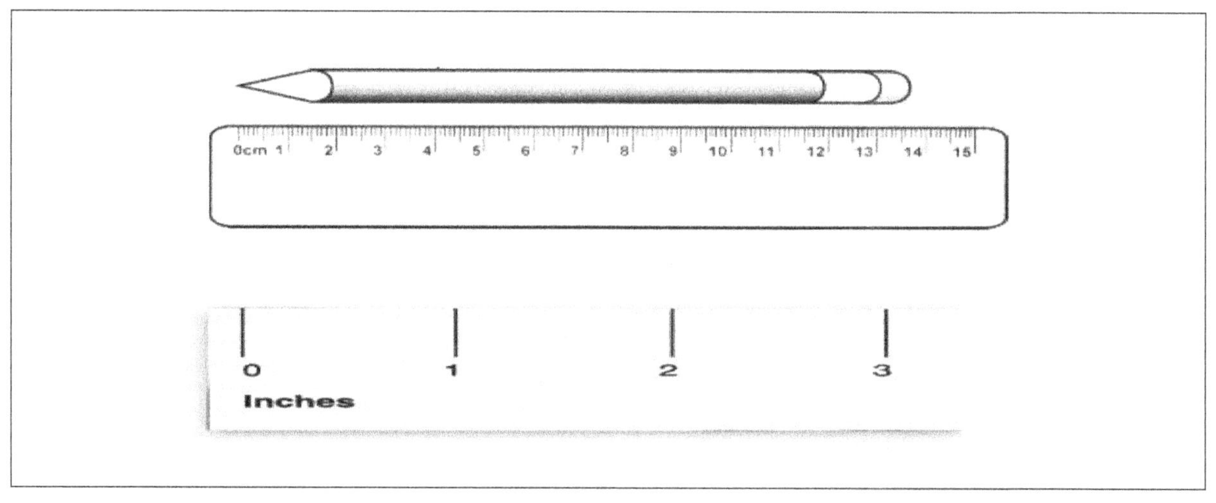

Figure 9.1 Rulers

The protractor

Students usually like to use circular angle measures if they are measuring bearings, and protractors to measure pie charts and angles in shapes. The angle measures seem to present fewer problems than the protractors.

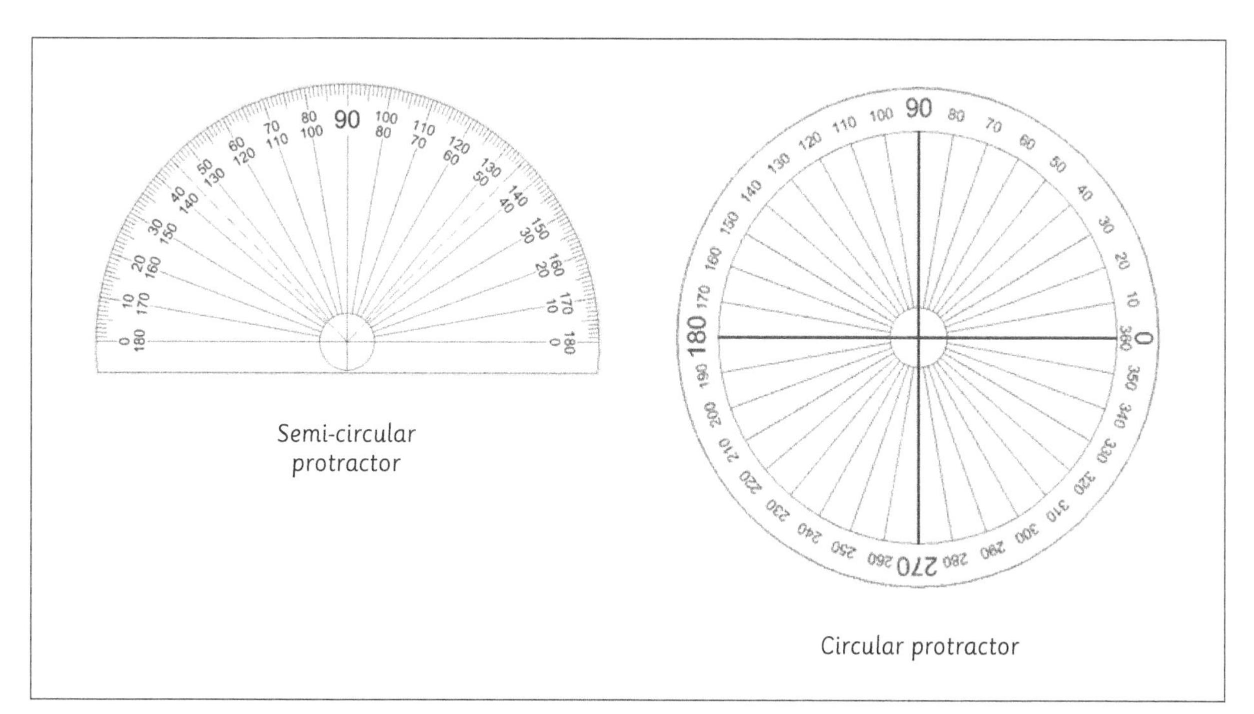

Figure 9.2 Protractors

One student kept going wrong when doing pie charts, even though we had revised the method and he appeared to be confident. With closer observation it was obvious that he was struggling with left, right, clockwise and anti-clockwise when using the protractor to measure the angles. Sometimes the inside scale, sometimes the outside scale was read so he was never sure which one to use. After our discussion I gave him specific notes to clearly show the method. He used these until the method became automatic to him. It is better to pre-empt this problem by spending enough time discussing the properties of the protractor. You could make a Memory card that will specifically help students using them.

Section C: Specific issues with shape, space and measures

Direction

Problems here often include:

- measuring the wrong angle, especially with bearings;
- confusion with 'clockwise' and 'anticlockwise' directions when using a protractor;
- confusion over directions generally (North, South, East and West);
- confusing left (West) and right (East).

You could make a memory card (number 17, see page 143) with the following mnemonics for directions:

'Naughty Elephants Squirt Water'

Talking about North and its exact opposite South is helpful; link this with the initials of the two remaining directions West and East that spell 'we'. This can be a better way for many students.

Language

Students can find words like horizontal, vertical, vertices and isosceles difficult to read, and it is also difficult for them to remember exactly what they mean. Introduce the main words they will come across. Encourage them to write them down on index cards with diagrams and, if necessary, put the list on a wall chart. The following points help with this topic.

- Point out and discuss words within the topic (see Table 9.1). Teachers should focus on specific words their students may need.

Table 9.1 Shape, space and measures vocabulary

height	length	width	depth	area
squared	bisect	volume	cubed	parallel
vertical	horizontal	cm^2	cm^3	units

Symbols used like the arrows indicating parallel lines, and those indicating that lines are of equal length, can cause difficulties (see Figure 9.3).

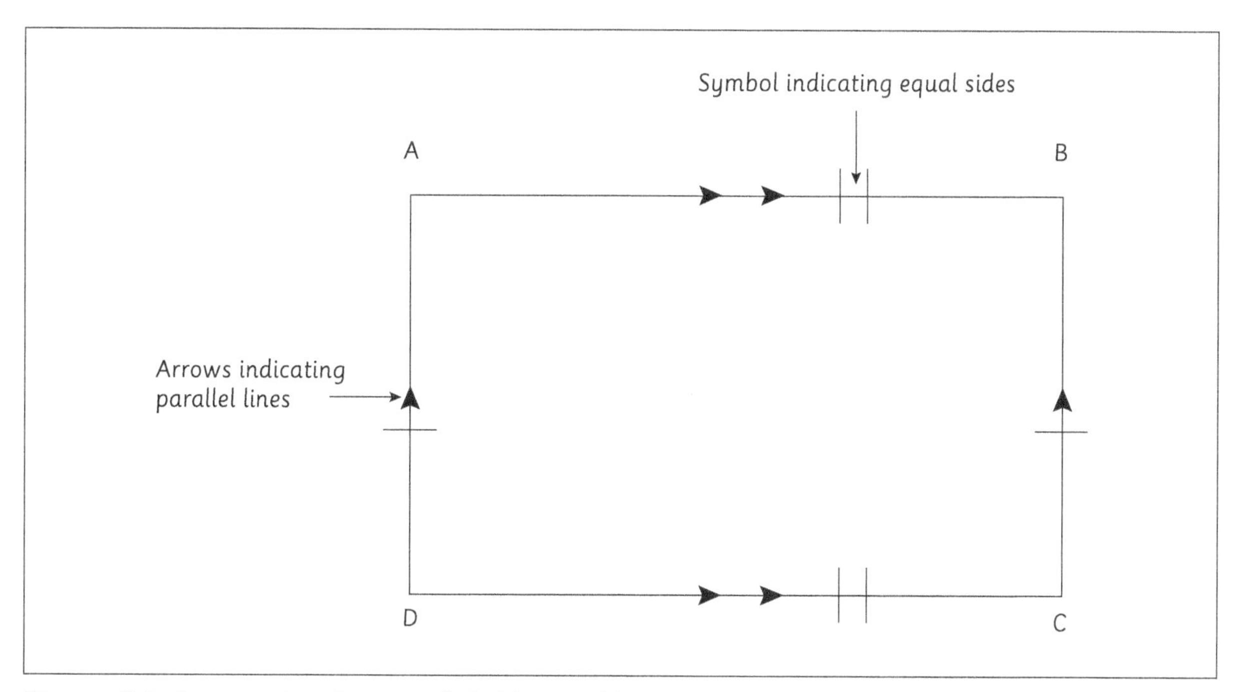

Figure 9.3 Arrows showing parallel sides and line symbols showing equal sides

- Explain that lines are identified by two letters, one at each end (see Figure 9.4).

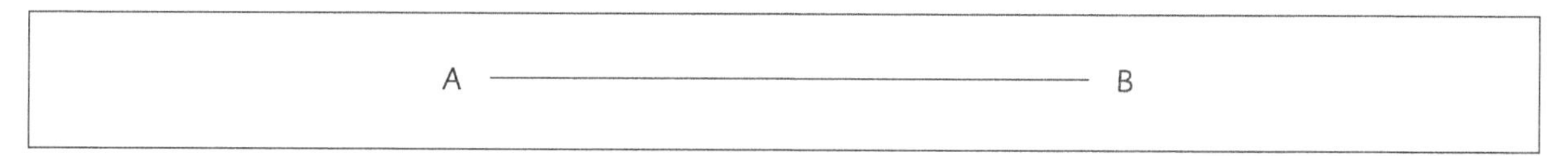

Figure 9.4 A named line – AB

Angles are identified usually by three letters. The middle one refers to the angle, and the other two to the ends of the lines that make the angle (see Figure 9.5).

Angle XYZ or $\angle$ XYZ

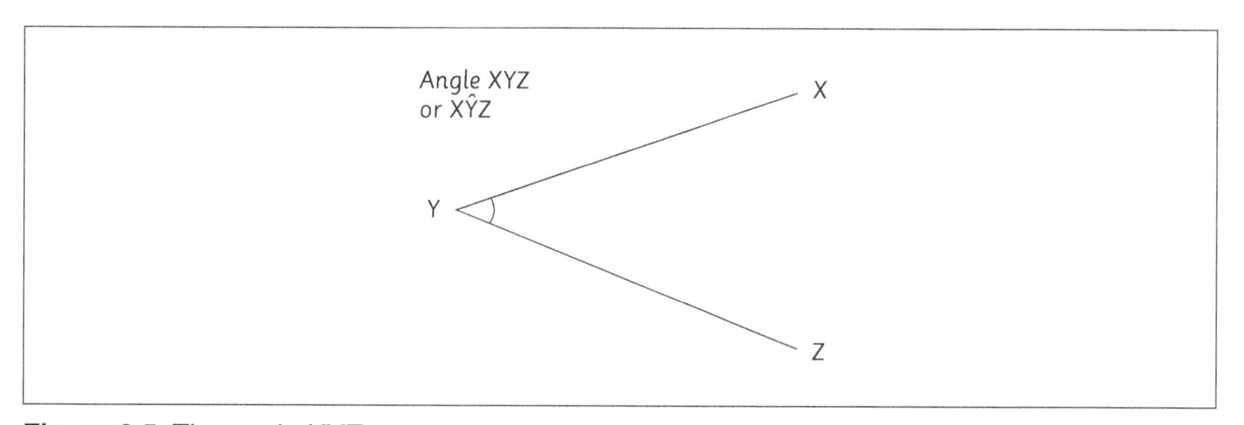

Figure 9.5 The angle XYZ

Section D: Properties of angles and shapes

Many of the figures in this chapter show different shapes and their properties. These visual representations usually help students to remember the shapes, their names and their properties. Copy them onto A4 paper so they are readily available. Students are then able to add their own explanatory notes if necessary. The shapes can also be photocopied onto card, and mobiles can be made and hung from the ceiling. Using the same idea, three-dimensional shapes can be made showing the properties of each shape and again made into mobiles.

Index cards should be made for each shape with the correct words shown clearly. Provide accompanying notes using key words, if required, and diagrams showing worked examples of area and volume. It is important to remember that each student has varying demands from notes, so their format must be governed by the individual's needs.

Properties of angles

See page 143 for the memory cards referred to here.

- Copy, cut out, stick onto card and turn these angle pictures and facts into a memory card (number 18, see page 143).
- Always read the symbol ° as degree or degrees.

Acute angle

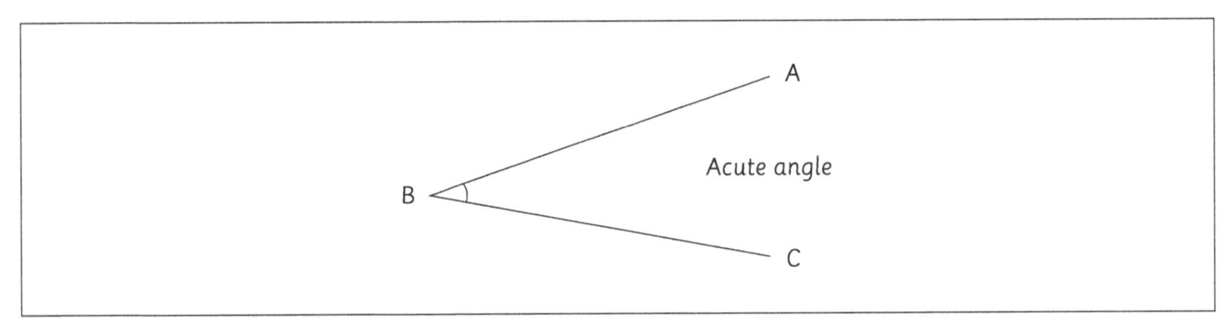

Figure 9.6 Acute angles (sharp, pointed: less than 90°)

Right angle

Note that these do not always point to the right, so show diagrams with the right angle in different places.

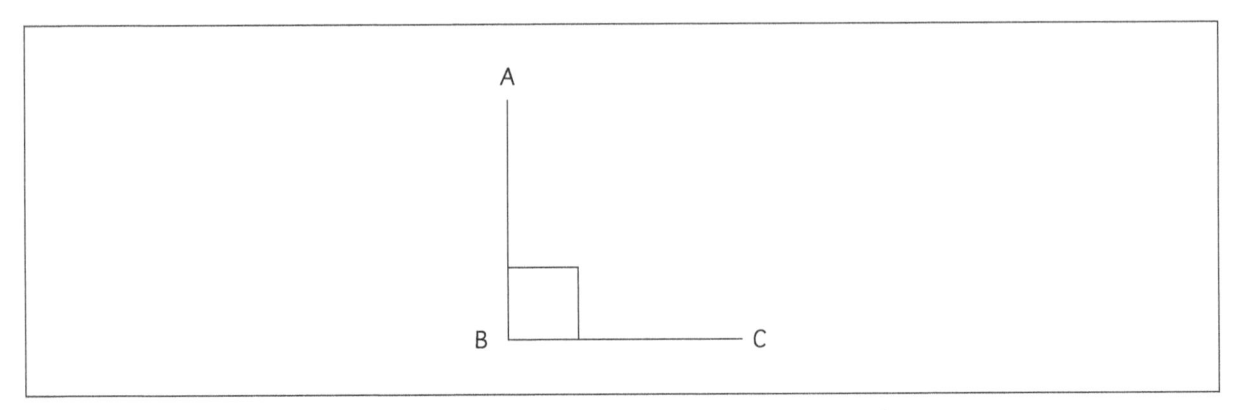

Figure 9.7 Right angles are exactly 90° (but not always on the right)

Obtuse angle

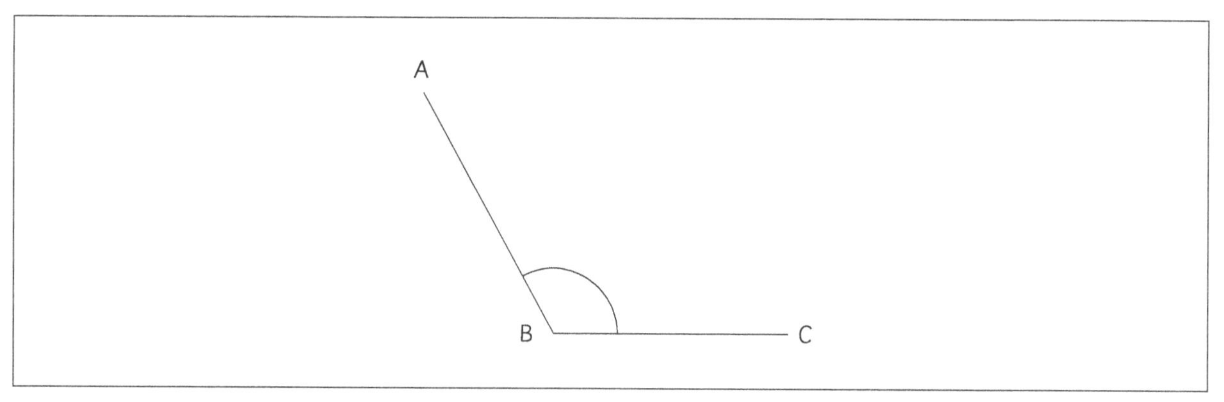

Figure 9.8 Obtuse angles are more than 90° but less than 180°

Straight angle

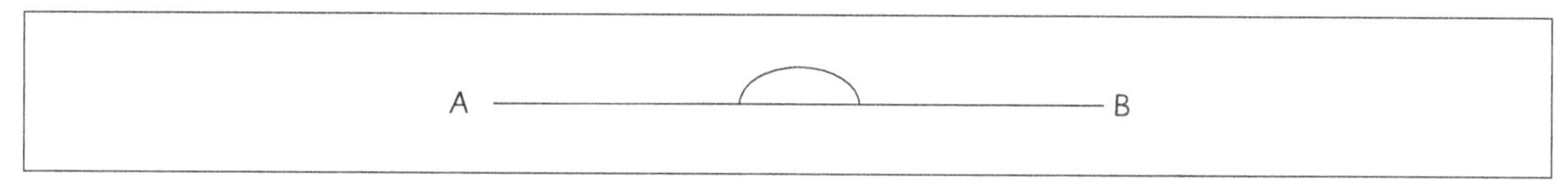

Figure 9.9 Straight angles are exactly 180°

Reflex angle

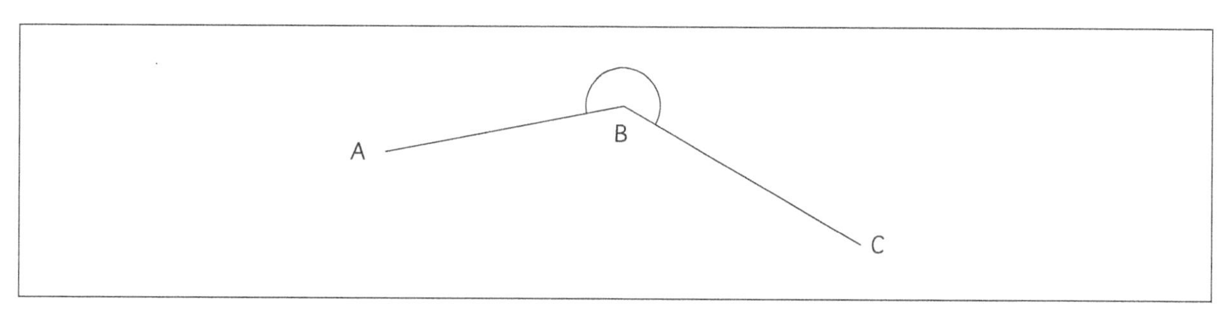

Figure 9.10 Reflex angles are more than 180° but less than 360°

Properties of triangles

- Copy, cut out, stick onto card and turn these shapes into a memory card (number 19, see page 144).
- Explain that the angles in all triangles add up to 180°.

A *scalene triangle*: has no equal sides or angles.

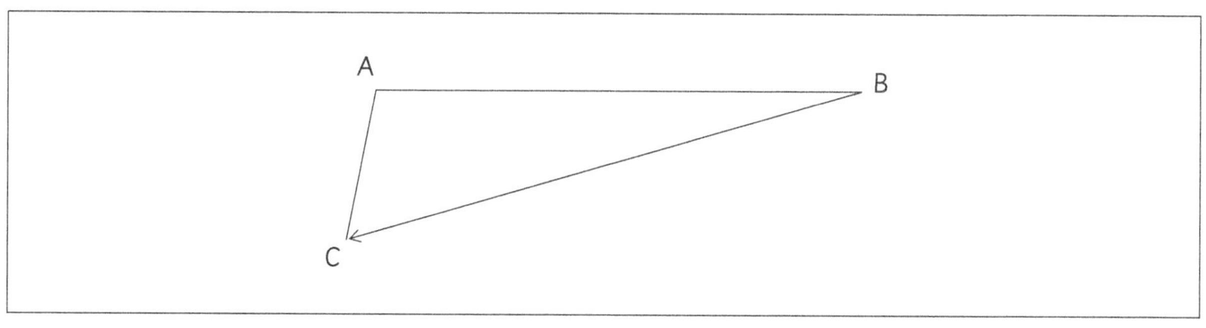

Figure 9.11 A scalene triangle with no equal sides or angles

An *isosceles triangle* has two equal sides and two equal angles opposite them.

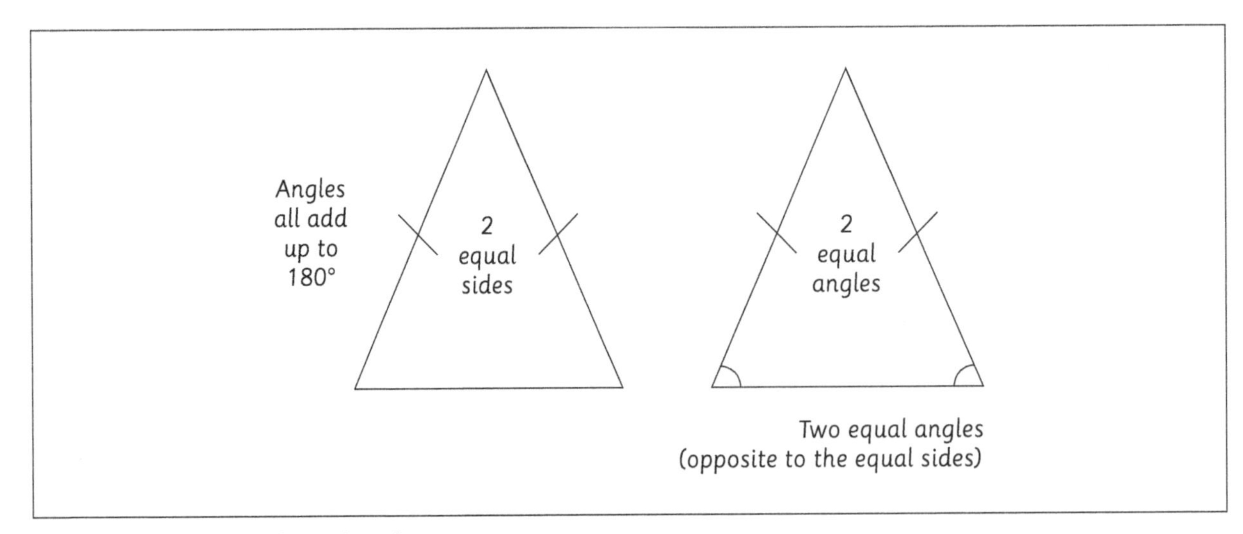

Figure 9.12 Isosceles triangle

An *equilateral triangle* has all sides of equal length and all angles of equal size (60°).

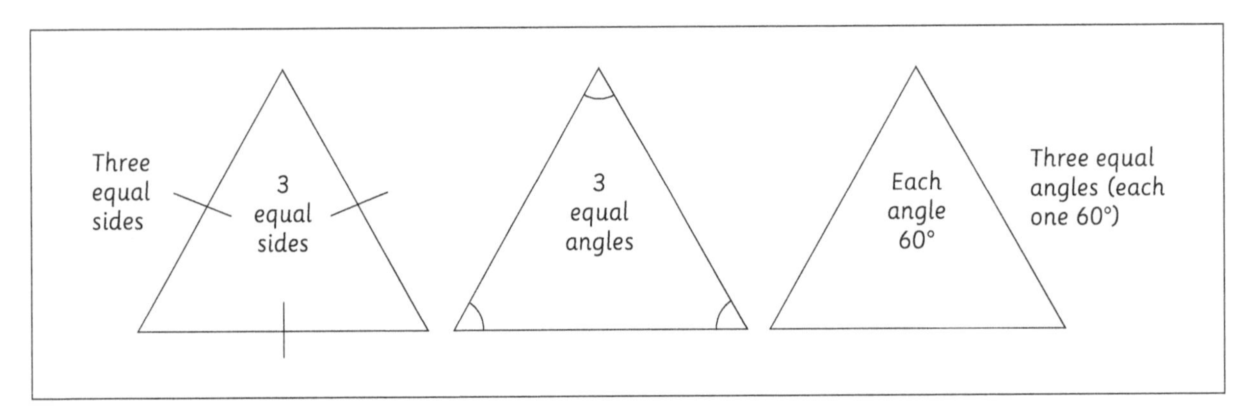

Figure 9.13 Equilateral triangle

Properties of shapes

Squares

- Copy, cut out, stick onto card and turn the angle pictures and facts given into a memory card (number 20, see page 144).

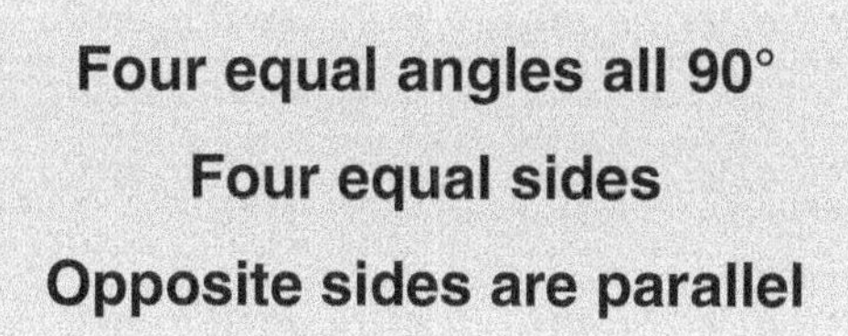

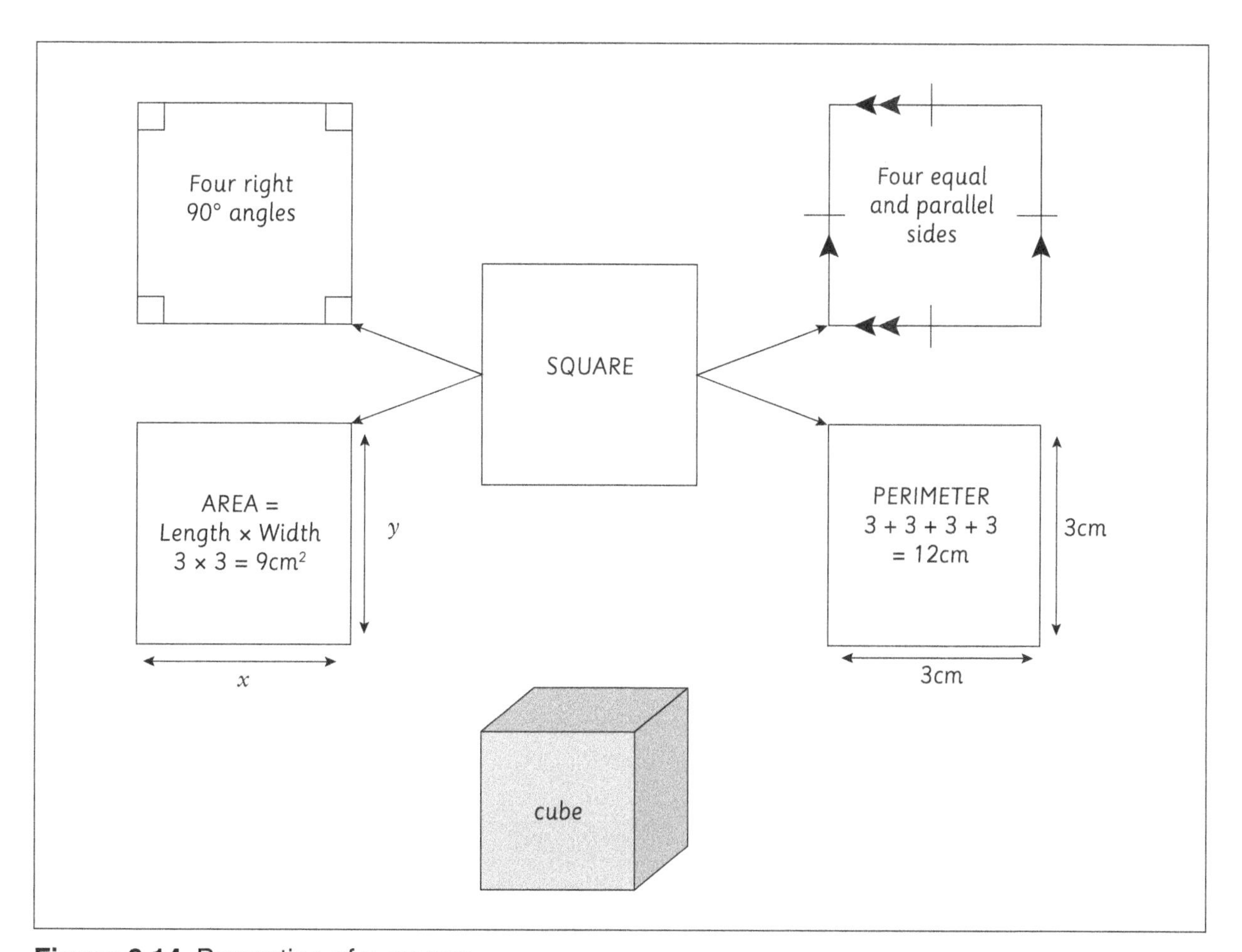

Figure 9.14 Properties of a square

- Explain that a 3D shape with square sides is a cube.

Rectangles

- Copy, cut out, stick onto card and turn the angle pictures and facts given into a memory card (number 21, see page 144).

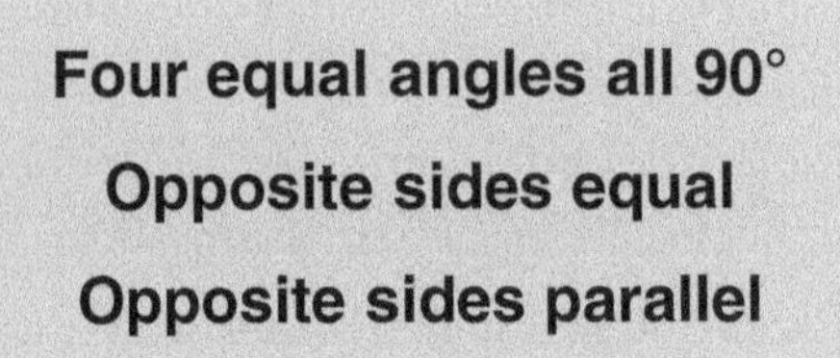

Four equal angles all 90°

Opposite sides equal

Opposite sides parallel

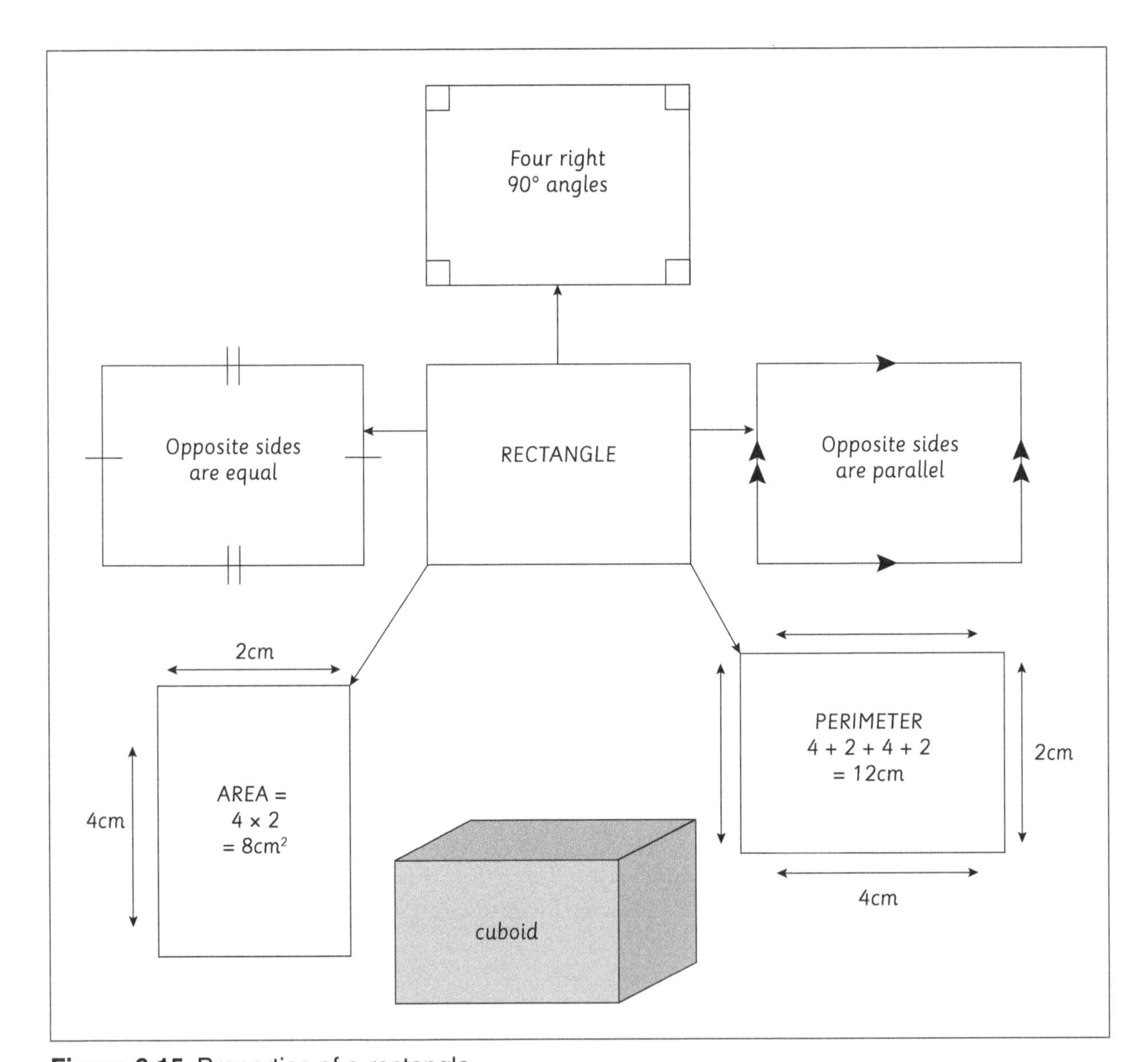

Figure 9.15 Properties of a rectangle

- Explain that a 3D shape with rectangular sides is a cuboid.

Circles

- Copy, cut out, stick onto card and turn the angle pictures and facts given into a memory card (number 22, see page 144).
- Use colour to show the:
  radius – r, diameter – D, circumference – C.

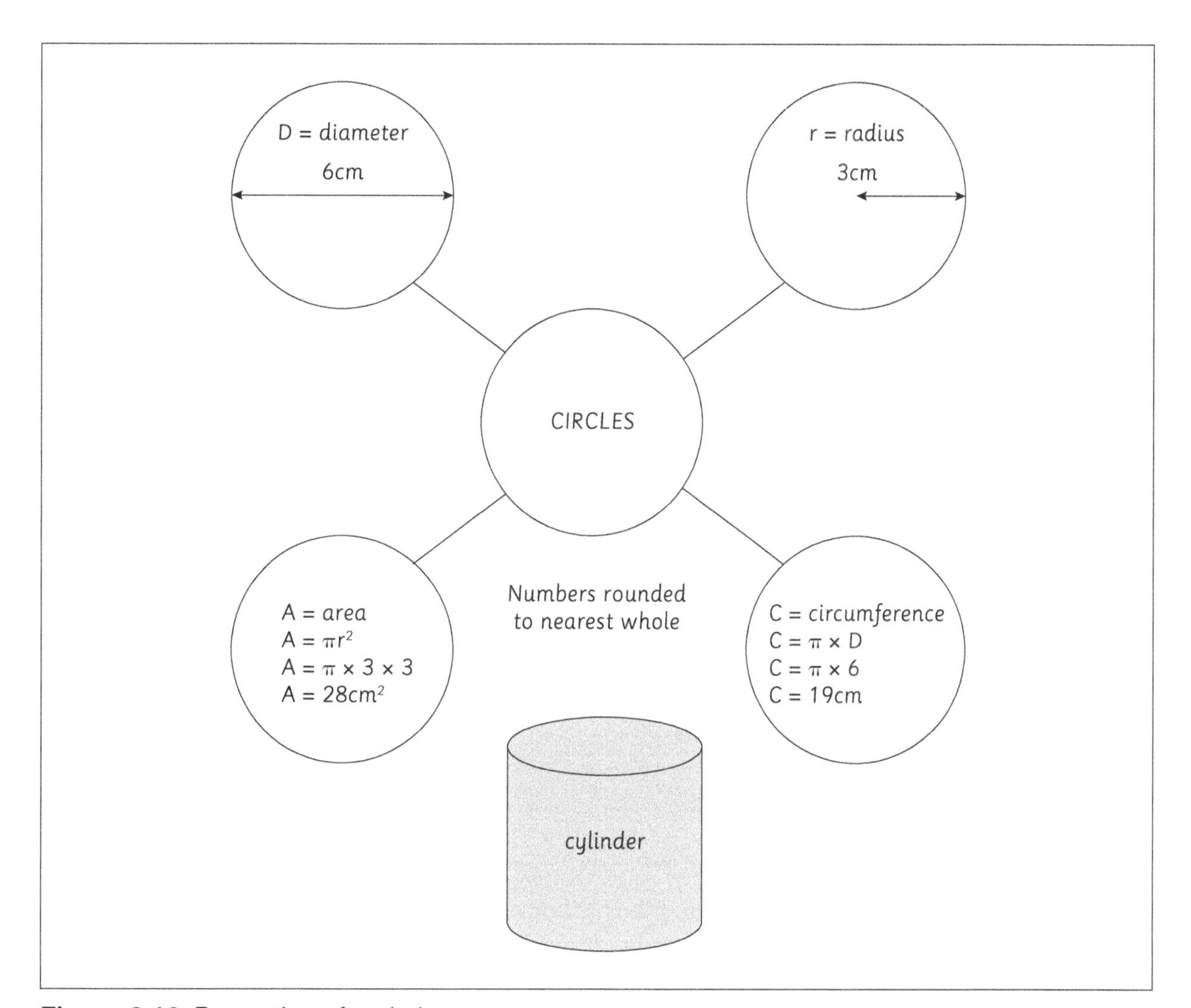

Figure 9.16 Properties of a circle

Circle facts

- The circumference is the perimeter of a circle.
- The diameter is twice the length of the radius.
- The radius is half the length of the diameter (divide D by 2).
- Pi π (pronounced pie) is important.
- Pi π has a value of 3.142.
- Press EXP on the calculator to use π.
- A 3D shape with circular top and bottom is a cylinder.

To find the circumference of a circle: (answer is in units)

$\pi \times D$ or $\pi \times 2r$

A rhyme to help:

Fiddle de-dum, Fiddle de-dee
The ring round the moon is π times D.

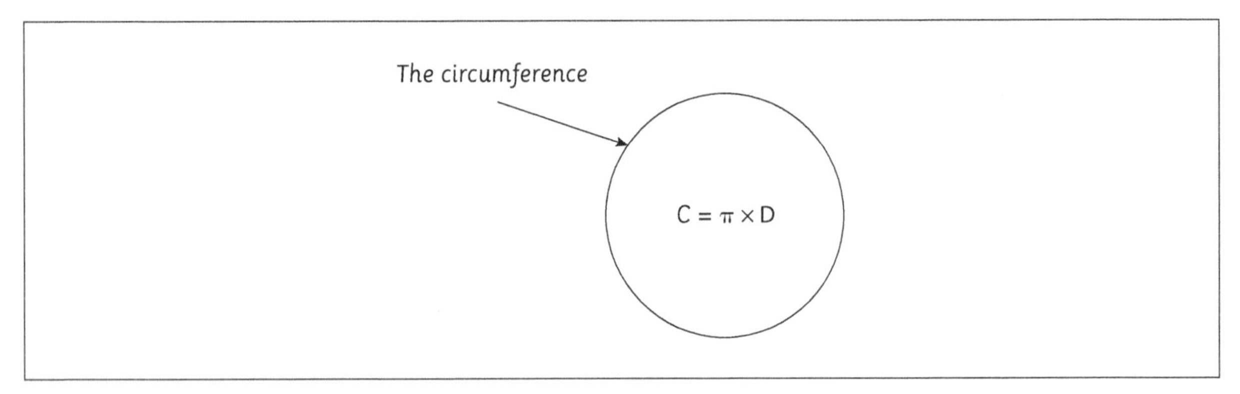

Figure 9.17 How to find the circumference of a circle

To find the area of a circle (answer is in units^2)

$\pi \times$ radius $\times$ radius which is written πr^2

A rhyme to help:

A round hole in my sock
Has just been repaired.
The area mended
Is pi r squared.

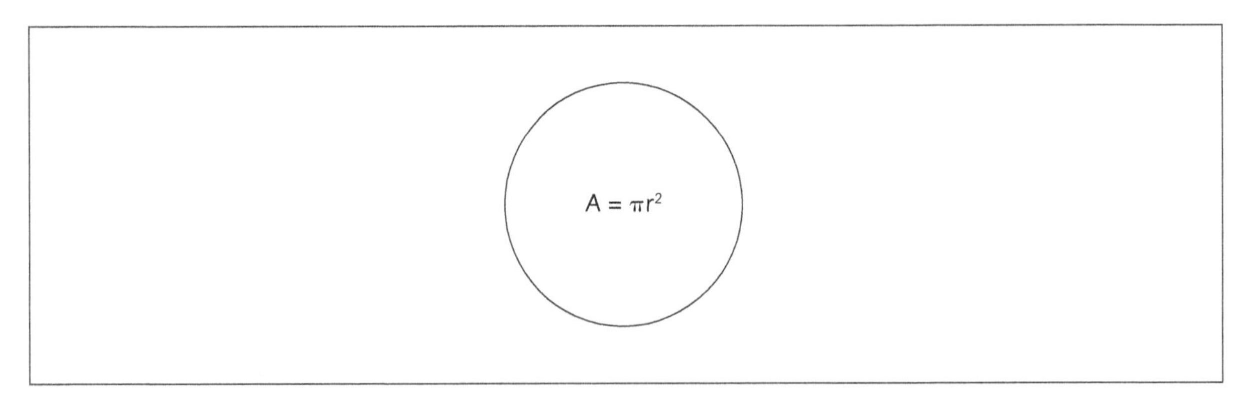

Figure 9.18 How to find the area (A) of a circle

Polygons

- Copy, cut out, stick onto card and turn the angle pictures and facts given into a memory card (number 23, see page 144).
- Multi-sided figures are generally called polygons. They have individual names depending on the number of sides, but many students find these difficult to remember.

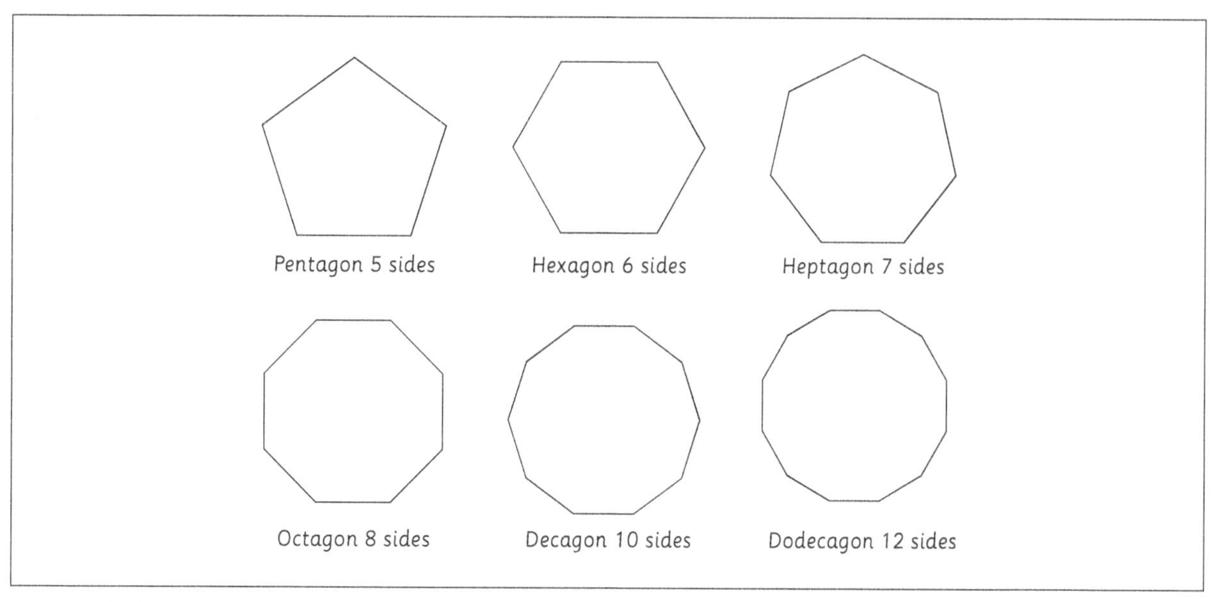

Figure 9.19 Polygons

Section E: Co-ordinates

The two straight lines at right angles to each other on a graph are called the axes. Coordinates are a pair of numbers, usually in brackets, which describe the precise location of a point on the axes. The one which is horizontal is called the x-axis (because x is a cross) and the vertical line is called the y-axis. The first number indicates the x-axis value (across the hall) and the second number indicates the y-axis value (up the stairs).

For example:

(3, 5) means 3 units across to the right and 5 units up.

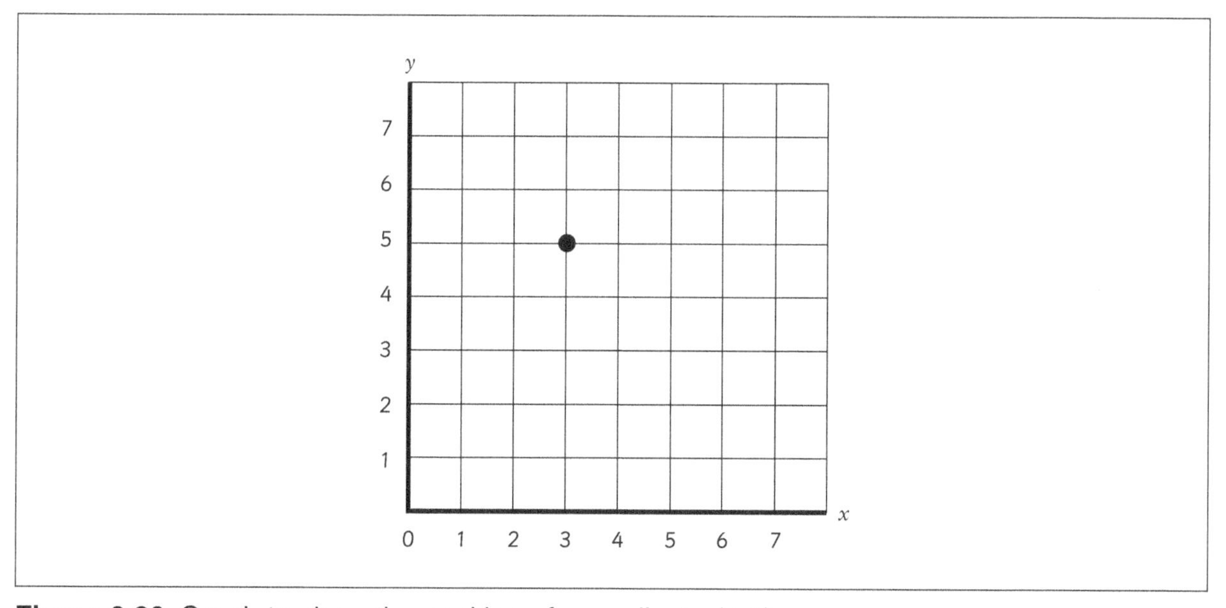

Figure 9.20 Graph to show the position of co-ordinate (3,5)

Section F: Rotational symmetry

This is the description given when a pattern is rotated around a point to identify the number of times the pattern is repeated. The centre is called the point of symmetry, and the shape is described as having rotational symmetry. If you use tracing paper to copy the pattern and turn it around a point it allows a pupil to identify the rotational symmetry of the pattern.

Order of symmetry

The pattern is given the following descriptions:

- If it is repeated four times it has rotational symmetry to the order of 4 (i.e. the angle it turns at the centre is 90°).
- If it is repeated three times it has rotational symmetry to the order of 3 (i.e. the angle it turns at the centre is 120°).
- If it is repeated two times it has rotational symmetry to the order of 2 (i.e. the angle it turns at the centre is 180°).
- If it is not repeated it has rotational symmetry to the order of 1 (i.e. the angle it turns at the centre is 360°).

Section G: Direction and bearings

Students often have difficulty with direction, confusing up with down, right with left, before with after and nearest with furthest.

How to help

- Draw a North line at the point you are starting from. This is most important.
- Measure your angle in a clockwise direction.
- Answer in three figures.
- Numbers under 10 begin 00, e.g. 8° is written 008°.
- Numbers 10 to 99 begin 0, e.g. 86° is written 086°.
- Numbers above 100 are the same, e.g. 267 is written 267°.

Section H: The Pythagorean theorem

Pythagoras, a Greek mathematician, lived in the sixth century BC and discovered the connection between the length of the hypotenuse (the side opposite the right-angled in a right-angled triangle) and the lengths of the other two sides. The theorem is used to find the length of a side in a right-angled triangle when the lengths of the other two sides are known.

The theorem states:

In a right-angled triangle the area of the square on the hypotenuse is equal to the sum of the areas of the squares on the other two sides.

How to help

- Find a picture or drawing depicting Pythagoras and talk about the man. Often students cannot remember the word Pythagoras on its own but they remember the picture and with a little prompting remember his theorem.
- Make a memory card (number 24, see page 144) to show that the longest side, the hypotenuse, is always opposite to the right angle.
- Present the triangle in different ways.

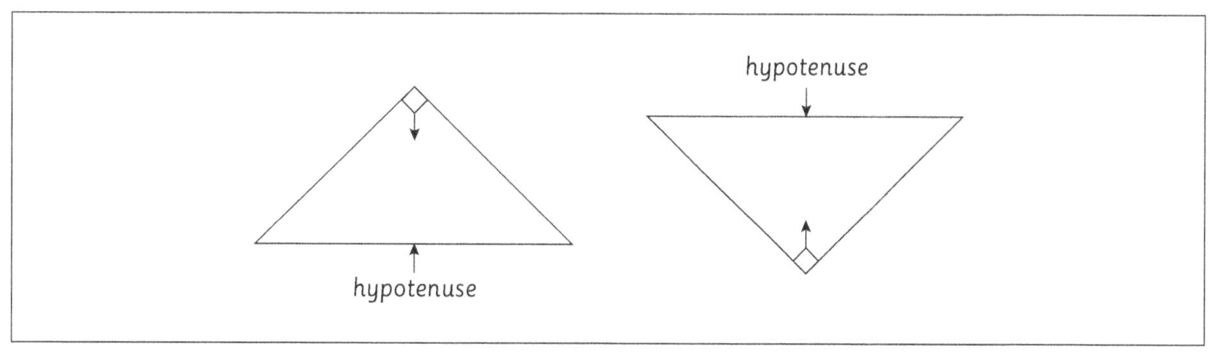

Figure 9.21 A right-angled triangle presented in different way to show the hypotenuse

A good multi-sensory exercise is to draw a triangle with the two smaller sides with lengths of 3 cm and 4 cm so that the hypotenuse will be 5 cm. Draw squares on the three sides. Cut the 9 cm into 1 cm squares and fit these around the 16 cm square to make a 25 cm square.

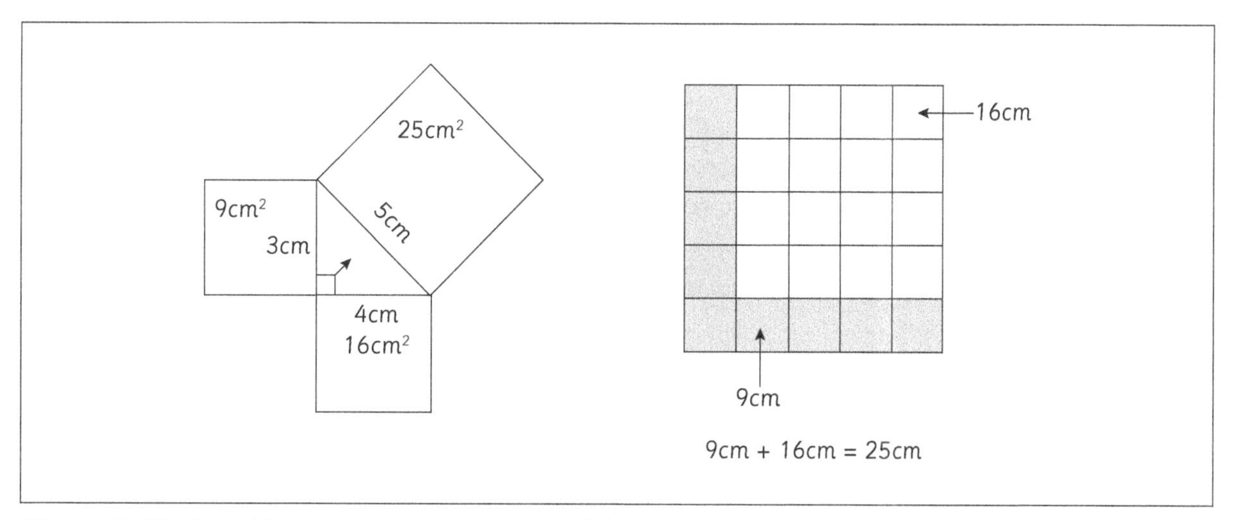

Figure 9.22 A multi-sensory exercise to explain the Pythagorean theorem

To find the length of the hypotenuse of a triangle when the other two sides are known.

- Square the numbers (multiply them by themselves).
- Add the numbers.
- Take the square root to get the answer.

Section I: Trigonometry

Abbreviations

O = opposite side	A = adjacent side	H = hypotenuse
S = sine (angle)	C = cosine (angle)	T = tangent (angle)

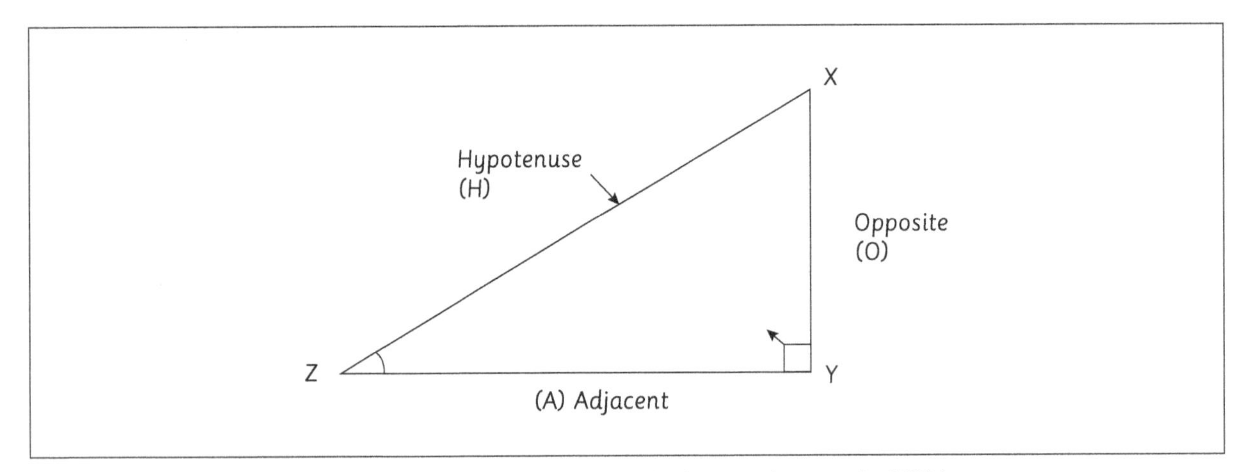

Figure 9.23 Identify the sides of the triangle in relation to the angle XZY

How to help

- Identify the sides of the triangle, discussing which sides are adjacent and which are opposite. This seemingly simple item can take a great deal of time as many students cannot connect up angles and lines easily.
- Indicate with an arrow the hypotenuse.
- The following mnemonic may help:

Some **O**fficers **H**ave	SOH means Sin	$= \frac{\text{Opposite}}{\text{Hypotenuse}}$
Curly **A**uburn **H**air	CAH means Cos	$= \frac{\text{Adjacent}}{\text{Hypotenuse}}$
To **O**ffer **A**ttraction	TOA means Tan	$= \frac{\text{Opposite}}{\text{Adjacent}}$

10 Handling data

Section A: Graphical representation

Initially when children begin to collect and record data it is usually a fun time, with picture graphs being made with practical apparatus. Pictograms always use pictures to represent data, but if they are to make sense to children there needs to be a key. Children should be shown where to find the key and the meaning of its value explained.

For example, Figure 10.1 shows who collected the most car numbers in the class.

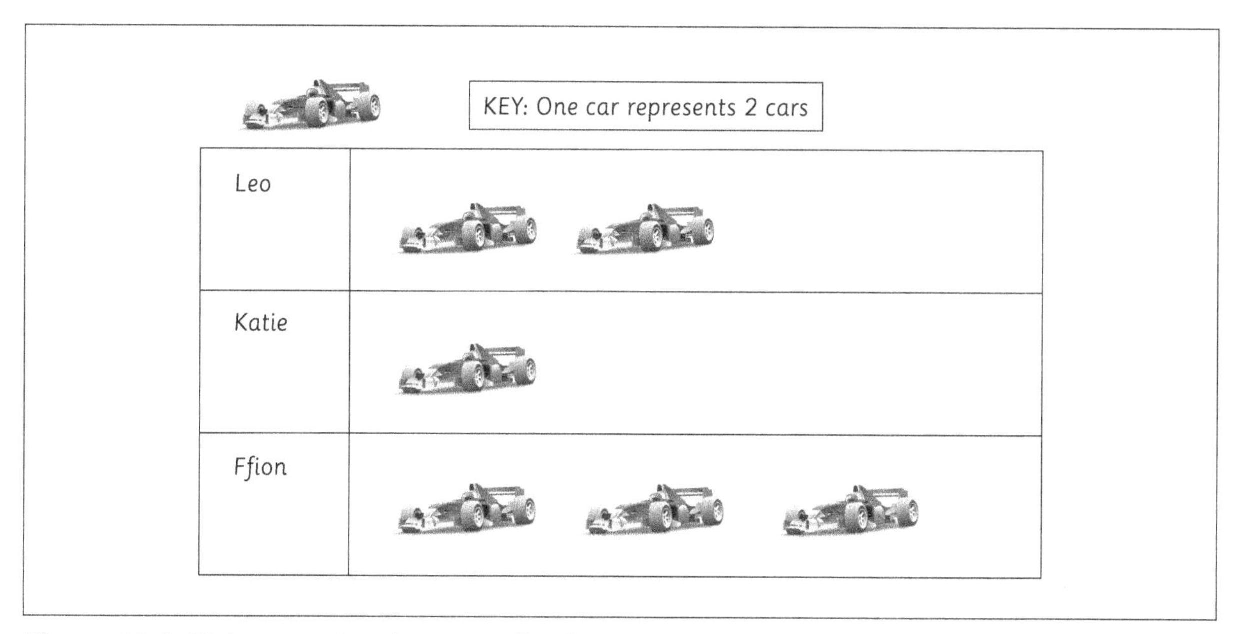

Figure 10.1 Pictogram showing car collection

Later other graphs are used, and children need to discover that some are better than others for representing data. In cross-curricular subjects they will be able to select the best graph to illustrate the information they have collected, which could be a bar chart.

Example: Callum conducts a survey to find the number of people in each of the cars arriving at his school gate between 8.00 am and 9.00 am. His results are shown in the bar chart in Figure 10.2.

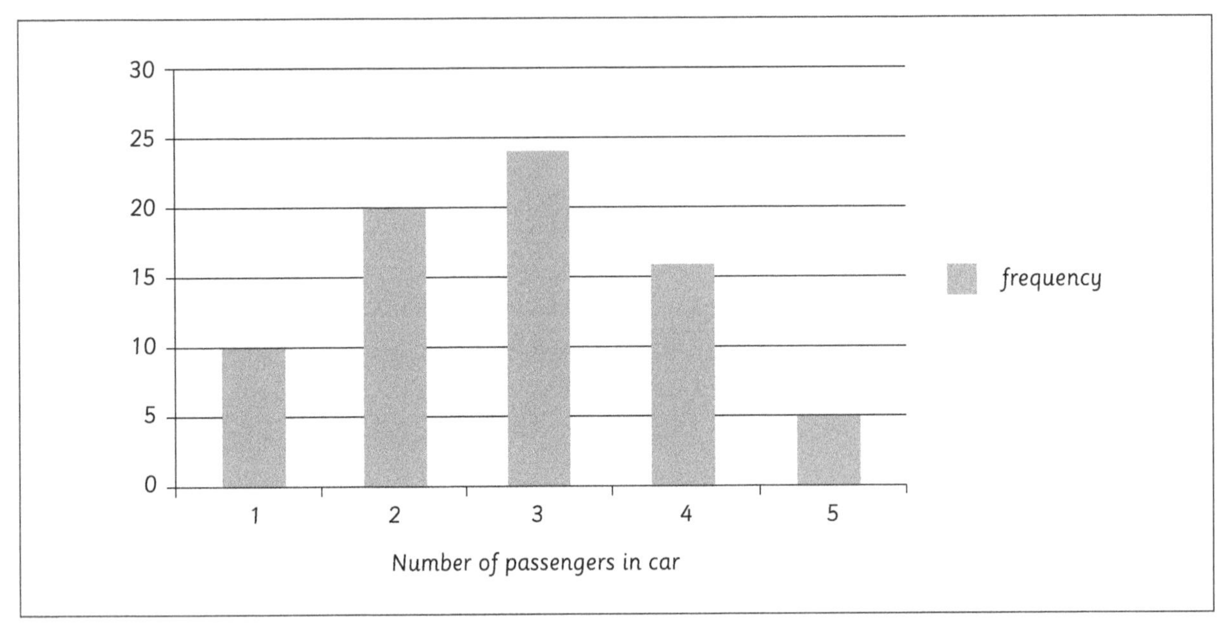

Figure 10.2 School survey

From this children can be asked questions such as:

- How many cars carried one passenger?
- How many cars carried two passengers?
- How many cars had more than three passengers?

Pie charts

Although a variety of graphs will be used by students, they seem to need most assistance with pie charts. It is important for teachers to consult other teachers working in different faculty areas so that all can agree on methods that are appropriate. In this way students do not feel threatened when asked to draw or read a pie chart in a subject other than mathematics.

Example: See the traffic survey shown in Table 10.1.

Table 10.1 Traffic survey

Type of vehicle	Number of vehicles
Cars	80
Buses	10
Lorries	8
Vans	40
Motorbikes	22

How to draw a pie chart (for a traffic survey)

- Count up the total number of vehicles.
- Divide the number of each type of vehicle by the total number of vehicles.
- Multiply that answer by 360 to find out how many degrees will represent the data in the pie chart.
- For example, if 80 out of 160 vehicles are cars, we will represent this on the circle as a segment with an angle of: $(^{80}/_{160}) \times 360 = 180$ degrees.

The reason for these steps is because each part of the data has to be represented as a proportion of 360, because there are 360 degrees in a circle.

This will give the results shown in Table 10.2.

Table 10.2 Chart showing degrees of a circle

Type of vehicle	Number of vehicles	Calculation	Degrees of a circle
Cars	80	$(^{80}/_{160}) \times 360$	180
Buses	10	$(^{10}/_{160}) \times 360$	23
Lorries	8	$(^{8}/_{160}) \times 360$	17
Vans	40	$(^{40}/_{160}) \times 360$	90
Motorbikes	22	$(^{22}/_{160}) \times 360$	50

This data is represented on the pie chart in Figure 10.3.

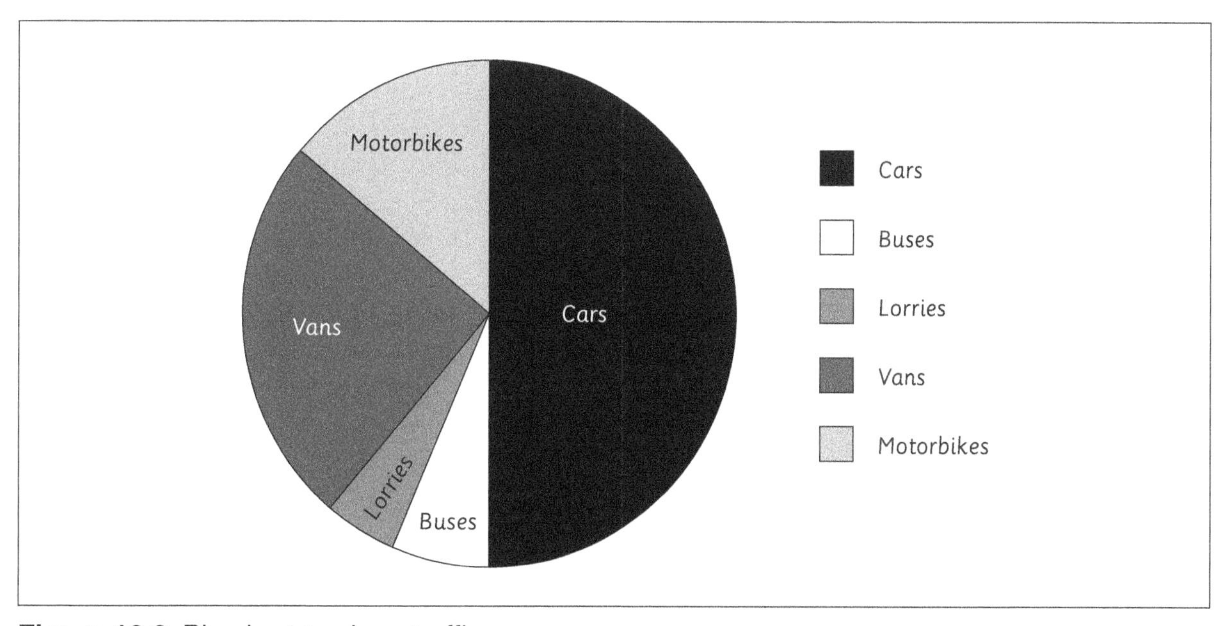

Figure 10.3 Pie chart to show traffic survey

Tally charts

Collecting information is fun and students usually enjoy this activity, but making a tally of the results can cause difficulties. Students forget how to write the five symbol which looks like this 𝍸

Checking a list of data means that students are working vertically and horizontally so the ensuing directional difficulties cause problems for them.

Table 10.3 Tally chart

1	I
2	II
3	III
4	IIII
5	𝍸

How to help

- Make wall charts, memory cards and ceiling charts of the words used within this topic, for example axis /axes, continuous, coordinates, distribution, frequency, scale.
- Use pictures to identify particular graphs, e.g. block charts, tally charts, bars, histograms, columns, pie charts, scatter graphs. The Excel program that is on most computers offers students easy access to all these different graphs clearly identified by their names.
- Discuss which axis relates to which piece of data (horizontal or vertical).
- Talk about the exact values represented on the axes.
- Discuss how to choose a scale that will not only fit the information but also fit onto the page.

Different types of graphs

It is beneficial if students are given the time to experiment with different types of graphs to illustrate data. They are able to draw graphs on squared paper, colour them, cut them out and paste them into books. In this way they will compile a clear record of the different types of graphs available. Obviously this comparison can easily be done on the computer but sometimes the cutting and pasting can mean that the image is remembered better.

For example Table 10.4 shows the shoe sizes for 24 members of a class, and Table 10.5 puts this information into a tally chart. Students could discuss whether this is the most appropriate format for this information.

Table 10.4 Shoe sizes

1	2	3	4	5	2
3	2	4	5	4	4
3	1	4	4	1	2
2	2	3	2	2	4

Table 10.5 Tally chart of shoe sizes

Size	Tally chart	Frequency
1	III	3
2	~~IIII~~ III	8
3	IIII	4
4	~~IIII~~ II	7
5	II	2

Section B: Probability

Probabilities range from 0 (impossible) to 1 (certain).

The words for children to get to know include:

impossible unlikely evens (even chance) very likely certain

How to help with memorising probability words

Discuss with the children the following statements and use the above words to describe them.

- Tomorrow the sun will rise.
- My mother will go shopping on Saturday.
- I will be 20 metres tall by tonight.
- It will snow next winter.
- If I spin a coin it will be a 'head'.

More probability

Probability is abbreviated as P.

Students are able to use probability to reinforce their skills in cancelling fractions.

How to help

If both top and bottom are even they can be divided by two:

$$P = \frac{12 \div 2}{52 \div 2} = \frac{6 \div 2}{26 \div 2} = \frac{3}{13}$$

If there are numbers ending in 5 or 0, then they can be divided by 5

$$P = \frac{25 \div 5}{40 \div 5} = \frac{5}{8}$$

If there are numbers in which the digits add up to 3, 6 or 9, they can be divided by 3.

$$P = \frac{21 \quad (2 + 1 = 3) \quad \div 3}{132 \quad (1 + 3 + 2 = 6) \quad \div 3} = \frac{7}{44}$$

Spinning a coin

When spinning a coin there are only two outcomes possible: it will land with tails (T) or heads (H) uppermost.

The probability of a tail is 1 out of 2, written as P (tail) $= \frac{1}{2}$

The probability of a head is 1 out of 2, written as P (head) $= \frac{1}{2}$

Throwing dice

When throwing a die there are six sides so there are six outcomes.

The probability of getting a 2 is 1 out of 6, written as P (2) $= \frac{1}{6}$

Other probability exercises

A bag with elastic around the top is useful for experiments with probability.

Example 1

Put numbered cards 1 to 20 in the bag with even numbers coloured red and odd numbers coloured black. After talking about odd and even numbers up to 20, students divide the cards into two piles, with ten red even numbers in one pile and ten black odd numbers in the other. Some students will work out mentally that there are ten even and ten odd numbers.

Ask:

- What is the probability that a card with an even number will be pulled out?

The probability of pulling out an even number is 10 out of 20

written as P (even) $= \frac{10}{20}$ cancelled down is $\frac{1}{2}$

Example 2

What is the probability that a prime number will be pulled out?
Discuss prime numbers and have the class write down the primes up to 20: 2, 3, 5, 7, 11, 13, 17, 19
Students will see that there are eight prime numbers which are written as

P (prime) $= \frac{8}{20}$ cancelled down is $\frac{2}{5}$

What is the probability that you will pull out a multiple?

A multiple of 2 — Answer is $P(2) = \frac{10}{20} = \frac{1}{2}$

A multiple of 5 — $P(5) = \frac{4}{20} = \frac{1}{5}$

A multiple of 6 — $P(6) = \frac{3}{20}$

As well as helping with probability, this technique allows you to check whether students understand other basic concepts such as odd and even numbers, primes and multiples. This is especially useful if they are older students who were taught these concepts some time before. Subtle techniques are needed to assess their knowledge of basics.

Probability exercises using marbles

For this exercise, put four green, three red and five blue marbles in a bag. Then ask:

- What is the probability of pulling out a green marble?

  P (green) $= \frac{4}{12} = \frac{1}{3}$

- What is the probability that you will *not* pull out a green marble?

  P (not green) $= \frac{2}{3}$

- What is the probability of pulling out a marble that is red?

  P (red) $= \frac{3}{12} = \frac{1}{4}$

Students are able to test this outcome by experimenting. Ask them to pull three single marbles out of the bag and make a note of the colour each time. This procedure is repeated several times. Then they should count up the number of times a red has been pulled out and divide it by the total number of times the experiment has been done. This should reinforce the original calculation.

Probability exercises using a pack of cards

There are several ways of splitting up a pack of 52 cards, as shown in Table 10.6.

Table 10.6 A pack of cards

4 suits	Diamonds red 13 cards	Clubs black 13 cards	Hearts red 13 cards	Spades black 13 cards
Face or picture cards	Ace King Queen Jack	Ace King Queen Jack	Ace King Queen Jack	Ace King Queen Jack
9 other cards	2 to 10	2 to 10	2 to 10	2 to 10

Questions to ask are, if you draw a single card:

- What is the probability of getting the 6 of spades? P (6 of spades) $= \frac{1}{52}$

- What is the probability of getting an ace? P (ace) $= \frac{4}{52}$

- What is the probability of getting a face card?

$$P\ (\text{face cards}) = \frac{12}{52}$$

- What is the probability of getting a club?

$$P\ (\text{club}) = \frac{13}{52}$$

Sample spaces

A sample space (see Table 10.7) can show several outcomes. It can be used, for example, if two dice are thrown and the sum of their numbers is found. Count up specific numbers to find probability.

Table 10.7 A sample space

+	1	2	3	4	5	6
1	2	3	4	5	6	7
2	3	4	5	6	7	8
3	4	5	6	7	8	9
4	5	6	7	8	9	10
5	6	7	8	9	10	11
6	7	8	9	10	11	12

Questions to ask with this exercise are, for example:

- What is the probability of getting a 6?

$$P\ (6) = \frac{5}{36}$$

- What is the probability of getting an even number?

$$P\ (\text{even}) = \frac{18}{36} = \frac{1}{2}$$

- What is the probability of getting a number that is a multiple of 3?

$$P\ (\text{multiple of } 3) = \frac{12}{36} = \frac{1}{3}$$

Many other probabilities can be worked out using the sample space. Students find the visual representation helpful. Once basic probability has been grasped, pupils appear to progress easily to more complicated problems.

Section C: Averages

To find the average, add up all the amounts given and divide the answer by the number of amounts added together.

For example:

- Find the average of: 6, 7, 4, 8, and 10
  6 + 7 + 4 + 8 + 10 = 35
  35 ÷ 5 = 7 The average is 7

Section D: Mode, median, mean and range

Dyslexic students find the first three of these words confusing because they all begin with the same letter 'm', but dyscalculic students also find this topic complicated and struggle to make sense of the questions. Make separate memory cards to help, using colour and word meanings.

How to help

- Always arrange numbers in order of size.
- Explain that **mode** and most mean the same – the mode is the most frequent number.
- Explain that **median** is related to medium – middle size, so if you have a range large – medium – small, it is the middle number.
- The word **mean** is difficult because of all its other meanings – humble, inferior, shabby and so on. If averages have already been covered, then give a clear definition, that finding the mean is exactly the same as finding the average.
- **Range** is another difficult word because of its multiple meanings. Discuss the other meanings and then focus on exactly what is required by the mathematical word and write it down: that is, you take the smallest number from the biggest number, and the range is the difference between them.
- Eventually, when students have practised using each one of these concepts, make a memory card that shows all the words and their definitions.

Example to show how to calculate the mode, median, mean and range

Find the mode, median, mean and range of the following numbers. 14, 12, 2, 4, 11, 8

- Rearrange the numbers in order:
  2, 4, 8, 11, 12, 12, 14
- Mode: 12 (most frequent);
- Median: 11 (middle number);
- Mean: 2 + 4 + 8 + 11 + 12 + 12 + 14 = 63 divided by 7 = 9 (the average);
- Range: 14 – 2 = 12 (biggest number minus smallest number).

11 Dyslexia, dyscalculia and technology

Computer technology

Children use modern technology in the shape of iPads, DS consoles, mobile phones and Kindle readers from early childhood, so the new generations do not have any fear of these machines. The idea of logging on and reading a computer screen is much more agreeable for many children than reading a book, so incorporating computers into maths lessons can only be beneficial. The flexibility of this technology – the ability to change the colour and background of screens, alter font size and line spacing, remove any background distractions or sounds according to the preference of the user – make this mode of working ideal for both dyslexic and dyscalculic learners. Children can work on their own at their own pace, self-checking work, retracing their steps to do the work again if they have made mistakes, or they can work in pairs, sharing ideas and thoughts but again working at a pace that suits them. In addition, if the school has a website, then children can continue their work at home without being too fazed at the thought of homework.

Maths lessons are more exciting if computers and interactive white boards are used together to prepare materials suited to the needs of the class, and indeed of individuals within the class. Texts can be projected onto the screens and at the touch of a key a voice will read the specific words. Diagrams, pictures and scale drawings can all be added to make the lesson dynamic. Teachers can prepare lessons with specific examples for the white board, children work out the answers on their own individual white boards then answers are transferred to the teacher's own interlinked computer, so that children within the group who need more help are identified. All of this coupled with the wonder of the Internet can only bring magic to children as they learn with the aid of computer technology.

Teachers are able to download lessons and resources from the National Strategies site, as well as simply logging onto the many other sites available for almost any topic in mathematics syllabus. Over the last years there has been such vast progress with computers that it is difficult to keep pace with the changing technology involved, so it is difficult to recommend specific software to help dyslexic/dyscalculic children with mathematics. However details of some useful software and websites can be found in the Useful contacts and addresses section (page 147).

Thomas West suggests in his book *In The Mind's Eye* (1991) that it is when we reach the age where the world is governed by technology that dyslexic and dyscalculic people with different kinds of brains will be able to benefit the world with their talents.

Learning differences

Thoreau said:

If a man does not keep pace with his companions,
Perhaps it is because he hears a different drummer.
Let him step to the music he hears,
However measured or far away.

Leonardo da Vinci, Michael Faraday, James Maxwell and Albert Einstein, to name a few, were great men who had difficulties in their early school lives. These included problems with reading, writing, spelling, calculating and memory. Often those with talents in higher levels of mathematics prove to have struggled with simple arithmetic. It seems obvious that those people who struggle in one sphere of learning might learn with ease in another. It is essential that those who have trouble learning mathematics have teachers who are able to recognise strengths in learners, and also have the patience to help them achieve.

> *To put the matter another way, if there is bad practice it seems likely that intelligent non-dyslexics may in many cases survive it without any major disaster, whereas its effect, even on the most intelligent dyslexics is likely to be catastrophic.*
>
> **(Miles and Miles, 2004)**

Mathematical skills develop continuously in all students, but the rate at which they develop varies enormously. Some children learn quickly while others, especially those with specific learning difficulties, learn slowly, regardless of how motivated they are. Children vary in the skills which they are able to use well, so different methods, materials, books and pedagogical styles appeal to different individuals. It is the challenge of providing for these varying conditions of learning which makes teaching dyslexic and dyscalculic children so exciting and rewarding.

Appendix: memory cards

1

My thinking style

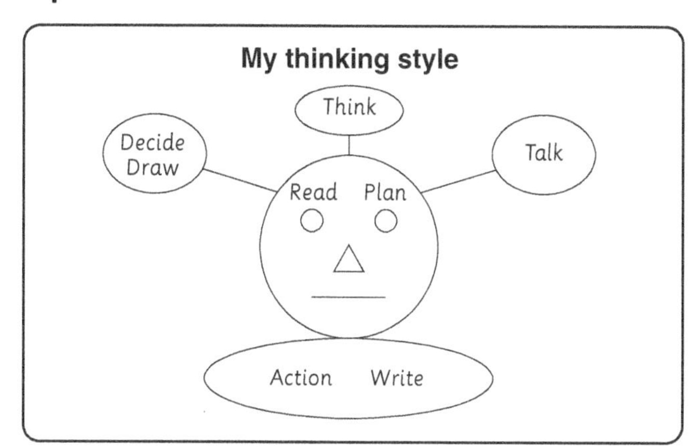

2

Difficult words

scales	fair	die
alternative	generalise	investigate
predict	methodically	record
maximum	minimum	precise
	theory	

3

Number patterns

3 + 6 = 9	9 – 6 = 3
3 + 16 = 19	19 – 16 = 3
3 + 26 = 29	29 – 26 = 3
3 + 36 = 39	39 – 36 = 3
3 + 46 = 49	49 – 46 = 3
3 + 56 = 59	59 – 56 = 3

4

How to problem solve

Read through problem, then re-read it
Highlight important information/key words
Underline important numbers
Break information into manageable chunks
Discuss problem, decide on a method
Decide which symbol + – × ÷ to use
Estimate an answer (use easy numbers)
Calculate answer (use pictures or diagrams)
Check against the estimate
Check against the original question

5

Important numbers

1	one	11	eleven	30	thirty		
2	two	12	twelve	40	forty		
3	three	13	thirteen	50	fifty		
4	four	14	fourteen	60	sixty		
5	five	15	fifteen	70	seventy		
6	six	16	sixteen	80	eighty		
7	seven	17	seventeen	90	ninety		
8	eight	18	eighteen	100	hundred		
9	nine	19	nineteen	1000	thousand		
10	ten	20	twenty	1000000	million		

6

How to read big numbers

Example: to read the number 23768054

From the right split 23768054 into groups of three digits, put in commas to be read as following:

23,	768,	054
23 million	768 thousand	and 54

© 2012, *Dyslexia, Dyscalculia and Mathematics*, London: Routledge

7

Symbols with words

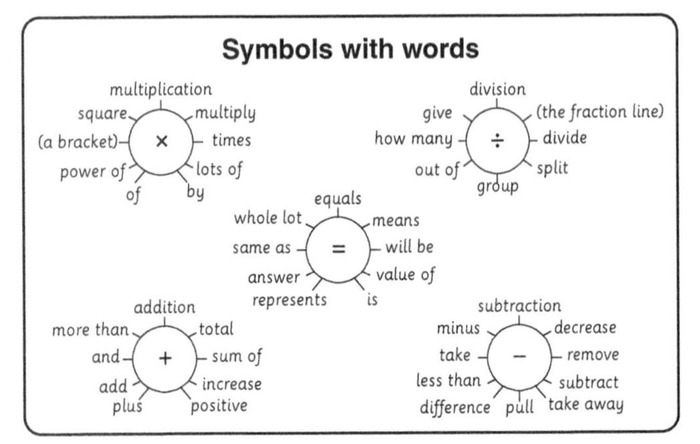

8

Greater than/less than

The Greedy Robot eats the biggest number

2 4

4 is greater than 2

2 < 4

9

Prime numbers up to 20

2	3	5	7	9
11	13		17	19

10

Percentages (1)

To find:

10% divide by 10

20% divide by 5

25% divide by 4

50% divide by 2

75% divide by 4 then multiply by 3

11

Percentages (2)

To find:

30% divide by 10 then multiply by 3

40% divide by 10 then multiply by 4

60% divide by 10 then multiply by 6

70% divide by 10 then multiply by 7

80% divide by 10 then multiply by 8

90% divide by 10 then multiply by 9

12

Percentages/decimal fractions

2% = 0.02

8% = 0.08

16% = 0.16

35% = 0.35

72% = 0.72

© 2012, *Dyslexia, Dyscalculia and Mathematics*, London: Routledge

13

How to use a calculator to find percentages

When using a calculator the decimal fraction must always be followed by the multiplication sign
(followed by ×)

Colour 'followed by ×' in red

Example: Find 2% of 800

Enter 0.02 × 800 = 16

14

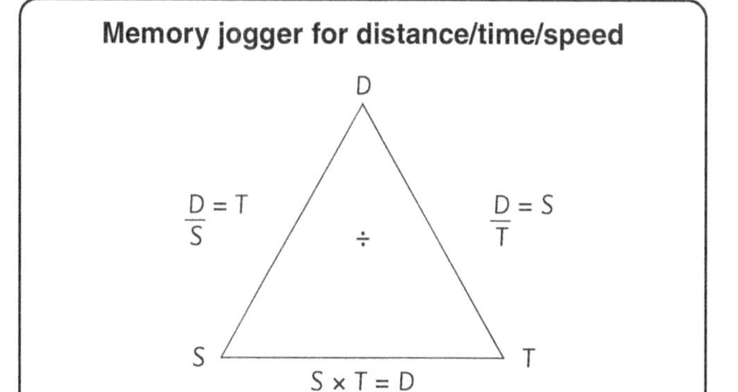

15

Positive and negative number line

Negative	Positive
Smaller	Bigger
Lower	Higher
Colder	Hotter
Less	More

–5 –4 –3 –2 –1 0 +1 +2 +3 +4 +5

16

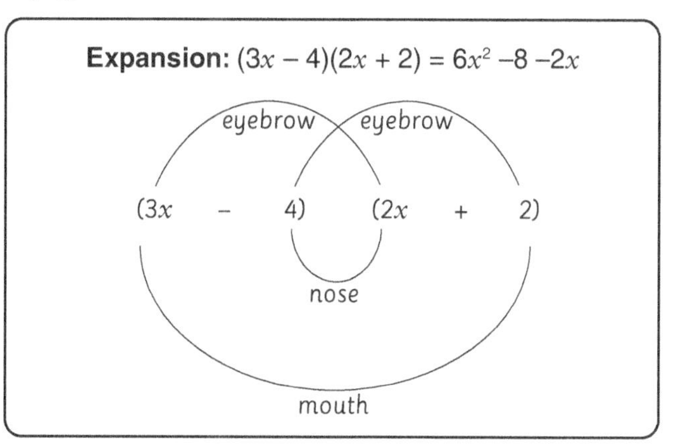

17

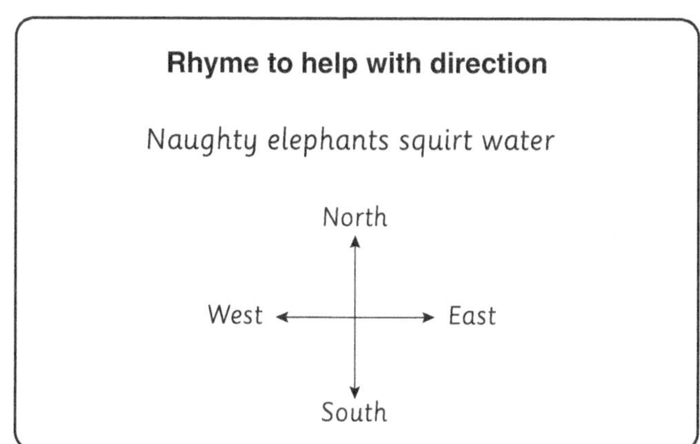

18

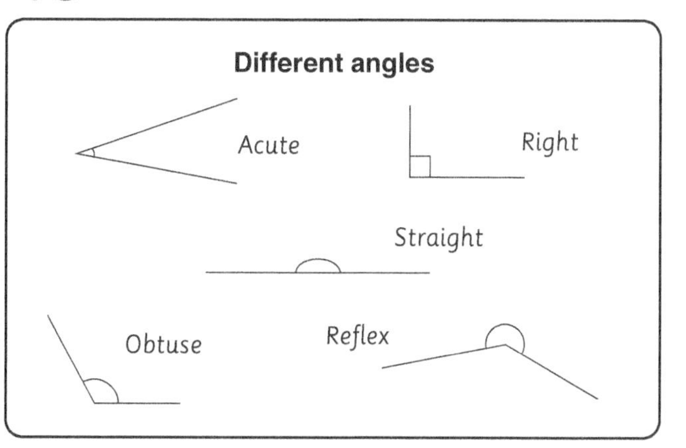

© 2012, *Dyslexia, Dyscalculia and Mathematics*, London: Routledge

19

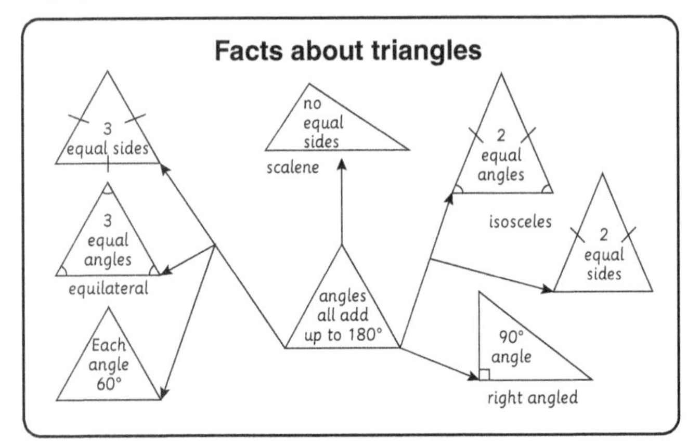

20

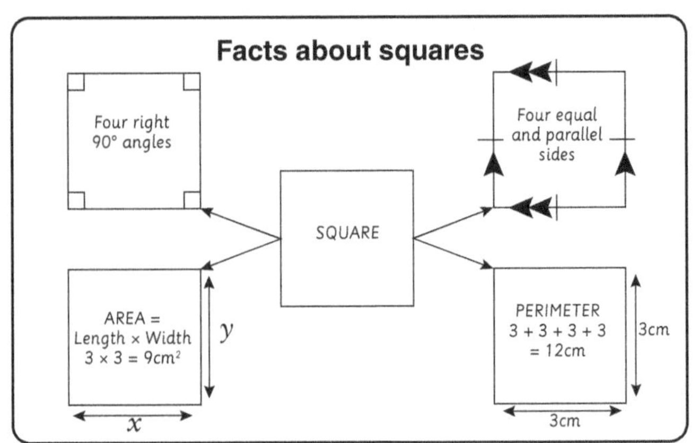

21

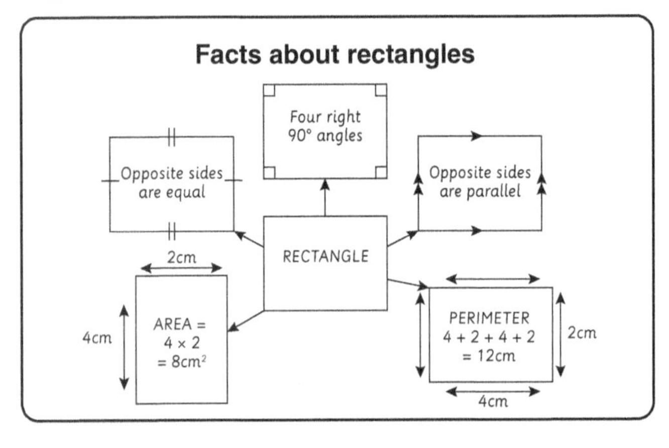

22

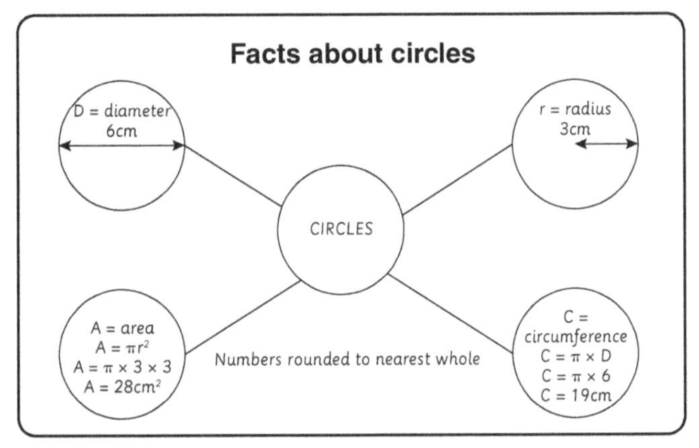

23

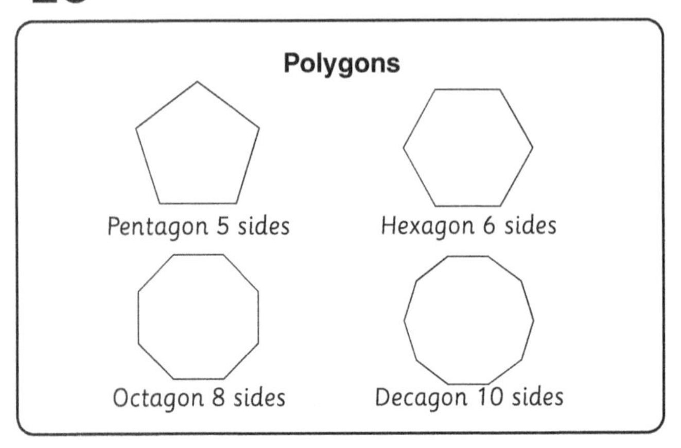

24

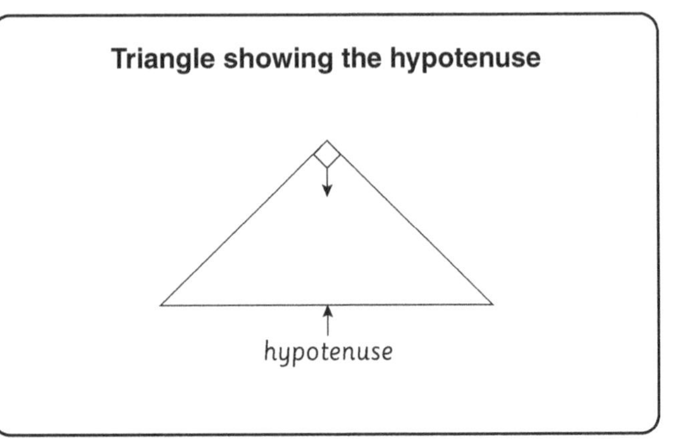

© 2012, *Dyslexia, Dyscalculia and Mathematics*, London: Routledge

References and suggested reading

References

Atkinson, R., Tacon, R. and Haseler, M. (2011) *Numicon Diagnostic Assessment.* Oxford: Oxford University Press.

Atkinson, R., Tacon, R. and Haseler, M. (2011) *Numicon Planning Signposts, Teaching and Assessing Guidance.* Oxford: Oxford University Press.

Bath, J. B., Chinn, S. J. and Knox, D. E. (1984) *Dyslexia: Research and its Application to the Adolescent*, rev. edn. Bath: Better Books.

Borthwick, A. and Harcourt-Heath, M. (2010) 'Calculation strategies used by Year 5 children.' *Proceedings of the British Society for Research into Learning Mathematics*. Norwich: University of East Anglia.

British Dyslexia Association (2011) Information from website: www.bdadyslexia.org.uk

Butterworth, B. (2003) *Dyscalculia Screener*. London: nfer Nelson.

Butterworth, B. (2011) Contributions to *All in the Mind. That does not compute: the hidden affliction of dyscalculia.* 29 January Transcript Australia: ABC National Radio.

Chinn. S. (2007) *Dealing with Dyscalculia, Sum Hope²*. London: Souvenir Press.

Denvir, H. and Bibby,T. (2002) *Diagnostic Interviews in Number Sense*. London: BEAM Education.

Dowker, A. (2004) *What Works for Children with Mathematical Difficulties?* Research report no: 554. Nottingham: DfES Publications.

Dowker, A. (2009) *What Works for Children with Mathematical Difficulties? The Effectiveness of Intervention Schemes*. London: DCSF.

Every Child Counts Team (2008) *Every Child Counts*. Edge Hill: Edge Hill University.

Grauberg, E. (1998) *Elementary Mathematics and Language Difficulties*. London: Whurr.

Gross, J. (2007) 'Supporting children with gaps in their mathematical understanding.' *Educational and Child Psychology*, 24, 146–56.

Miles, T. R. and Miles, E. (2004) *Dyslexia and Mathematics*. London: RoutledgeFalmer.

Ostler, C. (1991) *Dyslexia, A Parents' Guide*. Godalming: Ammonite Books.

Oxford Dictionary (2012) Web dictionary: http://oxforddictionaries.com

Reeve, R. (2011) Contributions to *All in the Mind. That does not compute: the hidden affliction of dyscalculia.* 29 January. Australia: ABC National Radio.

Reid, G. (1996). *Dimensions of Dyslexia, Vol. 2: Literacy, Language and Learning*. Edinburgh: Moray House Publications.

Rose, J. (2009) *Review of Mathematics in Early Years Settings.* Nottingham: DCSF Publications.

Sharron, H. (1987) *Changing Children's Minds*. London: Souvenir Press.

West, T. G. (1991) *In the Mind's Eye*. New York: Prometheus Books.

William, P. (2008) *Independent Review of Mathematics Teaching in Early Years Settings and Primary Schools: Final Report*. Nottingham: Department for Children, Schools and Families (DCSF).

Suggested reading

Bird, R. (2007) *The Dyscalculia Toolkit: Supporting Learning Difficulties in Maths.* London: Paul Chapman.

Burr, T. (2008) *Mathematics Performance in Primary Schools: Getting the Best Results.* London: National Audit Office/DCSF.

Dowker, A. (2009) *What Works for Children with Mathematical Difficulties? The Effectiveness of Intervention Schemes.* London: DCSF.

Gifford, S. (2005) *Young Children's Difficulties in Learning Mathematics: Review of Research in Relation to Dyscalculia.* London: Qualifications and Curriculum Authority.

Haseler, M. (2008) 'Making intervention in numeracy more effective in schools.' In A. Dowker (ed.), *Mathematical Difficulties: Psychology and Intervention* (pp. 225–41). London: Elsevier.

Henderson, A. and Miles, E. (2001) *Basic Topics in Mathematics for Dyslexics.* London: Whurr.

Wing, T. and Tacon, R. (2007) 'Teaching number skills and concepts with the Numicon materials.' *Down Syndrome Research and Practice*, 12(1).

Useful contacts and addresses

Contacts for intervention strategies

Every Child Counts: Numbers Count	dowrickn@edgehill.ac.uk
Catch Up Numeracy	graham@catchup.org.uk
Mathematics Recovery	jrmartland@btopenworld.com
Making Maths Magic	Rebecca.Lewis@eastriding.gov.uk
Moving on in Maths, Luton	Juliet.parker@luton.gov.uk
Snap-on Maths in Surrey	Kathy.burr@vtplc.com

Assessment tests

Wechsler Objective Numerical Dimensions (WOND). The Psychometrics Centre, University of Cambridge PPSIS, Free School Lane, Cambridge CB2 3RQ

Sandwell Early Numeracy Test (revised version 2009) Sandwell Metropolitan Borough Council. Contact@psychometrics.cam.ac.uk

MaLT (Mathematics assessment for Learning and Teaching) Hodder Tests, Hodder Education, University of Manchester

Useful web addresses

BEAM Mathematics	www.beam.co.uk
British Dyslexia Association	www.bdadyslexia.org.uk
Dyslexia Institute	www.dyslexiainst.org.uk
Helen Arkell Dyslexia Centre	www.arkellcentre.org.uk
Miles Dyslexia Centre	www.dyslexia.bangor.ac.uk
National Strategies/Primary	www.education.gov.uk
Numbers Count	www.edgehill.ac.uk/ecc
Numdrum	www.numdrum.com
Numicon	www.numico.com
Primary Framework for Mathematics	www.cumbriagridforlearning.org.uk
Taskmaster	www.taskmaster.co.uk

Useful websites for software

www.4mation.co.uk
www.educationcity.com
www.espresso.co.uk
www.coxhoeprimaryschool.com
www.priorywoods.middlesbrough.sch.uk
www.schooljotter.com/showpage
www.dynamomaths.com
www.risingstars.com
www.ictgames.com
www.interactivegames.com
www.wordshark.co.uk
www.mathsproject.com
www.sherston.com
www.semerc.com

Index